VOCABULARY

for the High School Student

FOURTH EDITION

HAROLD LEVINE

Chairman Emeritus of English,
Benjamin Cardozo High School, New York

NORMAN LEVINE

Associate Professor of English,
City College of the City University of New York

ROBERT T. LEVINE

Professor of English,
North Carolina A & T State University

Amsco School Publications, Inc.
315 Hudson Street, New York, N.Y. 10013

Text and Cover Design: One Dot Inc.
Composition: Brad Walrod/High Text Graphics, Inc.

Please visit our Web site at: *www.amscopub.com*

When ordering this book, please specify:
Either **R 788 W** *or*
VOCABULARY FOR THE HIGH SCHOOL STUDENT

ISBN: 978-1-56765-115-7
NYC Item 56765-115-6
Copyright © 2004, 1994, 1982, 1967 by Amsco School Publications, Inc.

Printed in the United States of America

6 7 8 9 10   10 09 08 07 06

Preface

The principal aim of this updated and enlarged edition is to help high school students build a superior vocabulary and learn the skills of critical thinking, close reading, and concise writing. The exercises in this edition have been written expressly to teach these and other desirable skills at the same time as vocabulary.

Like its predecessors, this edition involves students in a variety of vocabulary-enriching activities in chapter after chapter.

Learning New Words From the Context (Chapter 1) presents one hundred sixty short passages in which unfamiliar words can be defined with the help of clues in the context. By teaching students how to interpret such clues, this chapter provides them with an indispensable tool for vocabulary growth and, at the same time, *makes them better readers*.

Enlarging Vocabulary Through Central Ideas (Chapter 2) teaches twenty groups of related words. In the EATING group, students learn *condiment, glutton, palatable, succulent, voracious,* and other *eating* words. Each word studied in such a group helps students learn other words in the group.

Enlarging Vocabulary Through Anglo-Saxon Prefixes (Chapter 3) teaches words beginning with eight Anglo-Saxon prefixes, like FORE-, meaning "before," "beforehand," or "front." Knowing FORE-, students can more readily understand *forearm, forebear, foreboding, foreshadow, foreword,* etc.

Enlarging Vocabulary Through Latin Prefixes (Chapter 4) does the same with twenty-four Latin prefixes. It is easier for students to understand *discontent, discredit, disintegrate, dispassionate,* and *disrepair* when they know that the prefix DIS- means "opposite of."

Enlarging Vocabulary Through Latin Roots (Chapter 5) teaches words derived from twenty Latin roots. If students, for example, know that the root HERE- means "stick," they can better understand *adhere* ("stick to"), *cohere* ("stick together"), *incoherent* ("not sticking together"; "disconnected"), etc.

Enlarging Vocabulary Through Greek Word Elements (Chapter 6) teaches derivatives from twenty Greek elements, like AUTO-, meaning "self." Among the ten AUTO- words taught in this chapter are *autocrat* (ruler exercising self-derived power), *automation* (technique for making a process self-operating), and *autonomy* (self-government).

Expanding Vocabulary Through Derivatives (Chapter 7) teaches students how to convert one newly learned word into several—for example, *literate* into *illiterate, semiliterate, literacy, illiteracy,* etc. The chapter also provides an incidental review of some basic spelling rules.

Understanding Word Relationships and Word Analogies (Chapter 8) supplements the numerous explanations and hints given throughout the book on dealing with analogy questions. This chapter is principally for students who are unfamiliar with analogy questions, or are having difficulty with them.

Dictionary of Words Taught in This Text is intended as a tool of reference and review.

Whenever something is learned, it is likely soon to be forgotten unless it is used. Therefore, students must be encouraged to use—in their writing and class discussions—the words and skills they are learning in this book. If a wordy paragraph can be made more concise or if undesirable repetition can be avoided by use of a synonym—they should be expected to do so because they have been using these very same skills hundreds of times in the exercises of this book. When a strange word can be understood from a knowledge of its root or prefix—or from clues in the context—they should be challenged to define it and to verify their definition in the dictionary. Above all, they should be encouraged to own a good dictionary and to develop the dictionary habit.

—The Authors

Vocabulary books by the authors

A Scholarship Vocabulary Program, Books I–III

Vocabulary and Composition Through Pleasurable Reading, Books I–V

Vocabulary for Enjoyment, Books I–III

Vocabulary for the High School Student, Books A, B

Vocabulary for the High School Student

Vocabulary for the College-Bound Student

The Joy of Vocabulary

Contents

Chapter 2 Enlarging Vocabulary Through Central Ideas 78

Chapter 3 Enlarging Vocabulary Through Anglo-Saxon Prefixes   127

Chapter 4 Enlarging Vocabulary Through Latin Prefixes   152

Chapter 5 Enlarging Vocabulary Through Latin Roots 209

What is a root? 209
Why study roots? 209
Purpose of this chapter 209

1

Learning New Words From the Context

What is the context?

The context is the part of a passage in which a particular word is used and which helps to explain that word. Suppose you were asked for the meaning of *bear.* Could you give a definite answer? Obviously not, for *bear,* as presented to you, has no context.

But if you were asked to define *bear* in the phrase "polar bear," you would immediately know it refers to an animal. Or, if someone were to say, "Please stop that whistling—I can't bear it," you would know that in this context *bear* means "endure" or "stand."

Why is the context important?

An important point for those of us who want to enlarge our vocabularies is this: the context can give us the meaning not only of familiar words like *bear,* but also of unfamiliar words.

Suppose, for example, you were asked for the meaning of *valiant.* You might not know it, unless, of course, you already had a fine vocabulary. But if you were to meet *valiant* in the following context, you would have a very good chance of discovering its meaning:

"Cowards die many times before their deaths; The valiant never taste of death but once."

—WILLIAM SHAKESPEARE

From the above context, you can tell that the author is contrasting two ideas—"cowards" and "the valiant." Therefore, "the valiant" means the opposite of "cowards," namely "brave people." *Valiant* means "brave."

In what ways will this chapter benefit you?

This chapter will show you how to get the meaning of unfamiliar words from the context. Once you learn this skill, it will serve you for the rest of your life in two important ways: (1) it will keep enlarging your vocabulary, and (2) it will keep making you a better and better reader.

Part
1

Contexts With Contrasting Words

Pretest 1

Each passage below contains a word in italics. If you read the passage carefully, you will find a clue to the meaning of this word in an opposite word (antonym) or a contrasting idea.

Below each passage, write (a) the clue that led you to the meaning and (b) the meaning itself. The answers to the first two passages have been inserted as examples.

1. It is the responsibility of every driver to be entirely *sober* at all times. Drunk drivers pose a danger to themselves, to their passengers, and to everyone else on the road.

   a. CLUE: _____ **sober is the opposite of "drunk"**

   b. MEANING: _____ **sober means "not drunk"**

2. One sandwich for lunch usually *suffices* for you, but for me it is not enough.

   a. CLUE: _____ **suffices is in contrast with "is not enough"**

   b. MEANING: _____ **suffices means "is enough"**

3. Plastic dishes last a long time because they are unbreakable. Ordinary china is very *fragile*.

   a. CLUE: _____ opposite of unbreakable

   b. MEANING: _____ "can break easily"

4. Our tennis coach will neither *confirm* nor deny the rumor that she is going to be the basketball coach next year.

   a. CLUE: _____ doesn't mean deny

   b. MEANING: _____ prove true

5. Don't *digress*. Stick to the topic.

   a. CLUE: _____ opposite of to stick to something

   b. MEANING: _____ go to another topic

6. Your account of the fight *concurs* with Joanne's but differs from the accounts given by the other witnesses.

   a. CLUE: _____ opposite of differ

   b. MEANING: _____ agree

7. "I greatly fear your presence would rather increase than *mitigate* his unhappy fortunes."
   —JAMES FENIMORE COOPER
   a. CLUE: _opposite of unhappy fortunes_
   b. MEANING: _soften_

8. Roses in bloom are a common sight in summer, but a *rarity* in late November.
   a. CLUE: _opposite of common_
   b. MEANING: _uncommon_

9. The tables in the restaurant were all occupied, and we waited more than ten minutes for one to become *vacant*.
   a. CLUE: _opposite of occupied_
   b. MEANING: _empty_

10. There are few theaters here, but on Broadway there are theaters *galore*.
    a. CLUE: _opposite of few_
    b. MEANING: _plentiful_

11. "I do not *shrink* from this responsibility; I welcome it."—JOHN FITZGERALD KENNEDY
    a. CLUE: _opposite of welcome_
    b. MEANING: _draw back_

12. Ruth is an experienced driver, but Harry is a *novice*; he began taking lessons just last month.
    a. CLUE: _opposite of experienced_
    b. MEANING: _a beginner_

13. A bank teller can usually tell the difference between genuine $100 bills and *counterfeit* ones.
    a. CLUE: _opposite of genuine_
    b. MEANING: _fake_

14. When I ask Theresa to help me with a *complicated* assignment, she makes it seem so easy.
    a. CLUE: _opposite of easy_
    b. MEANING: _complex_

15. On the wall of my room I have a copy of Rembrandt's "The Night Watch"; the *original* is in the Rijks Museum in Amsterdam.
    a. CLUE: _opposite of copy_
    b. MEANING: _prototype_

16. "Friends, Romans, countrymen, lend me your ears; / I come to bury Caesar, not to praise him. / The evil that men do lives after them; / The good is oft *interred* with their bones; / So let it be with Caesar."—WILLIAM SHAKESPEARE
    a. CLUE: opposite of praise
    b. MEANING: bury

17. In some offices, work comes to a halt at noon and does not *resume* until 1 P.M.
    a. CLUE: opposite of halt
    b. MEANING: begon again

18. When we got to the beach, my sister and I were *impatient* to get into the water, but Dad was not in a hurry.
    a. CLUE: opposite of hury
    b. MEANING: anxious

19. Off duty, a police officer may wear the same clothes as a *civilian*.
    a. CLUE: opposite of police officer
    b. MEANING: normal person

20. The candidate spoke for less than 20 minutes. At first, the audience appeared friendly and supportive, nodding and occasionally applauding. Before long, however, listeners turned *hostile*, voicing their disapproval with shouts and boos.
    a. CLUE: opposite of supportive
    b. MEANING: unfriendly

Study Your Lesson Words, **Group 1**

WORD	MEANING	TYPICAL USE
civilian (*n.*) sə-'vil-yən	person who is not a member of the military, or police, or firefighting forces	Eight of the passengers were soldiers and one was a marine; the rest were *civilians*.
complicated (*adj.*) 'käm-plə-,kā-təd	hard to understand; elaborate; complex; intricate	If some of the requirements for graduation seem *complicated*, ask your guidance counselor to explain them to you.
concur (*v.*) kən-'kər	agree; coincide; be of the same opinion	The rules of the game require you to accept the umpire's decision, even if you do not *concur* with it.

confirm (*v.*) kən-'fərm	state or prove the truth of; substantiate; verify	My physician thought I had broken my wrist, and an X-ray later *confirmed* his opinion.
confirmation (*n.*)	proof; evidence; verification	
digress (*v.*) dī-'gres	turn aside; get off the main topic; deviate	At one point, the speaker *digressed* to tell of an incident in her childhood, but then she got right back to the topic.
fragile (*adj.*) 'fra-jəl	easily broken; breakable; weak; frail	The handle is *fragile*; it will easily break if you use too much pressure.
galore (*adj.*) gə-'lór	aplenty; in abundance; plentiful; abundant (galore always follows the word it modifies)	There were no cabs on the side streets, but on the main street there were cabs *galore.*
genuine (*adj.*) 'jen-yə-wən	actually being what it is claimed or seems to be; true; real; authentic	The oil painting looked *genuine,* but it proved to be a copy of the original.
hostile (*adj.*) 'häs-təl	of or relating to an enemy or enemies; unfriendly; inimical	In the heat of battle, allies are sometimes mistaken for *hostile* forces.
impatient (*adj.*) im-'pā-shənt	not patient; not willing to bear delay; fretful; anxious	Five minutes can seem like five hours when you are *impatient.*
inter (*v.*) in-'tər	put into the earth; bury; entomb	Many American heroes are *interred* in Arlington National Cemetery.
interment (*n.*)	burial; entombment; sepulture	
mitigate (*v.*) 'mi-tə-,gāt	make less severe; lessen; alleviate; soften; relieve	With the help of novocaine, your dentist can greatly *mitigate* the pain of drilling.
novice (*n.*) 'nä-vəs	one who is new to a field or activity; beginner; apprentice; neophyte; tyro	There are two slopes: one for experienced skiers and one for *novices.*
original (*n.*) ə-'rij-ə-n°l	work created firsthand from which copies are made; prototype; archetype	This is a copy of THANKSGIVING TURKEY by Grandma Moses. The *original* is in the Metropolitan Museum of Art.
original (*adj.*)	1. belonging to the beginning; first; earliest; initial; primary 2. inventive; creative	Miles Standish was one of the *original* colonists of Massachusetts; he came over on the "Mayflower."
originality (*n.*)	freshness; novelty; inventiveness	
rarity (*n.*) 'rar-ə-tē	something uncommon, infrequent, or rare	Rain in the Sahara Desert is a *rarity.*

resume (*v.*) ri-'züm	1. begin again	School closes for the Christmas recess on December 24 and *resumes* on January 3.
	2. retake; reoccupy	Please *resume* your seats.
shrink (*v.*) 'shriŋk	1. draw back; recoil; wince	Wendy *shrank* from the task of telling her parents about the car accident, but she finally got the courage and told them.
	2. become smaller; contract	Some garments *shrink* in washing.
sober (*adj.*) 'sō-bər	1. not drunk; not intoxicated	Someone who has been drinking should not drive, even if he or she feels *sober*.
	2. earnest; serious; free from excitement or exaggeration	When he learned of his failure, George thought of quitting school. But after *sober* consideration, he realized that would be unwise.
suffice (*v.*) sə-'fīs	be enough, adequate, or sufficient; serve; do	I had thought that $60 would *suffice* for my school supplies. As it turned out, it was not enough.
vacant (*adj.*) 'vā-kənt	empty; unoccupied; tenantless; not being used	I had to stand for the first half of the performance because I could not find a *vacant* seat.
vacancy (*n.*)	unfilled position; unoccupied apartment or room	

Apply What You Have Learned

 **EXERCISE 1.1:** SENTENCE COMPLETION

Enter the required lesson word, as in 1, below.

1. The showers have just stopped, but they may soon _____resume_____.

2. Their directions were _____; yours were easy to follow.

3. Why are you _____ to me? Aren't we friends?

4. We hope to move in as soon as there is a(n) _____ apartment.

5. Experts can tell the difference between a copy and the _____.

6. How many more chairs do you need? Will five _____?

7. Paul doesn't play tennis as well as Amy; he is a(n) _____.

8. If you _____, you will waste our time. Stick to the topic.

9. There is only one _____ on the committee; the other members are all army officers.

10. It may be unpleasant, but we must not _____ from doing our duty.

11. Jobs, then, were not plentiful; now, there are openings _____.

12. Is there a way to _____ the pain? It is very severe.

13. What evidence do you have to _____ your claim?

14. These cups are _____; handle them with care.

15. Cemetery workers were instructed to _____ the deceased immediately after the service.

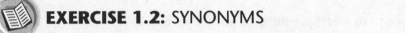 EXERCISE 1.2: SYNONYMS

Eliminate repetition by replacing the boldfaced word or words with a **synonym** from your lesson words. See 1 and 2, below.

<u>original</u>	1. Who lived here first? Were you the **first** tenant?
<u>sober</u>	2. He is not **drunk**; don't accuse him of drunkenness.
_____	3. I wanted to wait a day, but they were **unwilling to wait**.
_____	4. She has just begun to learn to swim, Are you a **beginner**, too?
_____	5. Stick to the topic. Don't **get off the topic**.
_____	6. A dozen is more than enough. Even six would **be enough**.
_____	7. I tried to be friendly, though they seemed **unfriendly**.
_____	8. You lack proof. There is no witness to **prove** your story.
_____	9. All rooms are occupied; not a single one is **unoccupied**.
_____	10. This is really a great buy. It's a **real** bargain.

EXERCISE 1.3: ANTONYMS

Enter the lesson word most nearly the **opposite** of the boldfaced word or words. See 1, below.

1. This **copy** is so good that it looks like the ____<u>original</u>____.

2. Trees were once a **common sight** here; now they are a(n) _____.

3. The carpenter is a **veteran**, but his helper is a(n) _____.

4. Her _____ attitude shows she is not **sympathetic** to our cause.

5. Is the auditorium **being used**, or is it _____.

6. Our opinions now _____; we no longer **disagree**.

7. I can neither _____ your statement nor **deny** it.

8. Say nothing to **intensify** his fears; try to _____ them.

9. Out of uniform, a **soldier** looks like an ordinary _____.

10. When we are **excited**, we are not capable of _____ judgment.

EXERCISE 1.4: CONCISE WRITING

Express the thought of each sentence in **no more than four words**, as in 1, below.

1. The people living next door to us were unwilling to put up with delay.

    Our neighbors were impatient.
    _____

2. People who are new to a field or activity need a great deal of help.

    _____

3. Rita misplaced the document from which the copies were made.

    _____

4. Which is the apartment that no one is living in at the present time?

    _____

5. Jones is not a member of the military, or police, or firefighting forces.

    _____

EXERCISE 1.5: SYNONYM SUMMARY

Each line, when completed, should have three words similar in meaning. Enter all missing letters, as in 1, below.

1. em **p** ty   ten **a** ntless   <u>v a c a n t</u>

2. abund __ nt   pl __ __ t __ ful   __ __ __ __ __ __

3. compl __ x   intr __ cate   __ __ __ __ __ __ __ __ __

4. pr __ __ f   ev __ dence   __ __ __ __ __ __ ation

5. b __ ry   ent __ __ b   __ __ __ __ __

6. neoph __ te   t __ ro   __ __ __ __ __

7. nov __ lty   inv __ ntiveness   __ __ __ __ __ __ __ __ ity

8. ser __ ous   __ __ rnest   __ __ __ __ __ __

9. an __ ious   fr __ tful   __ __ __ __ __ __ __ __

10. br __ __ kable   fr __ __ l   __ __ __ __ __ __ __

11. unfr __ __ ndly   inim __ cal   __ __ __ __ __ __ __

12. all __ viate   rel __ __ ve   __ __ __ __ __ __ __ __

13. ver __ fy   substant __ __ te   __ __ __ __ __ __ __

14. r __ __ l   __ __ thentic   __ __ __ __ __ __ __

15. rec __ __ l   w __ nce   __ __ __ __ __ __

16. proto __ __ pe   arch __ type   __ __ __ __ __ __ __ __

17. agr __ __   coin __ ide   __ __ __ __ __ __

18. anim __ sity   u __ fr __ __ __ dliness __ __ __ __ __ __ __ ity

19. entom __ ment   sep __ lture   __ __ __ __ __ __ ment

20. s __ rve   d __   __ __ __ __ __ __ __

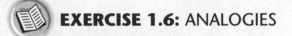 ## EXERCISE 1.6: ANALOGIES

Which lettered pair of words—*a, b, c, d,* or *e*—most nearly expresses the same relationship as the capitalized pair? Write the letter of your answer in the space provided. The first three analogy questions have been answered and explained to guide you.

Students who would like more help in answering analogy questions, should consult Chapter 8, pages 301–309.

__b__ 1. CONFIRM : DENY

    a. concur : agree   *b.* succeed : fail

    c. greet : welcome   *d.* disinter : unearth

    e. recoil : shrink

    Explanation: To **confirm** is the opposite of to **deny**. To **succeed** is the opposite of to **fail**.

__a__ 2. NEOPHYTE : EXPERIENCE

    a. fool : judgment   *b.* pedestrian : foot

    c. superstar : recognition *d.* motorist : license

    e. expert : skill

    Explanation: A **neophyte** lacks **experience**. A **fool** lacks **judgment**.

<u>e</u>   **3.** COMPLEX : UNDERSTAND

    a. painless : endure   *b.* tasty : consume

    c. inexpensive : afford   *d.* available : obtain

    e. vivid : forget

    Explanation: Something that is **complex** is hard to **understand**. Something that is **vivid** is hard to **forget**.

___   **4.** SOBER : INTOXICATED

    a. weak : frail   *b.* fretful : restless

    c. rude : impolite   *d.* inimical : friendly

    e. weird : strange

___   **5.** IMPATIENT : WAIT

    a. gossipy : talk   *b.* undecided : do

    c. stubborn : compromise   *d.* industrious : work

    e. obliging : assist

___   **6.** INTENSIFY : MITIGATE

    a. prohibit : permit   *b.* deviate : digress

    c. verify : substantiate   *d.* deny : contradict

    e. relieve : alleviate

___   **7.** FRAGILE : BREAK

    a. inflexible : bend   *b.* rubbery : chew

    c. rare : find   *d.* uncomplicated : grasp

    e. cumbersome : carry

___   **8.** CREATIVE : ORIGINALITY

    a. hostile : rancor   *b.* selfish : generosity

    c. sympathetic : ill will   *d.* unappreciative : gratitude

    e. frail : stamina

___   **9.** INTRICATE : SIMPLE

    a. vacant : unoccupied   *b.* abundant : scarce

    c. authentic : genuine   *d.* pleasant : agreeable

    e. uncommon : rare

___   **10.** CIVILIAN : COMBAT

    a. runner : marathon   *b.* accomplice : guilt

    c. passenger : navigation   *d.* singer : chorus

    e. guest : celebration

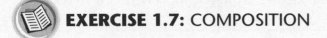

EXERCISE 1.7: COMPOSITION

Answer in a sentence or two.

1. Why should a person handling fragile objects always be sober?

   _____

   _____

2. When might you resume a friendship with someone who had been hostile to you?

   _____

   _____

3. How might the police confirm that someone had indeed been interred?

   _____

   _____

4. In what situation might you become impatient when someone begins to digress?

   _____

   _____

5. Would a novice mechanic suffice to work on a very complicated engine? Explain.

   _____

   _____

Pretest 2

Below each passage, write (a) the clue to the meaning of the italicized word and (b) the meaning itself.

21. "Then such a scramble as there is to get aboard, and to get ashore, and to take in freight and to *discharge* freight!"—MARK TWAIN

    a. CLUE: _____

    b. MEANING: _____

22. The owner is selling his gas station because the profit is too small. He hopes to go into a more *lucrative* business.

    a. CLUE: _____

    b. MEANING: _____

23. I tried reading Lou's notes but I found them *illegible*. However, yours were easy to read.

  a. CLUE: _____

  b. MEANING: _____

24. Debbie, who has come late to every meeting, surprised us today by being *punctual*.

  a. CLUE: _____

  b. MEANING: _____

25. As I hurried to the board, I *inadvertently* stepped on Alan's foot, but he thinks I did it on purpose.

  a. CLUE: _____

  b. MEANING: _____

26, 27. "When I was a boy, there was but one *permanent* ambition among my comrades in our village on the west bank of the Mississippi River. That was, to be a steamboatman. We had *transient* ambitions of other sorts.... When a circus came and went, it left us all burning to become clowns.... Now and then we had a hope that, if we lived and were good, God would permit us to be pirates. These ambitions faded out, each in its turn; but the ambition to be a steamboatman always remained."—MARK TWAIN

  a. CLUE: (*permanent*) _____

  b. MEANING: _____

  a. CLUE: (*transient*) _____

  b. MEANING: _____

28. When you chair a discussion, it is unfair to call only on your friends. To be *equitable,* you should call on all who wish to speak, without favoritism.

  a. CLUE: _____

  b. MEANING: _____

29. The only *extemporaneous* talk was Jerry's; all the other candidates gave memorized speeches.

  a. CLUE: _____

  b. MEANING: _____

30. "What's up" may be a suitable greeting for a friendly note, but it is completely *inappropriate* for a business letter.

  a. CLUE: _____

  b. MEANING: _____

31. If you agree, write "yes"; if you *dissent,* write "no."

  a. CLUE: _____

  b. MEANING: _____

32. "Mr. Hurst looked at her [Miss Bennet] with astonishment.
    "'Do you prefer reading to cards?' said he; 'that is rather singular [strange].'
    "'Miss Eliza Bennet,' said Miss Bingley, 'despises cards. She is a great reader, and has no pleasure in anything else.'
    "'I deserve neither such praise nor such *censure*,' cried Elizabeth; 'I am not a great reader, and I have pleasure in many things.'"—JANE AUSTEN

    a. CLUE: _____

    b. MEANING: _____

33. A child trying to squeeze through the iron fence became stuck between two bars, but luckily she was able to *extricate* herself.

    a. CLUE: _____

    b. MEANING: _____

34. When you let me take your bishop, I thought it was unwise of you; later I saw you had made a very *astute* move.

    a. CLUE: _____

    b. MEANING: _____

35. At first I was blamed for damaging Dad's computer, but when my sister said she was responsible, I was *exonerated*.

    a. CLUE: _____

    b. MEANING: _____

36. "If you once *forfeit* the confidence of your fellow citizens, you can never regain their respect and esteem."—ABRAHAM LINCOLN

    a. CLUE: _____

    b. MEANING: _____

37. Parking on our side of the street is *prohibited* on weekdays between 4 P.M. and 7 P.M. but permitted at all other times.

    a. CLUE: _____

    b. MEANING: _____

38. The caretaker expected to be praised for his efforts to put out the fire. Instead, he was *rebuked* for his delay in notifying the fire department.

    a. CLUE: _____

    b. MEANING: _____

39. If we can begin the meeting on time, we should be able to complete our business and *adjourn* by 4:30 P.M.

    a. CLUE: _____

    b. MEANING: _____

40. Before the new hotel can be constructed, the two old buildings now on the site will have
to be *demolished*.

  a. CLUE: _____

  b. MEANING: _____

Study Your Lesson Words, **Group 2**

WORD	MEANING	TYPICAL USE
adjourn (*v.*) ə-'jərn	close a meeting; suspend the business of a meeting; disband; recess	When we visited Washington, D.C., Congress was not in session; it had *adjourned* for the Thanksgiving weekend.
astute (*adj.*) ə-'stüt	1. shrewd; wise, perspicacious; sagacious	Marie was the only one to solve the riddle; she is a very *astute* thinker.
	2. crafty; cunning; sly; wily	An *astute* Greek tricked the Trojans into opening the gates of Troy.
censure (*n.*) 'sen(t)-shər	act of blaming; expression of disapproval; hostile criticism; rebuke; reprimand	Ali was about to reach for a third slice of cake but was stopped by a look of *censure* in Mother's eyes.
demolish (*v.*) di-'mä-lish	tear down; destroy; raze; smash; wreck	It took several days for the wrecking crew to *demolish* the old building.
demolition (*n.*)	destruction	
discharge (*v.*) dis-'chärj	1. unload	After *discharging* its cargo, the ship will go into dry dock for repairs.
	2. dismiss; fire	One employee was *discharged*.
dissent (*v.*) di-'sent	differ in opinion; disagree; object	There was nearly complete agreement on Al's proposal. Enid and Alice were the only ones who *dissented*.
dissension (*n.*)	discord; conflict; strife	
equitable (*adj.*) 'e-kwə-tə-bəl	fair to all concerned; just; impartial; objective; unbiased,	The only *equitable* way for the three to share the $600 profit is for each to receive $200.
inequitable (*n.*)	unfair; unjust	
exonerate (*v.*) ig-'zä-nə-rāt	free from blame; clear from accusation; acquit; absolve	The other driver *exonerated* Isabel of any responsibility for the accident.

extemporaneous (*adj.*)
,ek-,stem-pǝ-'rā-nē-ǝs

composed or spoken without preparation; offhand; impromptu; improvised

It was obvious that the speaker's talk was memorized, though she tried to make it seem *extemporaneous*.

extricate (*v.*)
'ek-strǝ-,kāt

free from difficulties; disentangle; disencumber; release

If you let your assignments pile up, you may get into a situation from which you will not be able to *extricate* yourself.

forfeit (*v.*)
'fȯr-fǝt

lose or have to give up as a penalty for some error, neglect, or fault; sacrifice

One customer gave a $150 deposit on an order of slipcovers. When they were delivered, she decided she didn't want them. Of course, she *forfeited* her deposit.

illegible (*adj.*)
i-'lej-ǝ-bǝl

not able to be read; very hard to read; not legible; undecipherable

It is fortunate that Miguel uses a computer to do his reports because his handwriting is *illegible*.

legible (*adj.*)

easy to read; readable

inadvertently (*adv.*)
,i-nǝd-'vǝr-t°nt-lē

not done on purpose; unintentionally; thoughtlessly; accidentally; carelessly

I finally found my glasses on the windowsill. I must have left them there *inadvertently*.

inappropriate (*adj.*)
,i-nǝ-'prō-prē-ǝt

not fitting; unsuitable; unbecoming; not appropriate; improper

Since I was the one who nominated Bruce, it would be *inappropriate* for me to vote for another candidate.

appropriate (*adj.*)

fitting; proper

lucrative (*adj.*)
'lü-krǝ-tiv

moneymaking; profitable; advantageous; remunerative

This year's school dance was not so *lucrative*; we made only $150 compared to $375 last year.

permanent (*adj.*)
'pǝr-mǝ-nǝnt

lasting; enduring; intended to last; stable

Write to me at my temporary address, the Gateway Hotel. As soon as I find an apartment, I shall notify you of my *permanent* address.

prohibit (*v.*)
prō-'hi-bǝt

forbid; ban; enjoin; interdict

The library's regulations *prohibit* the borrowing of reference books.

prohibition (*n.*)

ban; taboo; interdiction

punctual (*adj.*)
'pǝŋk-chǝ-wǝl

on time; prompt; timely

Be *punctual*. If you are late, we shall have to depart without you.

punctuality (*n.*)

promptness

rebuke (*v.*)
ri-'byük

express disapproval of; criticize sharply; censure severely; reprimand; reprove

Our coach *rebuked* the two players who were late for practice, but he praised the rest of the team for their punctuality.

| transient (*adj.*)
'tran(t)-zh(ē)-ənt | not lasting; passing soon; fleeting;
short-lived; momentary; ephemeral;
transitory | It rained all day upstate, but down
here we had only a *transient* shower;
it was over in minutes. |
| transient (*n.*) | guest staying for only a short time | The hotel's customers are mainly
transients; only a few are permanent
guests. |

Apply What You Have Learned

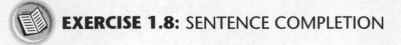 **EXERCISE 1.8:** SENTENCE COMPLETION

Fill each blank with the lesson word that best fits the meaning of the sentence, as in 1, below.

1. It is wrong to _____**rebuke**_____ Sam only, with not one word of _____**censure**_____ for the three others who are equally blameworthy.

2. As it was getting late, Lucy made a motion to _____ the meeting.

3. A boxer who deliberately uses tactics that the rules of the ring _____ will almost surely _____ the bout.

4. A letter with a(n) _____ address is undeliverable.

5. The complex has eighty unfurnished apartments to lease to _____ tenants and four furnished ones to accommodate _____ families.

6. It is illegal for a company to _____ toxic wastes into our state's rivers.

7. Those who _____ say they will not support the proposed settlement unless it is made more _____.

8. Her remarks were not _____; they had been prepared in advance.

9. The corporation's _____ new line of breakfast cereals should enable it to _____ itself from its financial difficulties.

10. Martha dashed out, _____ leaving her keys behind.

EXERCISE 1.9: SYNONYMS

Eliminate repetition by replacing the boldfaced word or words with a **synonym** from your lesson words.

_____ 1. Should we **ban** imports from nations that ban our products?

_____ 2. Cyclones **wreck** buildings, trapping victims in the wreckage.

_____ 3. The report clears them of blame, but it does not **clear** us.

_____ **4.** The firm has fired two employees and may soon **fire** some more.

_____ **5.** You are rarely on time; they are usually **on time**.

_____ **6.** Low profits are driving farmers into more **profitable** pursuits.

_____ **7.** Wait for a suitable occasion; this one is **not suitable**.

_____ **8.** The **lasting** peace we were supposed to have did not last long.

_____ **9.** Pat's handwriting is hard to read; Anita's is more **readable**.

_____ **10.** He is entangled in a web of lies and cannot **disentangle** himself.

EXERCISE 1.10: ANTONYMS

Enter the lesson word that is most nearly the **opposite** of the boldfaced word.

1. It makes no sense to _____ a structure we may soon need to **build** anew.

2. People insist on _____ treatment. **Unfair** practices must cease.

3. **Temporary** officers serve only until _____ ones are chosen.

4. Clothes **suitable** for leisure wear may be _____ for the office.

5. Many public places that used to **permit** smoking now _____ it.

6. **Commendation** is much more pleasing to our ears than _____.

7. The new owner turned an **unprofitable** business into a(n) _____ one.

8. I cannot **concur** with your conclusions. I must _____.

9. A **permanent** resident pays a lower daily rate than a(n) _____.

10. Our bus was **late** again today; it is seldom _____.

EXERCISE 1.11: CONCISE WRITING

Express the thought of each sentence in **no more than four words**, as in 1, below.

1. Jim strayed from the main topic without really intending to do so.

   Jim inadvertently digressed.
   _____

2. When are we going to bring our meeting to a close?

   _____

3. The laws by which we are governed must be fair to all concerned.

   _____

4. The comments she made were spoken on the spur of the moment, without any advance preparation.

_____

5. The notes that you took are very hard to read.

_____

EXERCISE 1.12: SYNONYM SUMMARY

Each line, when completed, should have three words similar in meaning. Enter all missing letters, as in 1, below.

1. disagr _e_ _e_   _o_ _b_ ject   _d_ _i_ _s_ sent

2. l __ se   sacr __ fice   forf __ __ t

3. shr __ __ d   w __ ly   __ __ tute

4. prom __ __   time __ __   pun __ __ __ __ __

5. __ reck   r __ ze   __ __ __ __ __ is __

6. last __ __ __   __ table   __ __ __ man __ __ __

7. b __ n   __ __ boo   pr __ hi __ __ tion

8. accident __ __ ly   care __ __ __ __ ly   __ __ __ __ __ __ __ tent __ __

9. impart __ __ __   __ __ bias __ __   __ quit __ __ __ __

10. f __ re   __ __ __ miss   __ __ __ charge

11. __ __ proper   __ __ becoming   __ __ appropriate

12. __ __ quit   __ __ solve   __ __ one __ __ __

13. fit __ __ __ __   prop __ __   __ __ prop __ __ __ __ __

14. __ __ cess   __ __ __ band   __ __ __ our __

15. moment __ __ __   fleet __ __ __   __ __ __ __ sit __ __ __

16. __ __ __ hand   __ __ prompt __   __ __ tempo __ __ __ __ __ __ __

17. profit __ ble   remuner __ tive   __ __ __ rat __ __ __

18. dis __ __ tangle   rel __ __ se   __ __ __ __ __ cat __

19. unread __ ble   undecipher __ ble   __ __ leg __ __ __ __

20. __ __ fair   __ __ just   __ __ __ __ __ __ __ table

EXERCISE 1.13: ANALOGIES

Which lettered pair of words—*a, b, c, d,* or *e*—most nearly expresses the same relationship as the capitalized pair? Write the letter of your answer in the space provided.

___ 1. ADJOURN : DISBAND
   a. win : lose
   b. differ : agree
   c. raise : lower
   d. bury : inter
   e. alleviate : intensify

___ 2. DEMOLISH : BUILD
   a. prohibit : interdict
   b. discharge : hire
   c. sacrifice : forfeit
   d. rebuke : reprimand
   e. absolve : exculpate

___ 3. ILLEGIBLE : DECIPHER
   a. audible : hear
   b. rare : find
   c. accessible : reach
   d. fragile : break
   e. visible : see
   Hint: Something **illegible** is hard to **decipher**.

___ 4. FOOL : ASTUTE
   a. coward : valiant
   b. inventor : creative
   c. imitator : unoriginal
   d. neophyte : inexperienced
   e. accomplice : blameworthy

___ 5. LUCRATIVE : UNREMUNERATIVE
   a. barren : unproductive
   b. scarce : unavailable
   c. becoming : inappropriate
   d. unjust : inequitable
   e. extemporaneous : impromptu

___ 6. EPHEMERAL : DURATION
   a. spacious : capacity
   b. priceless : value
   c. enormous : size
   d. lofty : height
   e. insignificant : importance
   Hint: Something **ephemeral** is of little **duration**.

___ 7. LATECOMER : PUNCTUAL
   a. liar : untrustworthy
   b. invalid : frail
   c. dictator : domineering
   d. gossip : talkative
   e. ally : inimical

___ **8.** OBJECTIVE : BIAS

    a. dependent : domination   *b.* vengeful : hate

    c. illiterate : ignorance   *d.* healthy : disease

    e. hesitant : doubt

    Hint: An **objective** person is free of **bias**.

___ **9.** FLEETING : STAY

    a. boiling : evaporate   *b.* stable : disappear

    c. complex : puzzle   *d.* amusing : entertain

    e. mitigating : relieve

    Hint: Something **fleeting** does not **stay**.

___ **10.** DYNAMITE : DEMOLITION

    a. food : agriculture   *b.* fog : atmosphere

    c. oil : heating   *d.* lumber : forest

    e. temperature : refrigeration

EXERCISE 1.14: COMPOSITION

Answer in a sentence or two.

1. Should a teacher rebuke a student for illegible writing? Explain.

    _____

    _____

2. Why wouldn't a boss discharge a worker for being punctual?

    _____

    _____

3. Give an example of inappropriate behavior that resulted in censure.

    _____

    _____

4. If the government must demolish houses, how can it do it in an equitable way?

    _____

    _____

5. Would an astute businessperson forfeit a lucrative contract? Explain.

    _____

    _____

Part

2

Contexts With Similar Words

This section will show you how you may discover the meaning of an unfamiliar word or expression from a similar word or expression in the context.

1. Do you know the meaning of *remuneration*? If not, you should be able to learn it from passage *a*:

   a. All school officials receive a salary except the members of the Board of Education, who serve without *remuneration*.

   Here, the meaning of *remuneration* is supplied by a similar word in the context, *salary*.

2. What is a *baker's dozen*? If you do not know, try to find out from passage *b*:

   b. "Mrs. Joe has been out a dozen times, looking for you, Pip. And she's out now, making it *a baker's dozen*."—CHARLES DICKENS

   A dozen plus one is the same as a *baker's dozen*. Therefore, a *baker's dozen* must mean "thirteen."

3. Let's try one more. Find the meaning of *comprehension* in passage *c*:

   c. I understand the first problem, but the second is beyond my *comprehension*.

   The clue here is *understand*. It suggests that *comprehension* must mean "understanding."

Note that you sometimes have to perform a small operation to get the meaning. In passage *c,* for example, you had to change the form of the clue word *understand* to *understanding*. In passage *b,* you had to do some adding: twelve plus one equals a *baker's dozen*. In passage *a,* however, you were able to use the clue word *salary,* without change, as the meaning of *remuneration*.

Pretest 3

Write the meaning of the italicized word or expression in the space provided. (*Hint:* Look for a *similar* word or expression in the context.)

1. "In the marketplace of Goderville was a great crowd, a mingled *multitude* of men and beasts."—GUY DE MAUPASSANT

   multitude means _____

2. When I invited you for a *stroll,* you said it was too hot to walk.

   stroll means _____

3. Jane's little brother has discovered the *cache* where she keeps her photographs. She'll have to find another hiding place.

   cache means _____

4. The *spine,* or backbone, runs along the back of human beings.

   spine means _____

5. "The king and his court were in their places, opposite the twin doors—those fateful *portals* so terrible in their similarity."—Frank R. Stockton

   portals means _____

6. Ellen tried her best to hold back her tears, but she could not *restrain* them.

   restrain means _____

7. Why are you so *timorous*? I tell you there is nothing to be afraid of.

   timorous means _____

8. Harriet's *version* of the quarrel differs from your account.

   version means _____

9. Our club's first president, who knew little about democratic procedures, ran the meetings in such a *despotic* way that we called him "the dictator."

   despotic means _____

10. "The 'Hispaniola' still lay where she had anchored, but, sure enough, there was the *Jolly Roger*—the black flag of piracy—flying from her peak."—Robert Louis Stevenson

    Jolly Roger means _____

11. The Empire State Building is a remarkable *edifice*; it has more than a hundred stories.

    edifice means _____

12. Some children who are *reserved* with strangers are not at all uncommunicative with friends.

    reserved means _____

13. The problems of the period we are living through are different from those of any previous *era.*

    era means _____

14. Why should I *retract* my statement? It is a perfectly true remark, and I see no reason to withdraw it.

    retract means _____

15. CELIA [urging Rosalind to say something]. Why, cousin! Why, Rosalind! . . . Not a word?
ROSALIND. Not one to throw at a dog.
CELIA. No, thy words are too precious to be cast away upon *curs*; throw some of them at me.
—WILLIAM SHAKESPEARE

curs means _____

16. Jerry thought he saw a ship in the distance. I looked carefully but could *perceive* nothing.

perceive means _____

17. Nina claims that I started the quarrel, but I have witnesses to prove that she *initiated* it.

initiated means _____

18. "He praised her taste, and she *commended* his understanding."—OLIVER GOLDSMITH

commended means _____

19. Students attending private schools pay *tuition*. In the public schools, however, there is no charge for instruction.

tuition means _____

20. "His facts no one thought of *disputing*; and his opinions few of the sailors dared to oppose."—RICHARD HENRY DANA

disputing means _____

Study Your Lesson Words, **Group 3**

WORD	MEANING	TYPICAL USE
cache (*n.*) 'kash	hiding place to store something	After confessing, the robber led detectives to a *cache* of stolen gems in the basement.
commend (*v.*) kə-'mend	praise; mention favorably; compliment	The volunteers were *commended* for their heroic efforts to save lives.
commendable (*adj.*)	praiseworthy; laudable	
cur (*n.*) 'kər	worthless dog	Lassie is a kind and intelligent animal. Please don't refer to her as a *cur*.
despotic (*adj.*) des-'pä-tik	characteristic of a despot (a monarch having absolute power); domineering; dictatorial; tyrannical; autocratic	The American colonists revolted against the *despotic* rule of George III.
despotism (*n.*)	tyranny; dictatorship	

dispute (*v.*)
di-'spyüt

argue about; debate; declare not true; call into question; oppose; challenge

Charley *disputed* my solution until I showed him definite proof that I was right.

disputatious (*adj.*)

argumentative; contentious

edifice (*n.*)
'e-də-fəs

building, especially a large or impressive building

The huge *edifice* under construction near the airport will be a hotel.

era (*n.*)
'ir-ə

historical period; period of time; age; epoch

The atomic *era* began with the dropping of the first atomic bomb in 1945.

initiate (*v.*)
i-'ni-shē-,āt

1. begin; introduce; originate; inaugurate

The Pilgrims *initiated* the custom of celebrating Thanksgiving Day.

2. put through the ceremony of becoming a member; admit; induct

Next Friday our club is going to *initiate* three new members.

initiation (*n.*)

induction; installation

Jolly Roger (*n.*)
'jä-lē-'rä-jər

pirates' flag; black flag with white skull and crossbones

The *Jolly Roger* flying from the mast of the approaching ship indicated that it was a pirate ship.

multitude (*n.*)
'məl-tə-,tüd

very large number of people or things; crowd; throng; horde; swarm

There was such a *multitude* outside the store waiting for the sale to begin that we decided to return later.

multitudinous (*adj.*)

many; numerous

perceive (*v.*)
pər-'sēv

become aware of through the senses; see; note; observe; behold; understand

When the lights went out, I couldn't see a thing, but gradually I was able to *perceive* the outlines of the larger pieces of furniture.

perception (*n.*)

idea; conception

portal (*n.*)
'pȯr-t°l

(usually plural) door; entrance, especially, a grand or impressive one; gate

The original doors at the main entrance have been replaced by bronze *portals*.

reserved (*adj.*)
ri-'zərvd

1. restrained in speech or action; reticent; uncommunicative; tight-lipped; taciturn

Mark was *reserved* at first but became much more communicative when he got to know us better.

2. unsociable; aloof; withdrawn

restrain (*v.*)
ri-'strān

hold back; check; curb; repress; keep under control

Mildred could not *restrain* her impulse to open the package immediately, even though it read, "Do not open before Christmas!"

retract (*v.*)
ri-'trakt

draw back; withdraw; take back; unsay

You can depend on Frank. Once he has given his promise, he will not *retract* it.

spine (*n.*) 'spīn	chain of small bones down the middle of the back; backbone	The ribs are curved bones extending from the *spine* and enclosing the upper part of the body.
spineless (*adj.*)	having no backbone; weak; indecisive; cowardly	
stroll (*n.*) 'strōl	idle and leisurely walk; ramble	It was a warm spring afternoon, and many people were out for a *stroll*.
timorous (*adj.*) 'ti-mə-rəs	full of fear; afraid; timid	I admit I was *timorous* when I began my speech, but as I went along, I felt less and less afraid.
tuition (*n.*) tü-'i-shən	payment for instruction	When I go to college, I will probably work each summer to help pay the *tuition*.
version (*n.*) 'vər-zhən	1. account or description from one point of view; interpretation	Now that we have Vera's description of the accident, let us listen to your *version*.
	2. translation	THE COUNT OF MONTE CRISTO was written in French, but you can read it in the English *version*.

Apply What You Have Learned

EXERCISE 1.15: SENTENCE COMPLETION

Fill each blank with the lesson word that best fits the meaning of the sentence, as in 1, below.

1. A(n) _____multitude_____ of desperate depositors gathered outside the closed
_____portal_____s of the ailing bank.

2. If you prove me wrong, I will gladly _____ my statement.

3. It is hoped that the settlement just reached will _____ a new
_____ of cooperation between labor and management.

4. Most of us would be too _____ to try sky-diving.

5. Since you _____ my _____ of what was said at today's
meeting, I am eager to hear your interpretation.

6. Many college students hold part-time jobs to help pay their _____.

7. In our _____ down Broadway, we passed one magnificent
_____ after another.

8. Sit up straight. Slouching tends to deform the _____.

9. It is hard to _____ why any people would prefer to keep their savings in a(n) _____ at home, instead of in an insured savings bank.

10. Why are you so _____ today? Don't you have anything to say?

EXERCISE 1.16: SYNONYMS

Eliminate repetition by replacing the boldfaced word or words with a **synonym** from your lesson words.

_____ 1. Her account of the incident is more believable than your **account.**

_____ 2. If he withdraws his objection to the plan, I will **withdraw** mine.

_____ s 3. The malls were crowded. I had never seen such **crowds** there.

_____ 4. Why are they afraid of our dog? There is no reason to be **afraid.**

_____ 5. That **large building** was built just a year ago.

_____ 6. Your cousins must love arguments; they **argue about** everything.

_____ 7. It is hard to communicate with you if you are **uncommunicative.**

_____ 8. I knew the **hiding place** where my brother hid his baseball cards.

_____ 9. Teachers often **praise** us when we do something praiseworthy.

_____ 10. **Curb** your appetite for snacks. If uncurbed, it may cause problems.

EXERCISE 1.17: ANTONYMS

Enter the lesson word that is most nearly the **opposite** of the boldfaced word or words.

1. A **valuable poodle** like Muffin is certainly not a(n) _____.

2. **Censure** them for their faults, but also _____ them for their merits.

3. Trained investigators _____ details that others may **fail to notice.**

4. Nonswimmers are _____ in a rowboat; swimmers are generally **unafraid.**

5. A **democratic** organization will not tolerate a(n) _____ president.

6. Be **sociable.** Mingle with the other guests. You are too _____.

7. They received **few** complaints, but we got a(n) _____ of them.

8. Please allow me to _____ the regrettable statement I **made** earlier.

9. **Let go.** Do not _____ me.

10. Nations that _____ hostilities may find it difficult to **end** them.

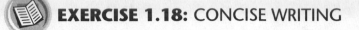 **EXERCISE 1.18:** CONCISE WRITING

Express the thought of each sentence in **no more than four words**.

1. A number of very large and impressive buildings are not being used.

_____

2. How much do you have to pay for the instruction that you are getting?

_____

3. I question the truth of the interpretation that they have presented.

_____

4. The supervisor that we worked for acted like an absolute monarch.

_____

5. Avoid injury to the chain of small bones that runs down the middle of your back.

_____

 **EXERCISE 1.19:** SYNONYM SUMMARY

Each line, when completed, should have three words similar in meaning.
Enter all missing letters, as in 1, below.

1. beh _o_ ld   _o_ _b_ serve   perc _e_ _i_ ve

2. q __ __ stion   challen __ __   dis __ __ __ __

3. c __ rb   ch __ ck   __ __ strain

4. cr __ wd   h __ rde   __ __ __ titude

5. pr __ __ se   compl __ ment   com __ __ __ __

6. dictator __ __ __ __   __ __ ranny   __ __ __ potism

7. orig __ nate   intr __ duce   init __ __ te

8. __ ge   epo __ __   __ __ a

9. tac __ turn   reti __ ent   res __ __ ved

10. w __ lk   __ amble   __ __ roll

11. afr __ __ d   __ __ __ ful   __ __ __ orous

12. acc __ __ nt   interpr __ tation   vers __ __ n

13. domin __ __ ring   __ __ tocratic   __ __ __ pot __ __

14. __ ate   entr __ nce   __ __ __ tal

15. __ __ say   with __ __ __ __   __ __ tract

16. __ __ ea   concept __ __ __   per __ e __ __ i __ __

17. __ __ duction   __ __ stallation   in __ __ __ __ tion

18. m __ ny   num __ __ __ __ __   __ __ __ __ __ __ tudinous

19. __ __ __ __ __ __ worthy   laud __ __ __ __   __ __ __ mend __ ble

20. arg __ mentative   conten __ __ ous   __ __ __ puta __ __ ous

 ## EXERCISE 1.20: ANALOGIES

Which lettered pair of words—*a, b, c, d,* or *e*—most nearly expresses the same relationship as the capitalized pair? Write the letter of your answer in the space provided.

___ 1. CUR : DOG
   a. calf : cow   *b.* lamb : sheep
   c. elk : deer   *d.* nag : horse
   e. tadpole : frog

___ 2. TUITION : INSTRUCTION
   a. dues : organization   *b.* interest : bank
   c. rent : shelter   *d.* fine : penalty
   e. tip : meal
   Hint: **tuition** is payment for **instruction.**

___ 3. STROLL : WALK
   a. hum : sing   *b.* drawl : speak
   c. gulp : swallow   *d.* dash : move
   e. snore : sleep
   Hint: To **stroll** is to walk **slowly.**

___ 4. DISPUTATIOUS : ARGUMENT
   a. obstinate : compromise   *b.* sociable : company
   c. restless : delay   *d.* indolent : exercise
   e. sober : exaggeration
   Hint: A **disputatious** person is fond of **argument.**

___ **5.** EDIFICE : BUILDING

    a. apron : garment   *b.* closet : storage

    c. canoe : vessel   *d.* glider : plane

    e. banquet : meal

___ **6.** CACHE : CONCEALMENT

    a. umbrella : rain   *b.* barrier : communication

    c. oven : fuel   *d.* showcase : privacy

    e. automobile : transportation

___ **7.** SPINELESS : WILLPOWER

    a. impartial : prejudice   *b.* enthusiastic : zeal

    c. inquisitive : curiosity   *d.* resentful : anger

    e. dauntless : courage

___ **8.** TACITURN : SAY

    a. disgruntled : complain   *b.* proficient : accomplish

    c. timid : fear   *d.* literate : know

    e. frank : conceal

    Hint: A **taciturn** person has **little** to say.

___ **9.** RESTRAINED : FREE

    a. enlightened : educated   *b.* reserved : withdrawn

    c. exonerated : guiltless   *d.* uninvited : welcome

    e. contented : satisfied

___ **10.** JOLLY ROGER : PIRACY

    a. green light : danger   *b.* full moon : illumination

    c. white flag : truce   *d.* red carpet : hostility

    e. yellow ribbon : cowardice

EXERCISE 1.21: COMPOSITION

Answer in a sentence or two.

1. How might people of the future perceive our current era?

_____

_____

2. When is it wise to restrain timorous feelings?

_____

_____

3. Should citizens dispute the policies of a despotic leader? Why or why not?

_____

_____

4. What type of portal might suit a grand edifice?

_____

_____

5. Why wouldn't you show your cache to a multitude?

_____

_____

Pretest 4

Write the meaning of the italicized word or expression in the space provided.
(Look for a *similar* word or expression in the context.)

21. "When all at once I saw a crowd,/A *host,* of golden daffodils."—WILLIAM WORDSWORTH

    host means _____

22. Choosing a career is a matter that calls for r*eflection,* but I haven't yet given it enough thought.

    reflection means _____

23. How can Alice *tolerate* your whistling while she is studying? I would never be able to bear it.

    tolerate means _____

24. We can't meet in the music room tomorrow because another group has reserved it. We shall have to *convene* somewhere else.

    convene means _____

25. Some of the students who arrive early gather near the main entrance, even though they are not supposed to *congregate* there.

    congregate means _____

26. "'Ah, so it is!' Edmond said, and, still keeping Mercédès' hand clasped in his, he held the other one out in all friendliness to the Catalan. Instead, however, of responding to this show of *cordiality,* Fernand remained mute and motionless as a statue."—ALEXANDRE DUMAS

    cordiality means _____

27. I can *dispense with* a midmorning snack, but I cannot do without lunch.

dispense with means _____

28. Up to now Diane has always started the disputes; this time Caroline is the *aggressor.*

aggressor means _____

29. Some pitchers try to *intimidate* batters by throwing fastballs very close to them, but they can't frighten a hitter like Joe.

intimidate means _____

30. "Rip now resumed his old walks and habits. He soon found many of his former *cronies,* though all rather the worse for the wear and tear of time; so Rip preferred making friends among the younger generation, with whom he soon grew into great favor."
—WASHINGTON IRVING

cronies means _____

31. The English Office is at one end of the hall, and the library entrance is at the other *extremity.*

extremity means _____

32. "'Slow, lad, slow,' he said. 'They might round upon us in a twinkle of an eye, if we was seen to hurry.'
"Very *deliberately,* then, did we advance across the sand...."—ROBERT LOUIS STEVENSON

deliberately means _____

33. Two hours ago the weather bureau predicted rain for tomorrow; now it is *forecasting* rain mixed with snow.

forecasting means _____

34. The old edition had a *preface.* The new one has no introduction at all.

preface means _____

35. Patricia's dog ran off with our ball and would not *relinquish* it until she made him give it up.

relinquish means _____

36. By noon we had climbed to a height of more than 2000 feet. From that *altitude,* the housetops in the town below seemed tiny.

altitude means _____

37. "He bade me observe it, and I should always find, that the *calamities* of life were shared among the upper and lower part of mankind; but that the middle station had the fewest disasters."—DANIEL DEFOE

calamities means _____

38. Yesterday it looked doubtful that I could finish my report on time. Today, however, it seems less *dubious*.

dubious means _____

39. People at the zoo usually draw back when the lion roars, but this time they did not *recoil*.

recoil means _____

40. Bears and bats *hibernate* in caves; frogs and lizards spend the winter in the earth, below the frost line.

hibernate means _____

Study Your Lesson Words, **Group 4**

WORD	MEANING	TYPICAL USE
aggressor (*n.*) ə-'gre-sər	person or nation that initiates hostilities or makes an unprovoked attack; assailant; invader	In World War II, Japan was the *aggressor*; its surprise attack on Pearl Harbor started the conflict in the Pacific.
aggression (*n.*)	unprovoked attack; assault; invasion	
altitude (*n.*) 'al-tə-,tüd	height; elevation; high position; eminence	Mount Washington, which rises to an *altitude* of 6,288 feet, is the highest peak in the White Mountains.
calamity (*n.*) kə-'la-mə-tē	great misfortune; catastrophe; disaster	The assassinations of John F. Kennedy and Martin Luther King, Jr. were national *calamities*.
calamitous (*adj.*)	disastrous; catastrophic	
congregate (*v.*) 'kä ŋ-gri-,gāt	come together into a crowd; assemble; gather	Some homeowners near the school do not like students to *congregate* on their property.
convene (*v.*) kən-'vēn	meet in a group for a specific purpose	The board of directors will *convene* next Tuesday to elect a new corporation president.
convention (*n.*)	treaty; agreement	
cordiality (*n.*) ,kȯr-jē-'a-lə-tē	friendliness; warmth of regard; amiability	Pam's parents greeted me with *cordiality* and made me feel like an old friend of the family.
cordial (*adj.*)	warm and friendly; gracious; hearty	

crony (*n.*) 'krō-nē	close companion; intimate friend; chum; associate	Some students socialize only with their *cronies* and rarely try to make new friends.
deliberately (*adv.*) di-'li-bə-rət-lē	1. in a carefully thought out manner; purposely; intentionally	We *deliberately* kept Glenda off the planning committee because we didn't want her to know that the party was to be in her honor.
	2. in an unhurried manner; slowly	The chef measured out the ingredients *deliberately,* wanting the amounts to be precise.
dispense (*v.*) di-'spen(t)s	1. deal out; distribute	Some charitable organizations *dispense* food to the needy.
	2. (followed by the preposition *with*) do without; get along without; forgo	When our club has a guest speaker, we *dispense* with the reading of the minutes to save time.
dubious (*adj.*) 'dü-bē-əs	doubtful; uncertain; questionable	There is no doubt about my feeling better, but it is *dubious* that I can be back at school by tomorrow.
extremity (*n.*) ik-'stre-mə-tē	very end; utmost limit; border	Key West is at the southern *extremity* of Florida.
forecast (*v.*) 'fȯr-,kast	predict; foretell; prophesy; prognosticate	The price of oranges has gone up again, as you *forecasted*.
hibernate (*v.*) 'hī-bər-,nāt	spend the winter in a dormant or inactive state, as some animals do	When animals *hibernate,* their heart rate drops sharply and their body temperature decreases.
host (*n.*) 'hōst	1. large number; multitude; throng; crowd; flock	The merchant had expected a *host* of customers, but only a few appeared.
	2. person who receives or entertains a guest or guests at home or elsewhere (Note also: *hostess*—a woman who serves as a *host*)	Dad treats his guests with the utmost cordiality; he is an excellent *host*.
intimidate (*v.*) in-'ti-mə-,dāt	frighten; influence by fear; cow; overawe; coerce	A few spectators were *intimidated* by the lion's roar, but most were not frightened.
preface (*n.*) 'pre-fəs	introduction (to a book or speech); foreword; prologue; preamble; exordium	Begin by reading the *preface*; it will help you to get the most out of the rest of the book.
preface (*v.*)	introduce or begin with a preface; usher in; precede	Usually, I get right into my speech, but this time I *prefaced* it with an amusing anecdote.

recoil (*v.*) ri-′kȯi(ə)l	draw back because of fear or disgust; shrink; wince; flinch	Marie *recoiled* at the thought of singing in the amateur show, but she went through with it because she had promised to participate.
reflection (*n.*) ri-′flek-shən	1. thought, especially careful thought; cogitation; deliberation	When a question is complicated, don't give the first answer that comes to mind. Take time for *reflection*.
	2. blame; discredit; aspersion; slur	Yesterday's defeat was no *reflection* on our players; they did their very best.
relinquish (*v.*) ri-′liŋ-kwish	give up; abandon; let go; release; surrender; cede	When an elderly man entered the crowded bus, one of the students *relinquished* her seat to him.
tolerate (*v.*) ′tä-lə-ˌrāt	endure; bear; put up with; accept; permit	Very young children will cry when rebuked; they cannot *tolerate* criticism.
tolerable (*adj.*)	bearable; endurable	

Apply What You Have Learned

EXERCISE 1.22: SENTENCE COMPLETION

Fill each blank with the lesson word that best fits the meaning of the sentence.

1. Many a(n) _____ has occurred in the Alps on the Matterhorn, an almost unscalable mountain that rises to a(n) _____ of 14,700 feet.

2. My teammates are confident of victory, but I am inclined to be _____.

3. We will _____ no more delays because our patience has already been stretched to its _____.

4. The author's _____ precedes the table of contents.

5. The United Nations has always called upon _____s to _____ the territories they have seized.

6. If you stop to feed one pigeon, a flock of them will soon _____ around you.

7. The candidate used to be a(n) _____ of mine, but since our dispute there has not been much _____ between us.

8. The _____ greeted each of his guests with a cordial handshake.

9. Since this matter is important, let us proceed _____ rather than hastily, with ample time for discussion and _____.

10. Lower winter air fares will probably encourage more Northerners to _____ in the South this year.

EXERCISE 1.23: SYNONYMS

Eliminate repetition by replacing the boldfaced word or words with a **synonym** from your lesson words.

_____ 1. They cannot **frighten** that reporter with threats; she is not easily frightened.

_____ 2. Cassandra was able to **predict** future events, but no one ever believed her predictions.

_____ 3. Will they **assemble** here or at some other place of assembly?

_____ 4. People have reluctantly put up with increases in taxes, but they refuse to **put up with** reductions in services.

_____ 5. The guest of honor was a **close friend** with whom she has been friendly since grade school.

_____ 6. Our neighbor speaks **in an unhurried way**; he is never in a hurry.

_____ 7. We do not question your facts, but we think your interpretation of them is **questionable**.

_____ 8. The two are supposed to be friends, but sometimes there is no **friendliness** between them.

_____ 9. That family has had great misfortunes, but never such a **great misfortune** as this one.

_____ 10. Many youngsters will gladly forgo vegetables but are most reluctant to **forgo** dessert.

EXERCISE 1.24: ANTONYMS

Enter the lesson word that is most nearly the **opposite** of the boldfaced word or words.

1. When David saw others _____ from the giant Goliath, he went out with his sling to **confront** him.

2. The crowds that _____ at the scene of an accident are often slow to **disperse**.

3. Don't _____ all your supplies; **keep** some for yourself.

4. I **inadvertently** neglected to say hello, but she thought I had done it
_____.

5. The first **guest** arrived with a small present for the _____.

6. The _____ is brief, but the **index** runs to more than six pages.

7. The **invaded nation** is fighting to repel the _____.

8. Sometimes what appears to be a(n) _____ turns out to be a **boon**.

9. Some animals that are **active in the summer** _____ when the weather turns cold.

10. We are **certain** about the election returns that have been verified, but we are
_____ about some of the others.

EXERCISE 1.25: CONCISE WRITING

Express the thought of each sentence in **no more than four words**.

1. I spoke without giving careful thought to what I was saying.

_____

2. The one who had invited us to her home as guests was warm and friendly.

_____

3. Has the individual who made the unprovoked attack offered an apology?

_____

4. What is it that made you draw back in disgust?

_____

5. Read the introduction to the book in an unhurried manner.

_____

EXERCISE 1.26: SYNONYM SUMMARY

Each line when completed, should have three words similar in meaning. Enter all missing letters, as in 1, below.

1. dou **b** tful   q u e stionable   dub i o u s

2. h __ __ ght   el __ vation   alt __ __ __ __ __

3. ab __ __ don   c __ d __   __ __ linquish

4. pred __ __ t   prophe __ y   __ __ __ __ cast

5. gath __ __   __ __ semble   __ __ __ gregate

6. b __ __ rable   __ __ durable   tol __ __ __ __ __ __

7. ch __ m   as __ __ ciate   __ __ ony

8. __ __ vasion   ass __ __ lt   ag __ __ __ __ __ __ __ __

9. grac __ __ __ __   h __ __ rty   cord __ __ l

10. thr __ __ g   __ __ __ titude   h __ __ t

11. dis __ __ trous   __ __ __ __ strophic   __ __ lam __ __ __ __ __

12. co __ rce   __ ow   __ __ timid __ __ __

13. ac __ ept   en __ __ __ e   __ __ lerate

14. p __ __ posely   __ __ tentionally   de __ __ __ __ erately

15. shr __ __ k   __ __ nce   rec __ __ l

16. __ __ liberation   cog __ tation   __ __ flec __ __ __ __ __

17. fr __ __ ndliness am __ __ bility   __ __ __ diality

18. agr __ __ ment   tr __ __ ty   __ __ __ vention

19. l __ mit   b __ __ der   ex __ __ __ __ ity

20. pre __ __ ble   ex __ __ dium   __ __ __ face

EXERCISE 1.27: ANALOGIES

Which lettered pair of words—*a, b, c, d,* or *e*—most nearly expresses the same relationship as the capitalized pair? Write the letter of your answer in the space provided.

___ 1. CALAMITY : MISFORTUNE
    a. hill : mountain   *b.* deluge : rainfall
    c. crime : misdemeanor   *d.* brook : river
    e. lake : ocean
    Hint: A **calamity** is a great **misfortune**.

___ 2. PREFACE : INDEX
    a. initiation : club   *b.* mouth : river
    c. appetizer : dessert   *d.* sunrise : noon
    e. lobby : edifice
    Hint: A **preface** is the first part of a book; an **index** is the last.

___ **3.** RELINQUISH : ABANDON

    a. wane : flourish
    b. convene : adjourn
    c. submit : defy
    d. repel : attract
    e. extinguish : quench

___ **4.** INVADER : AGGRESSION

    a. burglar : arson
    b. lawbreaker : arrest
    c. liar : perjury
    d. shoplifter : penalty
    e. swindler : greed

Hint: An **invader** commits **aggression**.

___ **5.** CONGREGATE : DISPERSE

    a. hesitate : waver
    b. prognosticate : foretell
    c. cow : coerce
    d. flinch : wince
    e. commend : reprimand

___ **6.** LOATHSOME : RECOIL

    a. incredible : believe
    b. irritating : relax
    c. spectacular : gasp
    d. interesting : yawn
    e. illegible : understand

Hint: Something that is **loathsome** makes us **recoil**.

___ **7.** ALTITUDE : DEPTH

    a. significance : importance
    b. confidence : doubt
    c. anxiety : worry
    d. mitigation : relief
    e. version : interpretation

___ **8.** INTOLERABLE : ENDURE

    a. intelligible : comprehend
    b. complicated : simplify
    c. palatable : consume
    d. inequitable : justify
    e. accessible : approach

___ **9.** COGITATION : BRAIN

    a. digestion : stomach
    b. air : lungs
    c. perspiration : exertion
    d. backbone : spine
    e. nutrition : food

___ **10.** HOST : MULTITUDE

    a. novice : veteran
    b. masterpiece : reproduction
    c. crony : chum
    d. cordiality : hostility
    e. guest : courtesy

EXERCISE 1.28: COMPOSITION

Answer in a sentence or two.

1. Why don't people show cordiality to an aggressor?

_____

_____

2. What calamity might occur to an airplane flying at a low altitude?

_____

_____

3. Give an example of a host whom you could not tolerate.

_____

_____

4. Why wouldn't a crony deliberately intimidate you?

_____

_____

5. Describe a time you felt dubious about a decision after giving it some reflection.

_____

_____

Commonsense Contexts

Do you know what *famished* means? If not, you should be able to tell from the following context:

> "The morning had passed away, and Rip felt *famished* for want of his breakfast."
>
> —WASHINGTON IRVING

How do you feel when the morning has gone by and you have not had breakfast? Very hungry, of course, even starved. Therefore, *famished* in the above context must mean "very hungry."

Note that the above context is different from those we have had so far. It has neither an opposite word nor a similar word to help with the meaning of *famished*. It does, however, offer a clue in the words "for want of his breakfast," so that you can get the meaning by using *common sense*.

Here is another commonsense context. Can you tell what *inundated* means in the sentence below?

> As a result of a break in the water main, many cellars in the area were *inundated*.

What happens to cellars when a nearby water main breaks? They become flooded, naturally. Therefore, *inundated* in the above context must mean "flooded."

Pretest 5

Here are some more commonsense contexts. Each contains a clue or clues to the meaning of the italicized word. Discover the meaning by using common sense, as in the previous examples. Then write the meaning in the space provided.

1. "Mrs. Linton's funeral was appointed to take place on the Friday after her *decease*."
   —EMILY BRONTË

   decease means _____

2. The race ended in a tie when Paul and Abe crossed the finish line *simultaneously*.

   simultaneously means _____

3. If you stand up in the boat, it may *capsize,* and we'll find ourselves in the water.

capsize means _____

4. I cannot tell you the secret unless you promise not to *divulge* it.

divulge means _____

5. "I now made one or two attempts to speak to my brother, but in some manner which I could not understand the *din* had so increased that I could not make him hear a single word, although I screamed at the top of my voice in his ear."—EDGAR ALLAN POE

din means _____

6. We had no use for our flashlights; the moon *illuminated* our path very clearly.

illuminated means _____

7. Sandra became *incensed* when I refused to return her library books for her, and she has not spoken to me since then.

incensed means _____

8. The President heads our national government, the Governor our state government, and the Mayor our *municipal* government.

municipal means _____

9. On February 12, 1809, in a Kentucky log cabin, there was born a boy who *subsequently* became the sixteenth President of the United States.

subsequently means _____

10. "All was dark within, so that I could *distinguish* nothing by the eye."—ROBERT LOUIS STEVENSON

distinguish means _____

11. There was a noise like the explosion of a firecracker when Karen *punctured* the balloon with a pin.

punctured means _____

12. President Franklin D. Roosevelt died in 1945, and his wife, Eleanor, in 1962; she *survived* him by seventeen years.

survived means _____

13. Every time you cross a busy street against the light, you are putting your life in *jeopardy.*

jeopardy means _____

14. By automobile, you can *traverse* the bridge in two minutes; on foot, it takes about half an hour.

traverse means _____

15. "I was witness to events of a less peaceful character. One day when I went out to my woodpile, or rather my pile of stumps, I observed two large ants, the one red, the other much larger, nearly half an inch long, and black, fiercely *contending* with one another."—HENRY DAVID THOREAU

contending means _____

16. The microscope is of the utmost importance in the study of biology because it can *magnify* objects too small to be seen by the naked eye.

magnify means _____

17. At one point during the hurricane, the winds reached a *velocity* of 130 miles an hour.

velocity means _____

18. Farmers will be in trouble unless the *drought* ends soon; it hasn't rained in six weeks.

drought means _____

19. The speaker should have used the microphone. Her voice was *inaudible,* except to those near the platform.

inaudible means _____

20. "However, at low water I went on board, and though I thought I had *rummaged* the cabin so effectually, as that nothing more could be found, yet I discovered a locker with drawers in it, in one of which I found two or three razors, and one pair of large scissors, with some ten or a dozen of good knives and forks...."—DANIEL DEFOE

rummaged means _____

Study Your Lesson Words, **Group 5**

WORD	MEANING	TYPICAL USE
capsize (*v.*) 'kap-ˌsīz or kap-'sīz	overturn; upset	When Sam's canoe *capsized,* I swam over to help him turn it right side up.
contend (*v.*) kən-'tend	1. compete; vie; take part in a contest; fight; struggle	Every spring some baseball writers try to predict which two teams will *contend* in the next World Series.
	2. argue; maintain as true; assert	Don't argue with the umpire. If she says you are out, it's no use *contending* you are safe.
contentious (*adj.*)	quarrelsome; belligerent	
decease (*n.*) di-'sēs	death; demise	Shortly after President Kennedy's *decease,* Vice President Johnson was sworn in as the new chief executive.

din (*n.*)
'din

loud noise; uproar; clamor; racket

I couldn't hear what you were saying because the plane passing overhead made such a *din*.

distinguish (*v.*)
di-'stiŋ-(g)wish

tell apart; differentiate; recognize

The twins are so alike that it is hard to *distinguish* one from the other.

divulge (*v.*)
də-'vəlj or dī-'vəlj

make known; reveal; disclose

Yesterday our teacher read us a composition without *divulging* the name of the writer.

drought (*n.*)
'draút

long period of dry weather; lack of rain; dryness

While some regions are suffering from *drought,* others are experiencing heavy rains and floods.

famish (*v.*)
'fa-mish

starve; suffer from extreme hunger; make extremely hungry

The missing hikers were *famished* when we found them; they had not eaten for more than twelve hours.

illuminate (*v.*)
i-'lü-mə-,nāt

light up; lighten; brighten

The bright morning sun *illuminated* the room; there was no need for the lights to be on.

inaudible (*adj.*)
i-'nȯ-də-bəl

incapable of being heard; not audible

The only part of your answer I could hear was the first word; the rest was *inaudible*.

incense (*v.*)
in-'sen(t)s

make extremely angry; enrage; madden; infuriate

Some of the members were so *incensed* by the way Tamar opened the meeting that they walked right out.

inundate (*v.*)
'i-,nən-dāt

flood; swamp; deluge

The rainstorm *inundated* a number of streets in low-lying areas.

jeopardy (*n.*)
'je-pər-dē

danger; peril

If you arrive late for a job interview, your chances of being hired will be in serious *jeopardy*.

jeopardize (*v.*)

endanger; imperil

magnify (*v.*)
'mag-nə-,fī

cause to be or look larger; enlarge; amplify; exaggerate

The bacteria shown in your textbook have been greatly *magnified*; their actual size is considerably smaller.

municipal (*adj.*)
myü-'ni-sə-pəl

of a city or town

Your mother works for the city? How interesting! My father is also a *municipal* employee.

puncture (*v.*)
'pəŋk-chər

make a hole with a pointed object; pierce; perforate

Our neighbor swept a nail off his curb, and later it *punctured* one of his own tires.

rummage (*v.*)
'rə-mij
search thoroughly by turning over all the contents; ransack
Someone must have *rummaged* my desk; everything in it is in disorder.

simultaneously (*adv.*)
,sī-məl-'tā-nē-əs-lē
at the same time; concurrently; together
The twins began school *simultaneously,* but they did not graduate at the same time.

subsequently (*adv.*)
'səb-si-,kwənt-lē
later; afterward; next
When I first saw that dress, it was $49.95; *subsequently* it was reduced to $29.95; now it is on sale for $19.95.

survive (*v.*)
sər-'vīv
live longer than; outlive; outlast
After landing at Plymouth, the Pilgrims suffered greatly; about half of them failed to *survive* the first winter.

traverse (*v.*)
tra-'vərs
pass across, over, or through; cross
The Trans-Siberian Railroad, completed in 1905, *traverses* the Asian continent.

velocity (*n.*)
və-'lä-sə-tē
speed; swiftness; celerity; rapidity
Do you know that light travels at a *velocity* of 186,000 miles a second?

Apply What You Have Learned

EXERCISE 1.29: SENTENCE COMPLETION

Fill each blank with the lesson word that best fits the meaning of the sentence.

1. If that beached whale is to _____, we must get him back into the water.

2. At its maximum _____, the new high-speed train can _____ the distance in less than two hours.

3. Though she has a strong voice, her words were almost _____d by the _____ of the chanting crowd.

4. While Sal _____d the attic, I _____ searched the basement, but we failed to find the old comic books.

5. After the boat _____d, we had to _____ with the strong current as we swam shoreward.

6. The _____ employees were _____d when the mayor refused to raise their salaries.

7. The doctor's _____ put the health of the community in _____ because no other physician was willing to practice in that remote area.

8. 1 know the Bakers well, but in their Halloween costumes I could not _____ them from the other guests.

9. Driving is difficult on a moonless night when there are no street lights to _____ the road.

10. The candidate attempted to _____ his achievements, but his exaggerations were _____d by the reporter's sharp questioning.

EXERCISE 1.30: SYNONYMS

Eliminate repetition by replacing the boldfaced word or words with a **synonym** from your lesson words.

_____ 1. Tanks can pass over terrain that civilian vehicles cannot **pass through**.

_____ 2. When he is in a rage, do not say anything that will **enrage** him further.

_____ 3. The forests are especially dry because we have had a **long period of dry weather**.

_____ 4. Those who drive today are putting their lives in **danger** because the roads are icy and dangerous.

_____ 5. If you lean over the side of the boat, you may **turn it over**.

_____ 6. Steve maintains that you started the fight, and you **maintain** that he did.

_____ 7. Even with flood control, the Mississippi will occasionally **flood** millions of acres.

_____ 8. The speeding vehicle was clocked at a **speed** of 90 miles an hour.

_____ 9. Many who had outlived previous earthquakes did not **outlive** this one.

_____ 10. The findings have not been disclosed; the committee will **disclose** them at the proper time.

EXERCISE 1.31: ANTONYMS

Enter the lesson word that is most nearly the **opposite** of the boldfaced word or words.

1. People whose main concern is for the **safety** of their money may not want to put their savings in _____ by investing in the stock market.

2. In the flood, eighty-four people **perished**, nine are missing, and eleven _____d.

3. Let us neither _____ our accomplishments nor **minimize** our failures.

4. The brightly _____d business district was momentarily **darkened** by a sudden power outage.

5. Skills **previously** acquired may _____ serve us in good stead.

6. I often **confuse** one twin with the other. How are you able to _____ them?

7. Admirers of the late leader faithfully observe the anniversaries of his **birth** and _____.

8. The **stillness** of the early morning was abruptly broken by the _____ of wailing sirens.

9. Angela was so _____d that she could not be **placated**.

10. The two letters were mailed **at different times**, but they arrived _____.

EXERCISE 1.32: CONCISE WRITING

Express the thought of each sentence in **no more than four words**.

1. The long period of dry weather has come to an end.

_____

2. Burglars searched through the cabinets, turning over all the contents.

_____

3. The charges that they were making made her extremely angry.

_____

4. Someone made a hole in that tank with a pointed instrument.

_____

5. Light from the moon lit up the path that we were following.

_____

EXERCISE 1.33: SYNONYM SUMMARY

Each line, when completed, should have three words similar in meaning. Enter all missing letters, as in 1, below.

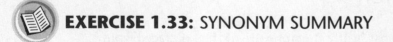

1. s _e_ _a_ rch   _r_ _a_ _n_ sack   rum _m_ _a_ _g_ _e_

2. per ___ l   dan ___ ___ ___   ___ ___ ___ pardy

3. sp __ __ d   __ __ lerity   __ __ __ __ city

4. __ __ set   __ __ __ __ turn   cap __ __ __ __

5. quarrel __ __ __ __ bel __ __ __ __ rent   conten __ __ __ __ __

6. d __ __ th   __ __ mise   __ __ cease

7. __ __ rage   __ __ furi __ __ __   in __ __ __ __ se

8. p __ __ rce   per __ __ __ __ __   punc __ __ __ __

9. clam __ r   __ __ roar   __ i __

10. bri __ __ ten   __ __ ght   __ __ lum __ __ __ __ __

11. arg __ __   __ __ sert   __ __ __ tend

12. __ __ gether   __ __ __ currently   __ __ __ __ __ taneously

13. sw __ mp   delu __ __   in __ __ date

14. different __ __ te   rec __ __ nize   disting __ __ sh

15. __ __ __ live   out __ __ st   surv __ __ __

16. rev __ __ l   __ __ __ close   di __ __ __ ge

17. __ __ terward   lat __ __   __ __ __ sequently

18. __ __ large   ampl __ fy   magn __ __ __

19. __ __ danger   imp __ __ __ __   j __ __ pard __ __ __

20. t __ __ n   __ ity   muni __ __ pal

EXERCISE 1.34: ANALOGIES

Which lettered pair of words—*a, b, c, d,* or *e*—most nearly expresses the same relationship as the capitalized pair? Write the letter of your answer in the space provided.

___ 1. AMPLIFY : ENLARGE

    a. ban : allow   *b.* survive : perish

    c. censure : commend   *d.* imperil : jeopardize

    e. specify : incense

___ 2. DROUGHT : RAIN

    a. curiosity : interest   *b.* famine : hunger

    c. aloofness : privacy   *d.* indifference : concern

    e. frankness : honesty

___ **3.** HARE : CELERITY

    a. lion : timidity   *b.* chicken : courage

    c. ant : industriousness   *d.* bat : vision

    e. spider : impatience

___ **4.** DECEASE : INTERMENT

    a. cloudburst : inundation   *b.* index : preface

    c. inauguration : election   *d.* evening : afternoon

    e. childhood : infancy

Hint: **Decease** is followed by **interment.**

___ **5.** CAPSIZE : RIGHT

    a. raze : demolish   *b.* suffice : do

    c. perforate : puncture   *d.* madden : incense

    e. damage : repair

Hint: To **capsize** is the opposite of to **right.**

___ **6.** TRESPASSER : TRAVERSE

    a. builder : construct   *b.* vendor : sell

    c. pedestrian : walk   *d.* transient : travel

    e. thief : take

Hint: A **trespasser traverses** another's property illegally.

___ **7.** RUMMAGE : SEARCH

    a. vanquish : defeat   *b.* scorch : burn

    c. simmer : boil   *d.* chill : freeze

    e. whisper : shout

___ **8.** CONTENDER : VIE

    a. emissary : send   *b.* aggressor : fear

    c. outcast : reject   *d.* victim : assault

    e. dissenter : object

___ **9.** SECRET : DIVULGE

    a. promise : keep   *b.* thorn : remove

    c. warning : ignore   *d.* defect : correct

    e. debt : pay

___ **10.** DIN : NOISE

    a. garment : shirt   *b.* vanilla : flavor

    c. coin : dime   *d.* color : purple

    e. tool : saw

Hint: A **din** is a **kind of noise.**

EXERCISE 1.35: COMPOSITION

Answer in a sentence or two.

1. Why might people in an agricultural country be famished after a long drought?

   _____

   _____

2. What information, divulged in a newspaper, could jeopardize a politician's career?

   _____

   _____

3. Is a din ever inaudible? Explain

   _____

   _____

4. What might help you survive a capsizing craft?

   _____

   _____

5. Describe a situation in which a citizen and a municipal employee might become contentious.

   _____

   _____

   _____

Pretest 6

By using the commonsense method, determine the meaning of the italicized words below.

21. "Now, the point of the story is this: Did the tiger come out of that door, or did the lady? The more we *reflect* upon this question, the harder it is to answer."—FRANK R. STOCKTON

   reflect means _____

22. According to the rules, as soon as you lose a match, you are *eliminated* from the tournament.

   eliminated means _____

23. In the midst of waxing the car, I became so *fatigued* that I had to stop for a rest.

fatigued means _____

24. Realizing that I was going the wrong way on a one-way street, I quickly *reversed* direction.

reversed means _____

25. "And he took care of me and loved me from the first, and I'll *cleave* to him as long as he lives, and nobody shall ever come between him and me."—GEORGE ELIOT

cleave means _____

26. My father is a sales agent, but I plan to go into some other *vocation*.

vocation means _____

27. Tenants usually do not stop complaining about the lack of heat until they are *content* with the temperature.

content means _____

28. The speaker kept the audience laughing with one *facetious* remark after another.

facetious means _____

29. Ms. Muldoon thought I was to blame for the whispering, unaware that the girl behind me was the true *culprit*.

culprit means _____

30. "We set out with a fresh wind...never dreaming of danger, for indeed we saw not the slightest reason to *apprehend* it."—EDGAR ALLAN POE

apprehend means _____

31. In your sentence, "She refused to accept my invitation to the party," omit the words "to accept"; they are *superfluous*.

superfluous means _____

32. In New York City, Philadelphia, Chicago, Los Angeles, and most other large *urban* centers, traffic is a serious problem.

urban means _____

33. Room 109 is too small for our club; it can *accommodate* only 35, and we have 48 members.

accommodate means _____

34. Everyone makes a mistake once in a while; no one is *infallible*.

infallible means _____

35. "Now, in the whale-ship, it is not every one that goes in the boats. Some few hands are reserved, called ship-keepers, whose *province* it is to work the vessel while the boats are pursuing the whale."—HERMAN MELVILLE

    province means _____

36. Don't dive there! The water is too *shallow*! Do you want to fracture your skull?

    shallow means _____

37. The detectives continued their search of the apartment, believing that the missing letter was *concealed* somewhere in it.

    concealed means _____

38. There are no clothing shops in the *vicinity* of the school; the nearest one is about a mile away.

    vicinity means _____

39. To halt the *pilfering* of construction materials, the builder has decided to hire security guards.

    pilfering means _____

40. "Then he advanced to the stockade, threw over his crutch, got a leg up, and with great vigor and skill succeeded in *surmounting* the fence and dropping safely to the other side." —ROBERT LOUIS STEVENSON

    surmounting means _____

Study Your Lesson Words, **Group 6**

WORD	MEANING	TYPICAL USE
accommodate (*v.*) ə-'kä-mə-,dāt	1. hold or contain without crowding or inconvenience; have room for	The new restaurant will *accommodate* 128 persons.
	2. oblige; do a favor for; furnish with something desired	I'm sorry I have no pen to lend you. Ask Norman. Perhaps he can *accommodate* you.
apprehend (*v.*) ,a-pri-'hend	1. anticipate (foresee) with fear; dread	Now I see how foolish I was to *apprehend* the outcome of the test. I passed easily.
	2. arrest	The escaped prisoners were *apprehended* as they tried to cross the border.
apprehension (*n.*)	alarm; uneasiness	
apprehensive (*adj.*)	fearful; afraid	

cleave (*v.*)
'klēv

stick; adhere; cling; be faithful

Some of the residents are hostile to new ways; they *cleave* to the customs and traditions of the past.

conceal (*v.*)
kən-'sēl

keep secret; withdraw from observation; hide; secrete

I answered all questions truthfully, for I had nothing to *conceal*.

content (*adj.*)
kän-'tent

satisfied; pleased

If you are not *content* with the merchandise, you may return it for an exchange or a refund.

culprit (*n.*)
'kəl-prət

one guilty of a fault or crime; offender; wrongdoer

The last time we were late for the party, I was the *culprit*. I wasn't ready when you called for me.

eliminate (*v.*)
i-'li-mə-,nāt

drop; exclude; remove; get rid of; rule out

The new director hopes to reduce expenses by *eliminating* unnecessary jobs.

facetious (*adj.*)
fə-'sē-shəs

given to joking; not to be taken seriously; witty; funny

Bea meant it when she said she was quitting the team. She was not being *facetious*.

fatigue (*v.*)
fə-'tēg

tire; exhaust; weary

Why not take the elevator? Climbing the stairs will *fatigue* you.

  fatigue (*n.*)

exhaustion; weariness

infallible (*adj.*)
,in-'fa-lə-bəl

incapable of being in error; sure; certain; absolutely reliable

When Phil disputes my answer or I question his, we take it to our math teacher. We consider her judgment *infallible*.

pilfer (*v.*)
'pil-fər

steal (in small amounts); purloin

The shoplifter was apprehended after *pilfering* several small articles.

province (*n.*)
'prä-vən(t)s

1. proper business or duty; sphere; jurisdiction

2. territory; region; domain

If your brother misbehaves, you have no right to punish him; that is not your *province*.

reflect (*v.*)
ri-'flekt

think carefully; meditate; contemplate

I could have given a much better answer if I had had the time to *reflect*.

reverse (*v.*)
ri-'vərs

turn completely about; change to the opposite position; revoke; annul

If found guilty, a person may appeal to a higher court in the hope that it will *reverse* the verdict.

  reverse (*n.*)

setback; defeat; reversal

In 1805, Napoleon's fleet met with a serious *reverse* at the Battle of Trafalgar.

  reversible (*adj.*)

able to be worn with either side out

shallow (*adj.*) 'sha-,lō	1. not deep	Nonswimmers must use the *shallow* part of the pool.
	2. lacking intellectual depth; superficial; uncritical	
superfluous (*adj.*) sủ-'pər-flü-əs	beyond what is necessary or desirable; surplus; needless	We already have enough volunteers; additional help would be *superfluous*.
surmount (*v.*) sər-'maủnt	conquer; overcome; climb over	At the end of the third quarter, the visitors were ahead by 18 points, a lead that our team was unable to *surmount*.
urban (*adj.*) 'ər-bən	having to do with cities or towns	In the United States today, the *urban* population far outnumbers the farm population.
vicinity (*n.*) və-'si-nə-tē	neighborhood; locality; region about or near a place	Katerina lost her keys in the *vicinity* of Pine Street and Wyoming Avenue.
vocation (*n.*) vō-'kā-shən	occupation; calling; business; trade; profession	Ruth will be studying to be an engineer. Bob plans to enter teaching. I, however, have not yet chosen a *vocation*.

Apply What You Have Learned

EXERCISE 1.36: SENTENCE COMPLETION

Fill each blank with the lesson word that best fits the meaning of the sentence.

1. Most _____ residents are _____ to live in the city, despite its many problems.

2. The warden's staff carefully searched the _____ of the zoo, hoping to _____ the escaped tiger.

3. Only after practicing law for three years did Deirdre realize that medicine was her true _____.

4. If you want your writing to be concise, you must _____ all _____ words.

5. The new auditorium can _____ three thousand people.

6. The police are empowered to arrest, but not to punish, an alleged _____ because punishment is the _____ of the courts.

7. The weary runner _____ed her exhaustion with a final burst of speed to win the six-mile race.

8. If building supplies are left unattended at the construction site, someone may _____ them.

9. After pausing to _____, the speaker _____d his position because he realized he had been completely wrong.

10. You shouldn't have taken me seriously when I boasted that my judgment is _____, for I was only being _____.

EXERCISE 1.37: SYNONYMS

Eliminate repetition by replacing the boldfaced word or words with a **synonym** from your lesson words.

_____ 1. Teaching children is not solely the **duty** of the schools; it is also a parental duty.

_____ 2. The new buses are roomier; they **have room for** thirty-six passengers.

_____ 3. There are no food shops in this neighborhood, but there are several in the **neighborhood** of the railroad station.

_____ 4. Even the experts are sometimes in error; no one is **absolutely incapable of error**.

_____ 5. A century ago, children generally followed the occupation of their elders, instead of choosing an **occupation** of their own.

_____ 6. It is not enough to get rid of spelling errors in your writing; you must also **get rid of** unnecessary words.

_____ 7. Prior to today's **defeat**, we were the only undefeated team in the league.

_____ 8. Physical exercise makes us very tired, though it does not seem to **tire** our gym instructor.

_____ 9. Progress is slow on the section of the highway near the city because of heavy **city** traffic.

_____ 10. The person initially blamed for the offense was not the real **offender**.

EXERCISE 1.38: ANTONYMS

Enter the lesson word that is most nearly the **opposite** of the boldfaced word.

1. Here, the water is _____, but a few feet out it is quite **deep**.

2. Weather forecasters are sometimes **wrong**; they are not _____.

3. Are more helpers **necessary**, or would they just be _____?

4. I felt **refreshed** by our stroll along the beach, but my companion was _____d.

5. Some are _____ with the outcome; others are **dissatisfied**.

6. The lawmakers decided to _____ some of the jobs they had just voted to **create**.

7. If you say you are famished after that filling seven-course dinner, you cannot be **serious**; you are being _____.

8. Let us _____ to the principles of law and justice; we cannot **abandon** them.

9. Facts that for years were _____ed from the public are now being **revealed**.

10. When the suspect was _____ed, her attorneys petitioned a judge to **release** her.

 EXERCISE 1.39: CONCISE WRITING

Express the thought of each sentence in **no more than four words**.

1. Are these coats able to be worn with either side out?

_____

2. The opinions that he expresses are lacking in intellectual depth.

_____

3. Most of the hotels have rooms for guests staying for only a short time.

_____

4. The remarks that she made were not intended to be taken seriously.

_____

5. We made a complete about-face and embraced the opposite point of view.

_____

EXERCISE 1.40: SYNONYM SUMMARY

Each line, when completed, should have three words similar in meaning. Enter all missing letters, as in 1, below.

1. t _i_ re ___ ex _h_ aust ___ fati _g_ _u_ _e_
2. conq __ __ r ___ __ __ __ __ come ___ __ __ __ mount
3. __ __ raid ___ fear __ __ __ ___ appre __ __ __ sive
4. occu __ __ tion ___ __ __ __ fession ___ __ __ cation
5. satisf __ __ d ___ pl __ __ sed ___ con __ __ __ __
6. n __ __ ghborhood ___ __ __ cality ___ vi __ __ __ ity
7. med __ tate ___ con __ __ __ plate ___ __ __ flect
8. h __ de ___ sec __ __ te ___ con __ eal
9. wit __ __ ___ fun __ y ___ face __ __ __ __ __
10. __ __ feat ___ __ __ __ back ___ __ __ verse
11. __ __ move ___ ex __ __ __ de ___ e __ __ __ inate
12. st __ __ l ___ __ __ __ loin ___ pilf __ __
13. need __ __ __ __ ___ surp __ __ s ___ su __ __ __ fluous
14. cl __ ng ___ __ __ here ___ cl __ __ ve
15. h __ ld ___ cont __ __ n ___ accom __ __ date
16. __ __ critical ___ superfi __ __ __ l ___ shal __ __ __
17. s __ re ___ cert __ __ n ___ in __ __ __ __ ible
18. of __ __ __ der ___ wrongd __ __ r ___ __ __ __ prit
19. d __ ty ___ b __ s __ ness ___ prov __ __ __ __
20. __ larm ___ __ __ easiness ___ ap __ __ __ hension

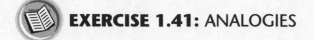

EXERCISE 1.41: ANALOGIES

Which lettered pair of words—*a, b, c, d,* or *e*—most nearly expresses the same relationship as the capitalized pair? Write the letter of your answer in the space provided.

___ 1. SHALLOW : DEEP
- *a.* remote : distant
- *b.* frigid : cold
- *c.* scarce : abundant
- *d.* transient : brief
- *e.* depressing : sad

___ 2. PROVINCE : COUNTRY
- *a.* story : edifice
- *b.* island : sea
- *c.* month : day
- *d.* hand : finger
- *e.* flock : bird

___ 3. OBLIGING : ACCOMMODATE
- *a.* timorous : complain
- *b.* reticent : gossip
- *c.* industrious : loaf
- *d.* contentious : argue
- *e.* obstinate : yield

___ 4. CULPRIT : REPRIMAND
- *a.* victim : suffer
- *b.* hostage : release
- *c.* tutor : instruct
- *d.* donor : give
- *e.* tenant : rent

___ 5. SHOPLIFTER : PILFER
- *a.* dissenter : concur
- *b.* scofflaw : obey
- *c.* transient : remain
- *d.* perjurer : lie
- *e.* vagrant : reside

___ 6. APPREHENSIVE : CONFIDENCE
- *a.* appreciative : gratitude
- *b.* cordial : warmth
- *c.* diplomatic : tact
- *d.* polite : manners
- *e.* spineless : determination

___ 7. CONTENT : DISSATISFIED
- *a.* normal : atypical
- *b.* lukewarm : tepid
- *c.* rare : extraordinary
- *d.* enthusiastic : zealous
- *e.* despotic : authoritarian

___ **8.** URBAN : CITY

    a. metropolitan : town   *b.* suburban : nation

    c. global : world   *d.* national : region

    e. municipal : state

___ **9.** MEDITATE : MIND

    a. grope : eyes   *b.* kneel : ground

    c. swelter : perspiration   *d.* speak : tongue

    e. yell : din

___ **10.** REFLECT : CONTEMPLATION

    a. confront : timidity   *b.* plan : confusion

    c. confess : guilt   *d.* swerve : collision

    e. intimidate : coercion

    Hint: When we **reflect**, we engage in **contemplation**.

EXERCISE 1.42: COMPOSITION

Answer in a sentence or two.

1. Why do stores try to apprehend people who pilfer?

_____

_____

2. Do workers feel apprehensive if their jobs may be eliminated? Why?

_____

_____

3. Tell what a culprit might try to conceal.

_____

_____

4. Why would it be superfluous to doubt an infallible person?

_____

_____

5. Does surmounting a problem make you feel content? Explain.

_____

_____

Mixed Contexts

This section deals with all types of contexts studied so far—those containing a contrasting word, a similar word, or a commonsense clue.

Pretest 7

1. "You shall hear how Hiawatha/Prayed and fasted in the forest,/Not for greater skill in hunting,/Not for greater *craft* in fishing...."—HENRY WADSWORTH LONGFELLOW.

   craft means _____

2. If you lose the key to your apartment, go to the superintendent. He has a *duplicate* of every key in our building.

   duplicate means _____

3. Geri didn't notice me in the crowd, but she spotted my brother, who is *conspicuous* because of his red hair.

   conspicuous means _____

4. Children who do not want their cereal should not be required to finish it against their *volition.*

   volition means _____

5. "Daring burglaries by armed men, and highway robberies, took place in the capital itself every night; families were publicly cautioned not to go out of town without removing their furniture to upholsterers' warehouses for *security.*"—CHARLES DICKENS

   security means _____

6. The team's uniforms were *immaculate* at the start of play, but by the end of the first quarter they were dirty with mud.

   immaculate means _____

7. Let's wait. It's raining too hard now. As soon as it *abates,* we'll make a dash for the car.

   abates means _____

8. Cows, pigs, and chickens are familiar sights to a *rural* youngster, but they are rarely seen by an urban child.

   rural means _____

9. A pound of *miniature* chocolates contains many more pieces than a pound of the ordinary size.

   miniature means _____

10. "Stubb was the second mate. He was a native of Cape Cod; and hence, according to local usage, was called a Cape-Codman. A happy-go-lucky; neither *craven* nor valiant."
    —HERMAN MELVILLE

    craven means _____

11. I expected the medicine to alleviate my cough, but it seems to have *aggravated* it.

    aggravated means _____

12. After their quarrel, Cynthia and Warren didn't talk to each other until Ann succeeded in *reconciling* them.

    reconciling means _____

13. "The Man Without a Country," by Edward Everett Hale, is not a true story; the incidents and characters are entirely *fictitious*.

    fictitious means _____

14. When traveling in Canada, you may exchange American money for Canadian *currency* at any bank.

    currency means _____

15. Some students would probably collapse if they had to run two miles; they don't have the *stamina*.

    stamina means _____

16. Donald was defeated in last year's election, but that won't *deter* him from running again.

    deter means _____

17. Several neutral countries are trying to get the *belligerent* nations to stop fighting.

    belligerent means _____

18. Company and union officials have been in conference around the clock in an attempt to reach an *accord* on wages.

    accord means _____

19. The fight might have been serious if a passerby had not *intervened* and sent the participants on their way.

    intervened means _____

20. Our band now has four players and, if you join, it will become a *quintet*.

    quintet means _____

Study Your Lesson Words, **Group 7**

WORD	MEANING	TYPICAL USE
abate (*v.*) ə-'bāt	1. become less; decrease; diminish; let up	The water shortage is *abating,* but it is still a matter of some concern.
	2. make less; reduce; moderate	Helen's close defeat in the tennis tournament has not *abated* her zeal for the game.
abatement (*n.*)	slackening; letup	
accord (*n.*) ə-'kȯrd	agreement; understanding	If both sides to the dispute can be brought to the conference table, perhaps they can come to an *accord*.
accord (*v.*)	agree; correspond	Check to see if your definition *accords* with the one in the dictionary.
aggravate (*v.*) 'a-grə-ˌvāt	make worse; worsen; intensify	If your sunburn itches, don't scratch; that will only *aggravate* it.
belligerent (*adj.*) bə-'li-jə-rənt	fond of fighting; warlike; combative	Bert still has a tendency to settle his arguments with his fists. When will he learn that it's childish to be so *belligerent*?
conspicuous (*adj.*) kən-'spi-kyə-wəs	noticeable; easily seen; prominent; striking	Among Manhattan's skyscrapers, the Empire State Building is *conspicuous* for its superior height.
craft (*n.*) 'kraft	1. skill; art; trade	The weavers of Oriental rugs are famous for their remarkable *craft*.
	2. skill or art in a bad sense; guile	The Greeks took Troy by *craft*; they used the trick of the wooden horse.
crafty (*adj.*)	sly; cunning	
craven (*adj.*) 'krā-vən	cowardly; dastardly; pusillanimous; gutless	Henry Fleming thought he would be a hero, but as the fighting began he fled from the field in *craven* fear.
craven (*n.*)	coward; dastard	
currency (*n.*) 'kər-ən(t)-sē	something in circulation as a medium of exchange; money; coin; bank notes	Some New England tribes used beads as *currency*.

deter (*v.*)
di-'tər

turn aside through fear; discourage; hinder; keep back

The heavy rain did not *deter* people from coming to the play. Nearly every seat was occupied.

duplicate (*n.*)
'dü-pli-kət

one of two things exactly alike; copy; reproduction

If the photocopying machine had been working, I could have made a *duplicate* of my history notes for my friend who was absent.

fictitious (*adj.*)
fik-'ti-shəs

1. made up; imaginary; not real

In JOHNNY TREMAIN, there are *fictitious* characters like Johnny and Rab, as well as real ones, like Samuel Adams and Paul Revere.

2. false; pretended; assumed for the purpose of deceiving

The suspect said she lived at 423 Green Street, but she later admitted it was a *fictitious* address.

immaculate (*adj.*)
i-'ma-kyə-lət

spotless; without a stain; absolutely clean; unblemished

The curtains were spotless; the tablecloth was *immaculate,* too.

intervene (*v.*)
,in-tər-'vēn

1. occur between; be between; come between

More than two months *intervene* between a president's election and the day he takes office.

2. come between to help settle a quarrel; intercede; interfere

Ralph is unhappy that I stepped into the dispute between him and his brother. He did not want me to *intervene*.

intervention (*n.*)

interference; interposition

miniature (*adj.*)
'mi-nē-ə-,chu̇r

small; tiny

Kim has a *miniature* stapler in her bag. It takes up very little room.

quintet (*n.*)
kwin-'tet

group of five

A basketball team, because it has five players, is often called a *quintet*.

reconcile (*v.*)
're-kən-,sīl

1. cause to be friends again; restore to friendship or harmony

Pat and Tom are friends again. I wonder who *reconciled* them.

2. settle; resolve

We are friends again; we have *reconciled* our differences.

rural (*adj.*)
'ru̇r-əl

having to do with the country (as distinguished from the city or town)

Six inches of snow fell in the city and up to fourteen inches in the *rural* areas upstate.

security (*n.*)
si-'kyu̇r-ə-tē

1. safety; protection

Guests are advised to deposit their valuables in the hotel's vault for greater *security*.

2. measures taken to assure protection against attack, crime, sabotage, etc.

Security has been tightened at airports.

stamina (*n.*) 'sta-mə-nə	strength; vigor; endurance	Swimming the English Channel is a feat that requires considerable *stamina*.
volition (*n.*) vō-'li-shən	act of willing or choosing; will; choice	Did the employer dismiss him, or did he leave of his own *volition*?

Apply What You Have Learned

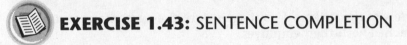 **EXERCISE 1.43:** SENTENCE COMPLETION

Fill each blank with the lesson word that best fits the meaning of the sentence.

1. Only when the United Nations _____d did the two _____ nations agree to stop fighting.

2. It is almost certain that the bitter rivals would not have reached a(n) _____ of their own _____.

3. Geraldine still lacks the _____ to go on a ski trip; her miserable cold has not _____d.

4. Since the assassination attempt, the _____ surrounding the prime minister has been particularly _____.

5. The two singers should _____ their differences; they made much better music together than they now do apart.

6. The jazz _____ has a drummer, a saxophonist, a bassist, a trumpeter, and a pianist.

7. At auction, the 1856 British Guiana one-penny postage stamp will command a huge price because it has no _____.

8. The _____ of stained-glass painting flourished during the thirteenth century.

9. I fear that my intervention will only _____ an already difficult situation.

10. Residents of the farming county insist that the construction of a large airport will not _____ with the _____ life they are determined to preserve.

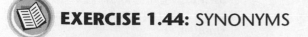

EXERCISE 1.44: SYNONYMS

Eliminate repetition by replacing the boldfaced word or words with a **synonym** from your lesson words.

_____ 1. We can settle our dispute without interference; please do not **interfere**.

_____ 2. Some urban residents who move to the country find it hard to adjust to **country** life.

_____ 3. A few of the strikers do not agree with the **agreement** tentatively reached with their employer.

_____ 4. Insert the original into the copier, and in seconds you will have a clear **copy**.

_____ 5. Antitheft devices that discourage an amateur thief may not **discourage** a professional burglar.

_____ 6. I could barely notice the moon an hour ago, but now it is much more **noticeable**.

_____ 7. The dining room is a model of cleanliness; the tablecloths and the curtains are **spotlessly clean**.

_____ 8. Since his recent excuses have been shown to be false, we suspect his earlier ones may have been **false**, too.

_____ 9. What can be done to **make** these two ex-friends **friendly again**?

_____ 10. The Armed Forces protect us. Without them we would have no **protection** against aggression.

EXERCISE 1.45: ANTONYMS

Enter the lesson word that is most nearly the **opposite** of the boldfaced word or words.

1. By no stretch of the imagination can a(n) _____ withdrawal be viewed as a **valorous** deed.

2. No _____ was reached; the meeting ended in **dissension**.

3. With a worrier, _____ problems sometimes assume **mammoth** proportions.

4. It is hard to understand why a **friendly** neighbor like Alicia should suddenly turn _____.

5. By reducing the occupants' exposure to **danger**, buckled seatbelts provide a measure of _____.

6. Employers began to **augment** their staffs as the recession _____d.

7. The stop sign was not _____; an overhanging tree limb made the warning sign **hard to see**.

8. At mealtime, an infant's _____ bib soon becomes **full of stains**.

9. Weak security does not _____ attack but tends to **encourage** it.

10. Intervention by outsiders may _____, rather than **alleviate**, the tension between the foes.

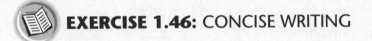

EXERCISE 1.46: CONCISE WRITING

Express the thought of each sentence in **no more than four words**.

1. The paper money that they have been using as a medium of exchange is not worth anything.

   _____

2. Hostile engagements are continuing to take place without any sign of letting up.

   _____

3. Living in the country does not cost a great deal of money.

   _____

4. The reputation that she has achieved with people in general does not have a single stain or blemish.

   _____

5. Are the measures that we have taken to protect ourselves against attack adequate to do the job?

   _____

EXERCISE 1.47: SYNONYM SUMMARY

Each line, when completed, should have three words similar in meaning. Enter all missing letters.

1. saf __ ty   __ __ __ tection   __ __ curity

2. notic __ __ ble   prom __ nent   conspic __ __ __ __

3. stain __ __ __ __   __ __ blemished   im __ __ __ __ late

4. sett __ __   __ __ solve   rec __ __ __ ile

5. disc __ __ rage   hind __ __   d __ t __ r

6. str __ __ __ th   vig __ __   stam __ __ __

7. combat __ __ __   __ __ __ like   bel __ __ __ erent

8. let __ p   slack __ __ ing   __ bat __ ment

9. interf __ __ __   in __ __ __ vene   __ __ terc __ __ __

10. __ ly   cun __ __ __ __   cr __ __ ty

11. __ gree   __ __ __ respond   __ __ cord

12. fal __ __   __ __ __ ginary   ficti __ __ __ __ __

13. __ ill   choi __ __   __ __ lition

14. gutl __ __ __   __ __ __ illanimous   __ rave __

15. wors __ __   intens __ __ __   __ __ grav __ __ __

16. sm __ __ __   __ __ ny   min __ __ ture

17. mon __ __   __ oi __   curr __ __ __ __

18. __ opy   __ __ prod __ __ tion   __ __ __ __ icate

19. dast __ __ __   cow __ __ __   __ __ __ ven

20. in __ __ __ ference   __ __ terpo __ __ tion __ __ __ __ __ vention

 ### EXERCISE 1.48: ANALOGIES

Which lettered pair of words—*a, b, c, d,* or *e*—most nearly expresses the same relationship as the capitalized pair? Write the letter of your answer in the space provided.

___ **1.** QUINTET : FIVE

    a. decade : year   *b.* dozen : gross

    c. score : twenty   *d.* liter : quart

    e. ounce : pound

___ **2.** RURAL : COUNTRY

    a. urban : population   *b.* local : vicinity

    c. initial : conclusion   *d.* terminal : beginning

    e. parallel : line

___ **3.** IMMACULATE : SPOT

    a. infinite : end   *b.* significant : meaning

    c. erroneous : fault   *d.* unanimous : support

    e. mute : silence

____ **4.** SENTINEL : SECURITY

    a. child : supervision   *b.* motorist : insurance

    c. coach : competition   *d.* proprietor : risk

    e. companion : company

____ **5.** PROMINENT : SEE

    a. cumbersome : carry   *b.* complex : understand

    c. fragile : break   *d.* inconspicuous : notice

    e. faint : hear

____ **6.** AGGRAVATE : WORSE

    a. facilitate : difficult   *b.* rectify : correct

    c. nullify : valid   *d.* elucidate : obscure

    e. complicate : simple

____ **7.** WRITING : CRAFT

    a. skill : reading   *b.* science : biology

    c. patience : virtue   *d.* education : ignorance

    e. sobriety : fault

____ **8.** BELLIGERENT : CONTENTION

    a. craven : valor   *b.* underhanded : deception

    c. frank : concealment   *d.* reserved : conversation

    e. honest : fraud

____ **9.** RECONCILE : ESTRANGE

    a. succeed : precede   *b.* vanquish : surmount

    c. abandon : neglect   *d.* abate : moderate

    e. accommodate : oblige

____ **10.** CHICKEN : PUSILLANIMOUS

    a. hawk: timid   *b.* tortoise : speedy

    c. swan : awkward   *d.* dove : warlike

    e. bat : blind

 EXERCISE 1.49: COMPOSITION

Answer in a sentence or two.

1. Describe how being belligerent might aggravate an argument.

_____

_____

2. If two friends weren't speaking to each other, how might you intervene to reconcile them?

_____

_____

3. Would making miniature dollhouse furniture require special craft? Explain.

_____

_____

4. What might families in a rural area do to guard their security?

_____

_____

5. Would you be making a fictitious claim if you said your bedroom was immaculate? Why or why not?

_____

_____

Pretest 8

Write the meaning of the italicized word in the space provided.

21. "...I doubted not that I might one day, by taking a voyage, see with my own eyes the little fields, houses, and trees, the *diminutive* people, the tiny cows...."—CHARLOTTE BRONTË

diminutive means _____

22. Walter left, saying he would return *presently,* but he was gone for a long time.

presently means _____

23. If you miss the bus, you have the choice of walking or waiting an hour for the next bus. There is no other *alternative.*

alternative means _____

24. My aim for this weekend is to finish my history and English assignments. I shall be disappointed if I cannot achieve this *objective.*

objective means _____

25. "In most books, the *I,* or first person, is omitted; in this it will be *retained*...."
—HENRY DAVID THOREAU

retained means _____

26. The Goodmans don't mind leaving their children in your *custody* because you are an excellent babysitter.

custody means _____

27. Is it fair for the partner who made the smaller investment to receive the *major* share of the profits?

major means _____

28. Most people will change their minds when shown they are wrong, but not Timothy. He is too *opinionated*.

opinionated means _____

29. Last year, I shared a gym locker with another student. Now I have one *exclusively* for myself.

exclusively means _____

30. "Perceiving myself in a *blunder,* I attempted to correct it."—EMILY BRONTË

blunder means _____

31. Some volcanoes have erupted in recent times; others have been *dormant* for many years.

dormant means _____

32. Frequent absences will make you fall behind in your work and *imperil* your chances of passing.

imperil means _____

33. There were no soft drinks. The only *beverages* on the menu were milk, coffee, tea, and hot chocolate.

beverages means _____

34. Two girls at the next table started quarreling, but I couldn't learn what their *controversy* was about.

controversy means _____

35. "As the news of my arrival spread through the kingdom, it brought *prodigious* numbers of rich, idle, and curious people to see me; so that the villages were almost emptied...."
—JONATHAN SWIFT

prodigious means _____

36. Everyone in the class must take the final examination to pass the course. No student is *exempt*.

exempt means _____

37. Don't put off what you should do today to "tomorrow," or "next week," or simply "later." Stop *procrastinating*.

procrastinating means _____

38. My fears of the dentist were *dispelled* when I had a relatively painless first visit.

dispelled means _____

39. Dad fell behind in his work at the office because of a *protracted* illness lasting several weeks.

protracted means _____

40. "For though Lorna's father was a nobleman of high and goodly *lineage*, her mother was of yet more ancient and renowned descent...."—Richard D. Blackmore

lineage means _____

Study Your Lesson Words, Group 8

WORD	MEANING	TYPICAL USE
alternative (*n.*) ȯl-'tər-nə-tiv	1. choice; one of two or more things offered for choice 2. other or remaining choice	If given the choice of making either an oral or a written report, I would pick the second *alternative*.
beverage (*n.*) 'bev-rij	drink; liquid for drinking	Orange juice is a healthful *beverage*.
blunder (*n.*) 'blən-dər	mistake or error caused by stupidity or carelessness	Have you ever committed the *blunder* of mailing a letter without a postage stamp?
controversy (*n.*) 'kän-trə-vər-sē	dispute; quarrel; debate; strife	The Republicans and the Democrats have been engaged in a *controversy* over which party is responsible for the increased taxes.
controversial (*adj.*)	arousing controversy; contentious; disputatious	
custody (*n.*) 'kəs-tə-dē	care; safekeeping; guardianship	The treasurer has *custody* of our club's financial records.
diminutive (*adj.*) də-'mi-nyə-tiv	below average size; small; tiny	To an observer in an airplane high over the city, even the largest buildings seem *diminutive*.
dispel (*v.*) di-'spel	drive away by scattering; scatter; disperse	The two officers were commended for their skill in *dispelling* the mob and preventing violence.

dormant (*adj.*) 'dȯr-mənt	inactive, as if asleep; sleeping; quiet; sluggish; resting	In early spring, new buds begin to appear on trees and shrubs that have been *dormant* all winter.
exclusively (*adv.*) iks-'klü-siv-lē	solely; without sharing with others; undividedly	Mrs. Lopez had bought the computer for all of her children, but the oldest behaved as if it were *exclusively* his.
exclusive (*adj.*)	sole; single; unshared	
exempt (*adj.*) ig-'zem(p)t	freed or released from a duty, liability, or rule to which others are subject	A certain portion of each person's income is legally *exempt* from taxation.
exemption (*n.*)	immunity; impunity	
imperil (*v.*) im-'per-əl	endanger; jeopardize	The fishing vessel was *imperiled* by high winds, but it managed to reach port safely.
lineage (*n.*) 'li-nē-ij	descent (in a direct line from a common ancestor); ancestry; family; extraction	A study of Franklin D. Roosevelt's *lineage* shows that he was descended from a Dutch ancestor who settled in America about 1638.
major (*adj.*) 'mā-jər	greater; larger; more important; principal	When the *major* companies in an industry raise prices, the smaller ones usually follow suit.
objective (*n.*) əb-'jek-tiv	aim or end (of an action); goal	Our fund has already raised $650; its *objective* is $1000.
objective (*adj.*)	involving facts, rather than personal feelings or opinions	College admissions committees consider two kinds of data: subjective evidence, such as letters of recommendation; and *objective* evidence, such as your scores on college-entrance tests.
opinionated (*adj.*) ə-'pin-yə-,nā-təd	unduly attached to one's own opinion; obstinate; stubborn	If you keep arguing that you are right, in the face of overwhelming objective evidence that you are wrong, you are *opinionated*.
presently (*adv.*) 'pre-zᵊnt-lē	in a little time; shortly; soon; before long	We won't have to wait long for our bus. It will be here *presently*.
procrastinate (*v.*) prə-'kras-tə-,nāt	put things off; delay; postpone; defer; dawdle	When a book is due, return it to the library promptly. Otherwise you will be fined 10¢ for every day you *procrastinate*.

prodigious (*adj.*) prə-'di-jəs	extraordinary in size, quantity, or extent; vast; enormous; huge; amazing	The average American city requires a *prodigious* amount of fresh milk daily.
prodigy (*n.*)	something extraordinary; wonder; phenomenon	
protract (*v.*) prō-'trakt	draw out; lengthen in time; prolong; extend	The visitors had planned to stay for a few hours only, but they were persuaded to *protract* their visit.
retain (*v.*) ri-'tān	keep; continue to have, hold, or use	The corporation will close its restaurants but *retain* its most profitable clothing stores.
retentive (*adj.*)	having the power to retain or remember; tenacious	Dora has a *retentive* memory.

Apply What You Have Learned

 EXERCISE 1.50: SENTENCE COMPLETION

Fill each blank with the lesson word that best fits the meaning of the sentence.

1. When Reuben learned Friday that the library would close for the weekend, he realized what a(n) _____ it was to have _____d with his research paper.

2. We must stop quarreling. If this committee spends another hour in _____ it will be unable to achieve its _____.

3. To _____ the workers' apprehensions of losing their jobs, the new employer promised to _____ all of them.

4. Most of the time, Pam has to share a swimming lane with others, but today she had one _____ for herself.

5. Though many of the secondary roads are impassable, the _____ highways have all been plowed.

6. Replacing the old bridge will cost a(n) _____ amount of money, but there is no practical _____.

7. Neither side is inclined to _____ the dispute much longer; a settlement is expected _____.

8. In the days of special privilege, individuals of royal _____ were generally _____ from taxation.

9. We stopped for a(n) _____ to quench our thirst.

10. When the parents are at work, the children are in the _____ of their grandparents.

EXERCISE 1.51: SYNONYMS

Eliminate repetition by replacing the boldfaced word or words with a **synonym** from your lesson words.

_____ 1. You can leave the dogs in Antoine's **care**; he will take excellent care of them.

_____ 2. Elections with only one choice are a farce because the voters have no **other choice**.

_____ 3. Grace cannot be held solely responsible if the accident was not **solely** her fault.

_____ 4. People make the common **mistake** of mistaking one of the twins for the other.

_____ 5. Two quarrelsome members are responsible for most of the **quarreling** in the club.

_____ 6. We decided not to **prolong** our conversation since we had been on the telephone long enough.

_____ 7. When asked what I wanted to drink, I asked for a cold **drink**.

_____ 8. You may have the original, and we will **keep** the copy.

_____ 9. She traces her ancestors back several generations, but I know little about my own **ancestry**.

_____ 10. People with an enormous appetite for knowledge usually do an **enormous** amount of reading.

EXERCISE 1.52: ANTONYMS

Enter the lesson word that is most nearly the **opposite** of the boldfaced word or words.

1. In spring, many living things that have been _____ all winter gradually become **active** again.

2. Unfortunately, _____ has developed; there had been a period of total **absence of strife**.

3. The residents _____ed by the flood are now **out of danger**.

4. When her term expires, she will **give up** the presidency but _____ her seat on the executive board.

5. We were planning to _____ our stay, when an unforeseen shortage of funds caused us instead to **curtail** it.

6. Some **minor** issues remain to be settled, but the _____ ones have all been resolved.

7. When that _____ blue spruce was planted a score of years ago, it was a **tiny** seedling.

8. Everything you buy is not necessarily **subject** to the sales tax; food purchases, for example, may be _____.

9. In the search for truth, _____ considerations are more reliable than those **based on feelings or opinions**.

10. For every person who does **not put off today's work to some other time**, there are many who _____.

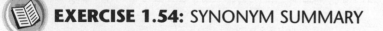 **EXERCISE 1.53:** CONCISE WRITING

Express the thought of each sentence in **no more than four words**.

1. Does this belong to you alone and to no one else?

_____

2. They will bring the meeting to a close in a little while.

_____

3. What are the choices that are being offered to us?

_____

4. The individuals on both sides are unduly attached to their own opinions.

_____

5. We presented evidence that is based on fact, rather than on what people think or feel.

_____

EXERCISE 1.54: SYNONYM SUMMARY

Each line, when completed, should have three words similar in meaning. Enter all missing letters.

1. d __ scent   an __ estry   lin __ __ ge

2. prol __ ng   __ __ tend   __ __ __ tract

3. err __ __   __ __ __ take   __ __ under

4. s __ __ n   __ __ ortly   __ __ __ sently

5. dr __ nk   liq __ __ d   __ ever __ __ __

6. go __ l   __ __ m   __ __ jective

7. s __ le   __ shared   ex __ __ __ sive

8. c __ re   __ ardianship   __ us __ __ __ __

9. d __ lay   d __ __ dle   __ __ __ __ __ __ __ tinate

10. d __ sp __ rse   __ cat __ __ __   __ __ spel

11. __ __ danger   __ __ __ pardize   __ __ peril

12. extr __ __ rdinary   __ norm __ __ __   __ __ __ dig __ __ us

13. __ mall   t __ ny   __ __ min __ tive

14. h __ ld   k __ __ p   __ __ tain

15. __ __ munity   imp __ nity   __ __ __ mption

16. stub __ __ __ __   __ __ stin __ te   opin __ __ nated

17. r __ sting   slug __ __ sh   dorm __ __ __

18. content __ __ __ __   dis __ __ tatious   __ __ __ troversial

19. l __ rger   princip __ __   __ __ jor

20. w __ nder   __ __ enomenon   __ __ __ digy

 EXERCISE 1.55: ANALOGIES

Which lettered pair of words—*a, b, c, d,* or *e*—most nearly expresses the same relationship as the capitalized pair? Write the letter of your answer in the space provided.

___   1. MILK : BEVERAGE

      a. utensil : fork   *b.* spider : web

      c. distance : mile   *d.* moccasin : shoe

      e. metal : aluminum

___   2. CONTROVERSY : HARMONY

      a. expertise : experience   *b.* shallowness : depth

      c. wealth : means   *d.* tact : judgment

      e. inundation : precipitation

___   3. OPINIONATED : LISTEN

      a. docile : obey   *b.* extravagant : squander

      c. alert : observe   *d.* submissive : yield

      e. suspicious : trust

___ **4.** PRODIGIOUS : AMAZEMENT
   a. irrational : admiration
   b. subjective : infallibility
   c. controversial : accord
   d. inconspicuous : attention
   e. outrageous : indignation

___ **5.** SCATTER : DISPEL
   a. adjourn : convene
   b. divulge : secrete
   c. expel : admit
   d. meddle : intervene
   e. disoblige : accommodate

___ **6.** TENACIOUS : HOLD
   a. belligerent : contend
   b. permissive : ban
   c. persistent : relinquish
   d. disputatious : assent
   e. reticent : inform

___ **7.** BLUNDER : IGNORANCE
   a. infection : fever
   b. flu : virus
   c. needle : perforation
   d. rumor : panic
   e. explosion : din

___ **8.** EXEMPTION : PRIVILEGE
   a. exclamation : sigh
   b. asset : liability
   c. interval : fortnight
   d. reading : skill
   e. vehicle : van

___ **9.** INDOLENT : PROCRASTINATE
   a. implacable : forgive
   b. conservative : change
   c. curious : inquire
   d. timid : protest
   e. indifferent : care

___ **10.** SHIFTLESS : OBJECTIVE
   a. crafty : cunning
   b. wary : caution
   c. disgruntled : complaint
   d. partial : prejudice
   e. callous : sympathy

EXERCISE 1.56: COMPOSITION

Answer in a sentence or two.

1. Can procrastinating imperil a student's success in school? How?

_____

_____

2. Do great writers and artists have diminutive or prodigious talents? Explain.

_____

_____

3. Why do opinionated people often find themselves in controversies?

_____

_____

4. Describe one of the major blunders of your life.

_____

_____

5. Is it better to dispel or retain fears about your ability to succeed? Why?

_____

_____

2

Enlarging Vocabulary Through Central Ideas

What is a central idea?

Examine these words: *devour, edible, glutton, luscious, palatable, voracious.* What do they have in common?

As you may have guessed, these words revolve around the idea of *eating.* We may therefore call *EATING* the central idea of this word group.

Every central idea discussed in this book has several words that we can associate with it. For example, under *DISAGREEMENT* we may *include antagonize, discord, discrepancy, dissent, irreconcilable,* and *wrangle.* Similarly, we may group *bulwark, dynamic, impregnable, invigorate, robust,* and *vigor* under the central idea *STRENGTH.*

In this chapter you will enlarge your vocabulary by learning words grouped under twenty central ideas like *EATING, DISAGREEMENT,* and *STRENGTH.*

Why study words through central ideas?

When you study vocabulary by the central-ideas method, you are dealing with groups of related words. Each word you learn helps you with some other word, or words, in the group. Consider, for example, the words *frugal* and *economize* that you will meet under POVERTY. *Frugal* means "thrifty" or "avoiding waste." To *economize* is to "cut down expenses" or to "be frugal." Notice that *economize* can strengthen your grasp of *frugal,* and vice versa. As a result, you should be better able to understand, as well as use, both *frugal* and *economize.* By the interesting central-ideas method, you can effectively learn many words in a short time.

How to use this vocabulary chapter

To get the most out of this chapter, follow these suggestions:

1. Notice the spelling. Then pronounce the word, using the pronunciation indicated below it.

2. Learn all the definitions in the MEANING column.

3. Pay particular attention to the TYPICAL USE column. Each sentence has been constructed to help you fix in mind the meaning and use of a new word. Follow up by constructing, at least in your mind, a similar sentence using your own context.

4. Do the exercises thoughtfully, not mechanically. Then review each word you have missed.

5. Make a point of *using* newly learned words whenever appropriate: in class discussions, informal conversations, compositions, and letters. A new word does not become a part of your vocabulary until you have *used* it a few times.

CENTRAL IDEAS 1–5

Pretest 1

Insert the *letter* of the best answer in the space provided.

1. If you are *versatile*, you _____.

   (A) like sports   (B) are easily angered   (C) can do many things well

2. You have no reason to be *apprehensive*. Stop _____.

   (A) boasting   (B) worrying   (C) arguing

3. When you are *rash*, you are _____.

   (A) taking risks   (B) not in a hurry   (C) too cautious

4. *Affluent* people are _____.

   (A) polite   (B) poor   (C) very wealthy

5. Since we have _____, we don't have to be *frugal*.

   (A) no means   (B) more than enough   (C) very little

THE ANSWERS ARE
1. C   2. B   3. A   4. C   5. B

As you work through Central Ideas 1–5, you will become familiar with several interesting and useful words, including the italicized words on which you have just been tested.

1. Skill

WORD	MEANING	TYPICAL USE
adroit (*adj.*) ə-'droit	expert in using the hands or mind; skillful; clever; deft; dexterous	Our *adroit* passing enabled us to score four touchdowns.
ambidextrous (*adj.*) ,am-bi-'dek-strəs	able to use both hands equally well	Ruth is an *ambidextrous* hitter; she can bat right-handed or left-handed.
apprentice (*n.*) ə-'pren-təs	person learning an art or trade under a skilled worker; learner; beginner; novice; tyro	Young Ben Franklin learned the printing trade by serving as an *apprentice* to his half brother James.
aptitude (*n.*) 'ap-tə-,tüd	natural tendency to learn or understand; bent; talent	Cindy is not clumsy with tools; she has mechanical *aptitude*.
craftsperson (*n.*) 'krafts-,pər-sᵊn	skilled worker; artisan	To build a house, you need the services of carpenters, bricklayers, plumbers, and electricians; each one must be a skilled *craftsperson*.
dexterity (*n.*) dek-'ster-ə-tē	skill in using the hands or mind; deftness; adroitness; expertise	You can't expect an apprentice to have the same *dexterity* as a skilled worker.
maladroit (*adj.*) ,ma-lə-'droit	clumsy; inept; awkward	A *maladroit* worker banged his thumb with a hammer.
versatile (*adj.*) 'vər-sə-tᵊl	capable of doing many things well; many-sided; all-around	Leonardo da Vinci was remarkably *versatile*. He was a painter, sculptor, architect, musician, engineer, and scientist.

EXERCISE 2.1: SKILL WORDS

Complete the partially spelled skill word, as in 1, below.

1. If you have musical a p t it u d e , you ought to learn to play an instrument.

2. A century ago, one learned a trade by serving as a(n) ___ ___ ___ **rent** ___ ___ ___.

3. Janet is a(n) ___ ___ ___ **sat** ___ ___ ___ athlete with letters in swimming, tennis, and volleyball.

4. When I injured my right hand, I realized what an advantage it must be to be ___ ___ **bid** ___ ___ ___ ___ ___ ___ ___.

5. A(n) ___ **rafts** ___ ___ ___ ___ ___ ___'s dexterity with tools is the result of years of experience.

2. *Poverty*

destitute (*adj.*)
ˈdes-tə-ˌtüt
not possessing the necessities of life, such as food, shelter, and clothing; needy; indigent
The severe earthquake killed hundreds of persons and left thousands *destitute*.

economize (*v.*)
iˈkä-nə-ˌmīz
reduce expenses; be frugal
Consumers can *economize* by buying their milk in gallon containers.

frugal (*adj.*)
ˈfrü-gəl
1. barely enough; scanty
The old man had nothing to eat but bread and cheese; yet he offered to share this *frugal* meal with his visitor.

2. avoiding waste; economical; sparing; saving; thrifty
My weekly allowance for lunches and fares isn't much, but I can get by on it if I am *frugal*.

impoverish (*v.*)
im-ˈpäv-rish
make very poor; reduce to poverty; bankrupt; ruin; pauperize
The increase in dues of only a dollar a year will not *impoverish* anyone.

indigence (*n.*)
ˈin-di-jən(t)s
poverty; penury
By hard work, countless thousands of Americans have raised themselves from *indigence* to wealth.

3. *Wealth*

affluent (*adj.*)
ˈa-flü-ənt
very wealthy; rich; opulent
The new wing to the hospital is a gift from an *affluent* humanitarian.

avarice (*n.*)
ˈa-və-rəs
excessive desire for wealth; greediness; cupidity
If manufacturers were to raise prices without justification, they could be accused of *avarice*.

avaricious (*adj.*)
ˌa-və-ˈri-shəs
greedy; grasping; covetous
An *avaricious* person likes to get and keep, but not to give or share.

covet (*v.*)
ˈkə-vət
desire; long for; crave, especially something belonging to another
Jorge *coveted* his neighbor's farm but could not get her to sell it.

dowry (*n.*)
ˈdau̇-rē
money, property, etc., that a bride brings to her husband
The *dowry* that his wife brought him enabled the Italian engraver Piranesi to devote himself completely to art.

financial (*adj.*)
fə-ˈnan(t)-shəl
having to do with money matters; monetary; pecuniary; fiscal
People who keep spending more than they earn usually get into *financial* difficulties.

fleece (*v.*) 'flēs	(literally, to remove the wool from a sheep or a similar animal) deprive or strip of money or belongings by fraud; charge excessively for goods or services; rob; cheat; swindle	If your sister paid $9000 for that car, she was *fleeced*. The mechanic says it is worth $5500.
hoard (*v.*) 'hȯrd	save and conceal; accumulate; amass	Aunt Bonnie had a reputation as a miser who *hoarded* every penny she could get her hands on.
lavish (*adj.*) 'la-vish	1. too free in giving, using, or spending; profuse; prodigal	The young heir was warned that he would soon have nothing left if he continued to be *lavish* with money.
	2. given or spent too freely; very abundant; extravagant; profuse	Vera's composition is good, but it doesn't deserve the *lavish* praise that Linda gave it.
lucrative (*adj.*) 'lü-krə-tiv	profitable; moneymaking	Because the gift shop did not produce a sufficient profit, the owner decided to go into a more *lucrative* business.
means (*n. pl.*) 'mēnz	wealth; property; resources	To own an expensive home, a yacht, and a limousine, you have to be a person of *means*.
opulence (*n.*) 'ä-pyə-lən(t)s	wealth; riches; affluence	Dickens contrasts the *opulence* of France's nobility with the indigence of her peasants.
sumptuous (*adj.*) 'səm(p)(t)-shə-wəs	involving large expense; luxurious; costly	The car with the leather upholstery and thick rugs is beautiful but a bit *sumptuous* for my simple tastes.

EXERCISE 2.2: POVERTY AND WEALTH WORDS

Complete the partially spelled poverty or wealth word.

1. As a(n) __ __ **flu** __ __ __ nation, the United States has given billions to aid the world's needy.

2. 18th-century France was impoverished by the __ __ __ __ **use** spending of her royal family.

3. It is not surprising that needy people __ __ **vet** the possessions of prosperous neighbors.

4. The bride is bringing her husband a large dowry, as her parents are people of __ __ **an** __.

5. If it does not begin to __ **con** __ __ __ __ __ , the nation will be in serious financial trouble.

4. Fear

apprehensive (*adj.*)
‚a-pri-'hen(t)-siv

expecting something unfavorable; afraid; anxious

Apprehensive parents telephoned the school when the class was late in getting home from the museum.

cower (*v.*)
'kau̇-ər

draw back tremblingly; shrink or crouch in fear; cringe; recoil

If you stand up to your bullying sister instead of *cowering* before her, she may back down.

dastardly (*adj.*)
'das-tərd-lē

cowardly and mean

It was *dastardly* of the captain to desert the sinking vessel and leave the passengers to fend for themselves.

intimidate (*v.*)
in-'ti-mə-‚dāt

make fearful or timid; frighten; force by fear; cow; bully

The younger children would not have given up the playing field so quickly if the older ones hadn't *intimidated* them.

poltroon (*n.*)
päl-'trün

thorough coward; dastard; craven

Like the *poltroon* that he was, Tonseten hid under a bed when he saw a fight coming.

timid (*adj.*)
'ti-məd

lacking courage or self-confidence; fearful; timorous; shy

If the other team challenges us, we should accept. Let's not be so *timid*!

trepidation (*n.*)
‚tre-pə-'dā-shən

nervous agitation; fear; fright; trembling

I thought Carol would be nervous when she made her speech, but she delivered it without *trepidation*.

5. Courage

audacious (*adj.*)
ȯ-'dā-shəs

1. bold; fearlessly daring

The *audacious* sea captain set a course for uncharted waters.

2. too bold; insolent; impudent

After we had waited for about twenty minutes, an *audacious* latecomer strolled up and tried to get in at the head of our line.

audacity (*n.*)
ȯ-'da-sə-tē

nerve; rashness; temerity

Oliver Twist, nine-year-old poorhouse inmate, was put into solitary confinement when he had the *audacity* to ask for a second helping of porridge.

dauntless (*adj.*)
'dȯnt-ləs

fearless; intrepid; very brave; valiant

The frightened sailors wanted to turn back, but their *dauntless* captain urged them to sail on.

exploit (*n.*) 'ek-,sploit	heroic act; daring deed; feat	Amelia Earhart won worldwide fame for her *exploits* as an aviator.
fortitude (*n.*) 'fȯr-tə-,tüd	courage in facing danger, hardship, or pain; endurance; bravery; pluck; backbone; valor	The officer showed remarkable *fortitude* in remaining on duty despite a painful wound.
indomitable (*adj.*) in-'dä-mə-tə-bəl	incapable of being subdued; unconquerable; invincible	The bronco that would not be broken threw all its riders. It had an *indomitable* will to be free.
plucky (*adj.*) 'plə-kē	courageous; brave; valiant; valorous	After two days on a life raft, the *plucky* survivors were rescued by a helicopter.
rash (*adj.*) 'rash	overhasty; foolhardy; reckless; impetuous; taking too much risk	When you lose your temper, you may say or do something *rash* and regret it afterward.

EXERCISE 2.3: FEAR AND COURAGE WORDS

Complete the partially spelled fear or courage word.

1. Don't think you can __ __ __ __ __ __ **date** us by shaking your fists at us!

2. Queen Elizabeth I knighted Francis Drake for his __ __ __ __ __ **its** at sea.

3. The champions looked __ __ __ __ __ __ **tab** __ __ when they took the field, but we beat them.

4. Who would have thought that a(n) __ __ **mid** sophomore like Sophie would have had the courage to address so large an audience?

5. It would be __ **as** __ to drop out of school because of failure in a single test.

Review Exercises

REVIEW 1: SENTENCE COMPLETION

Fill each blank with the word from the list below that best fits the context.
Use each word only once.

affluent	apprehensive	apprentice	aptitude	avarice
craftsperson	destitute	economize	exploit	financial
fortitude	frugal	hoard	impoverish	indigence
indomitable	intimidate	lavish	lucrative	opulence

1. Many unprofitable businesses have been made _____ by immigrants who were _____ when they first arrived in this country.

2. Sir Edmund Hillary and Tenzing Norgay showed amazing _____ in 1953 when they climbed Mt. Everest, a peak that had been _____.

3. Why are some people inclined to _____ even when they have accumulated more than enough? Can it be _____?

4. No one would expect a(n) _____ to have the expertise of a(n) _____.

5. Gertrude Ederle's early _____ for swimming marked her for future greatness. When she swam the English Channel—the first woman to do so—she broke the men's speed record for that swim. What a(n) _____!

6. The Wall Street crash of 1929 reduced countless investors from _____ to _____.

7. When _____ spenders suddenly lose their jobs, they may wish that they had been more _____ in managing their money.

8. The violent storm did not seem to _____ the crew, but it made the passengers _____.

9. Soaring outlays for employee pension and medical benefits can bring a(n) _____ corporation to the brink of _____ ruin.

10. If we do not _____ in the use of our precious natural resources, we will _____ our country.

REVIEW 2: SYNONYMS

Avoid repetition by replacing the boldfaced word with a **synonym** from the following list. See 1, below.

anxious	bent	indigent	fleece	pluck
pauperize	invincible	cow	lucrative	affluence

bent_____ 1. Cheryl is talented in many areas, but she has no **talent** for dramatics.

_____ 2. In a time of need, the **needy** look to the government for help.

_____ 3. Wealthy people tend to associate with people of **wealth**.

_____ 4. Conquerors often commit the blunder of believing they are **unconquerable**.

_____ 5. Don't let that bully **bully** you.

_____ 6. A sales tax is no way to fight poverty because it will more deeply **impoverish** whose who are already impoverished.

_____ 7. It has not been a **profitable** year. Profits are way down.

_____ 8. Don't be **afraid**. There is nothing to be afraid of.

_____ 9. The press lauded the courageous rescuers for their **courage**.

_____ 10. Know with whom you are dealing if you do not want to be cheated. A reputable firm will not **cheat** you.

REVIEW 3: ANTONYMS

Enter the word from the following list that is most nearly the **opposite** of the boldfaced word or words. See 1, below.

adroit	dastardly	destitute	economize	undercharge
frugal	enrich	unprofitable	rash	sumptuous

1. Dictators ___enrich___ themselves but **impoverish** their subjects.

2. An **inept** person cannot provide the _____ leadership that we need.

3. This is a time to _____, rather than to **increase expenses**.

4. When funds are low, one must be _____ to survive; **wasteful** spending cannot be tolerated.

5. Under questioning, the accused tend to be **cautious**, knowing that _____ answers can make problems for them.

6. Attacking unarmed civilians is a(n) _____ deed, but the aggressor considered it a **daring** act.

7. At first the thief claimed he stole from the **opulent** only to aid the _____.

8. The purchase of Alaska, which many had regarded as _____, turned out to be quite **lucrative**.

9. Investigation showed that the customers who thought they had been **fleeced** were in fact _____d.

10. Most gift shoppers look for items **that involve little expense**; they cannot afford _____ merchandise.

REVIEW 4: CONCISE WRITING

Express the thought of each sentence below in **no more than four words.**

1. There are millions of people who lack the basic necessities of life, such as food, shelter, and clothing.

_____

2. Employees who are in the process of learning a trade under the guidance of a skilled worker do not receive very high salaries.

_____

3. Those who practice the art of swindling charge their victims excessively for goods and services.

_____

4. There are occasions when people are inclined to do things that entail altogether too much risk.

_____

5. Those who have no confidence in themselves lack the courage to face danger, hardship, or pain.

_____

REVIEW 5: SYNONYM SUMMARY

Each line, when completed, should have three words similar in meaning. Supply the missing letters, as in 1, below.

1. p _a_ _u_ perize	bankr _u_ pt	_i_ _m_ poverish
2. f __ __ lhardy	impet __ ous	__ ash
3. mon __ tary	pec __ niary	finan __ __ al
4. n __ vice	t __ ro	apprent __ ce
5. n __ rve	tem __ rity	__ __ dacity
6. pr __ f __ se	prod __ gal	lav __ __ __
7. __ __ kward	in __ pt	maladr __ __ t
8. __ mass	accum __ late	h __ __ rd
9. val __ __ nt	__ __ trepid	d __ __ ntless
10. pov __ rty	pen __ ry	ind __ gence
11. cr __ ve	d __ sire	c __ v __ t
12. cr __ nge	__ __ coil	cow __ __
13. t __ lent	b __ nt	__ __ titude
14. gr __ __ diness	cup __ dity	av __ r __ ce
15. trem __ ling	__ right	tr __ p __ dation
16. l __ x __ rious	cost __ __	sum __ __ uous
17. unconq __ __ rable	invin __ __ ble	ind __ mit __ ble
18. gr __ sping	covet __ __ s	ava __ __ cious
19. __ __ rifty	__ __ __ nomical	fr __ g __ l
20. adr __ __ tness	exp __ rtise	dex __ __ rity

REVIEW 6: ANALOGIES

Which lettered pair of words—*a, b, c, d,* or *e*—most nearly expresses the same relationship as the capitalized pair? Write the letter of your answer in the space provided.

___ 1. PECUNIARY : MONEY

   a. lunar : sun
   b. meteorological : weather
   c. toxic : waste
   d. urban : nation
   e. vocational : leisure

___ 2. BUNGLER : MALADROIT

   a. scapegoat : blameworthy
   b. windbag : silent
   c. flatterer : sincere
   d. maverick : submissive
   e. jack-of-all-trades : versatile

___ 3. INTIMIDATE : COW

   a. ignore : badger
   b. praise : nag
   c. harass : hound
   d. outfox : help
   e. offend : please

___ 4. ASTRONAUT : INTREPID

   a. fact finder : objective
   b. apprentice : inattentive
   c. chauffeur : intoxicated
   d. custodian : unwary
   e. mediator : partial

___ 5. AUDACIOUS : MANNERS

   a. dauntless : courage
   b. vigorous : stamina
   c. indigent : means
   d. ambitious : goal
   e. competent : skill

___ 6. EXPLOIT : ADMIRATION

   a. blunder : self-esteem
   b. setback : prestige
   c. felony : crime
   d. repetition : interest
   e. calamity : dismay

   Hint: An **exploit** arouses **admiration**.

___ 7. ECONOMIZE : THRIFTY

   a. annoy : helpful
   b. sympathize : lukewarm
   c. worry : apprehensive
   d. bully : cordial
   e. tarry : punctual

___ 8. DEXTERITY : TRAIT
    a. whale : fish
    c. utensil : shovel
    e. bird : sparrow
    b. arrow : missile
    d. beverage : thirst

___ 9. AVARICE : PRODIGALITY
    a. enmity : hostility
    c. confidence : trust
    e. yearning : desire
    b. reluctance : unwillingness
    d. security : anxiety

___ 10. PALACE : OPULENCE
    a. prison : liberty
    c. paradise : discord
    e. sweatshop : drudgery
    b. hovel : comfort
    d. dove : belligerence

REVIEW 7: COMPOSITION

Answer in a sentence or two.

1. Would you prefer an adroit or maladroit craftsperson to build your new house? Why?

2. Why is it difficult for destitute people to economize?

3. Are avaricious parents likely to lavish money on their children? Why or why not?

4. Why would a timid child be more likely to cower than an audacious child?

5. If you were a soldier, would you prefer a leader who was plucky or rash? Why?

CENTRAL IDEAS 6–10

Pretest 2

Insert the *letter* of the best answer in the space provided.

1. An *estranged* friend is a friend _____.

   (A) you hardly know   (B) with whom you have quarreled   (C) who has moved away

2. If a criminal's name is *divulged,* it is _____.

   (A) made public   (B) kept secret   (C) legally changed

3. The two nations are old _____ because their goals almost always *correspond.*

   (A) allies   (B) rivals   (C) enemies

4. _____ is not a *condiment.*

   (A) Pepper   (B) Lettuce   (C) Mustard

5. Anything that is *latent* cannot be _____.

   (A) present   (B) hidden   (C) visible

THE ANSWERS ARE
1. B **2.** A **3.** A **4.** B **5.** C

The italicized words on which you were tested are a sample of the new vocabulary you are about to meet in Central Ideas 6–10.

6. Concealment

alias (*n.*)
ˈā-lē-əs

assumed name

Inspector Javert discovered that Monsieur Madeleine was not the mayor's real name but an *alias* for Jean Valjean, the ex-convict.

alias (*adv.*)

otherwise called; otherwise known as

Jean Valjean, *alias* Monsieur Madeleine, was arrested by Inspector Javert.

clandestine (*adj.*) klan-'des-tən	carried on in secrecy and concealment; secret; covert; underhand; undercover	Before the Revolutionary War, a patriot underground organization used to hold *clandestine* meetings in Boston.
enigma (*n.*) i-'nig-mə	puzzling statement; riddle; mystery; puzzling problem or person	I have read the sentence several times but cannot understand it. Maybe you can help me with this *enigma*.
enigmatic (*adj.*) e-,nig-'ma-tik	mysterious; puzzling; obscure	Her statement is *enigmatic*; we cannot make head or tail of it.
latent (*adj.*) 'lā-t°nt	present but not showing itself; hidden but capable of being brought to light; dormant; potential	A good education will help you discover and develop your *latent* talents.
lurk (*v.*) 'lərk	1. be hidden; lie in ambush 2. move stealthily; sneak; slink	Katherine called the police when she noticed a stranger *lurking* behind her neighbor's garage.
seclude (*v.*) si-'klüd	shut up apart from others; confine in a place hard to reach; hide; cloister; sequester	To find a quiet place to study, Amy had to *seclude* herself in the attic.
stealthy (*adj.*) 'stel-thē	secret in action or character; catlike; sly; furtive	The spy had to be very *stealthy* to get past the two guards without being noticed.

7. Disclosure

apprise (*v.*) ə-'prīz	inform; notify; advise	The magazine has *apprised* its readers of an increase in rates beginning May 1.
avowal (*n.*) ə-'vau̇-əl	open acknowledgment; frank declaration; admission; confession	The white flag of surrender is an *avowal* of defeat.
divulge (*v.*) də-'vəlj	make public; disclose; reveal; tell	I told my secret only to Margaret because I knew she would not *divulge* it.
elicit (*v.*) i-'li-sət	draw forth; bring out; evoke; extract	By questioning the witness, the attorney *elicited* that it was raining at the time of the accident.
enlighten (*v.*) in-'lī-t°n	shed the light of truth and knowledge upon; free from ignorance; inform; instruct	The newcomer was going in the wrong direction until someone *enlightened* him that his room was at the other end of the hall.

manifest (*v.*) 'ma-nə-ˌfest	show; reveal; display; evidence	I am surprised that Harriet is taking an art course because she has never, to my knowledge, *manifested* any interest in the subject.
manifest (*adj.*)	plain; clear; evident; not obscure; obvious	It is now *manifest* that the family across the street intends to move.
overt (*adj.*) ō-'vərt	open to view; not covert or hidden; public; manifest	The concealed camera recorded the *overt* acceptance of the bribe.

EXERCISE 2.4: CONCEALMENT AND DISCLOSURE WORDS

Complete the partially spelled concealment or disclosure word.

1. Price fluctuations are often __ __ __ __ **mat** __ __; we cannot tell why they occur.

2. Can I call without __ __ __ __ __ **gin** __ my identity?

3. He is confused. Will you please __ __ **light** __ __ him?

4. Two large companies were suspected of having made a **cove** __ __ agreement to fix prices.

5. It takes time for __ __ **tent** talents to show themselves.

8. *Agreement*

accede (*v.*) ak-'sēd	(usually followed by *to*) agree; assent; consent; acquiesce	When I asked my teacher if I might change my topic, he readily *acceded* to my request.
accord (*n.*) ə-'kȯrd	agreement; harmony	Though we are in *accord* on what our goals should be, we differ on the means for achieving them.
compact (*n.*) 'käm-ˌpakt	agreement; understanding; accord; covenant	The states bordering on the Delaware River have entered into a *compact* for the sharing of its water.
compatible (*adj.*) kəm-'pa-tə-bəl	able to exist together harmoniously; in harmony; agreeable; congenial	Arthur and I can't be on the same committee. We're not *compatible*.
compromise (*n.*) 'käm-prə-ˌmīz	settlement reached by a partial yielding on both sides	At first, the union and management were far apart on wages, but they finally came to a *compromise*.
conform (*v.*) kən-'fȯrm	be in agreement or harmony with; act in accordance with accepted standards or customs; comply; obey	When a new style in clothes appears, do you hasten to *conform*?

consistent (*adj.*) kən-'sis-tənt	keeping to the same principles throughout; showing no contradiction; in accord; compatible; consonant	By bringing up an unrelated matter you are not being *consistent* with your previous statement that we should stick to the topic.
correspond (*v.*) ,kär-ə-'spänd	be in harmony; match; fit; agree; be similar	The rank of second lieutenant in the Army *corresponds* to that of ensign in the Navy.
dovetail (*v.*) 'dəv-,tāl	to fit together with, so as to form a harmonious whole; interlock with	Gilbert's skill as a writer *dovetailed* with Sullivan's talent as a composer, resulting in the famous Gilbert and Sullivan operettas.
reconcile (*v.*) 're-kən-,sīl	cause to be friendly again; bring back to harmony	After their quarrel, Althea and Pat refused to talk to each other until I *reconciled* them.
relent (*v.*) ri-'lent	become less harsh, severe, or strict; soften in temper; yield	Serena gave her parents so many good reasons for letting her borrow the car that they finally *relented*.

9. Disagreement

altercation (*n.*) ,ȯl-tər-'kā-shən	noisy, angry dispute; quarrel, wrangle	We halted the *altercation* by separating the two opponents before they could come to blows.
antagonize (*v.*) an-'ta-gə-,nīz	make an enemy of; arouse the hostility of	The official *antagonized* the leader of her own party by not campaigning for him.
cleavage (*n.*) 'klē-vij	split; division; schism; chasm	We hope compromise will repair the *cleavage* in our ranks.
discord (*n.*) 'dis-,kȯrd	disagreement; dissension; strife	Billy Budd put an end to the *discord* aboard the "Rights-of-Man." He was an excellent peacemaker.
discrepancy (*n.*) dis-'kre-pən-sē	difference; disagreement; variation; inconsistency	Eighty people were at the dance but only seventy-four tickets were collected at the door. What accounts for this *discrepancy*?
dissent (*v.*) di-'sent	differ in opinion; disagree; object	The vote approving the amendment was far from unanimous; six members *dissented*.

embroil (*v.*) im-'bròil	draw into a conflict	My enthusiastic support for Lynette's candidacy soon *embroiled* me in a debate with her opponents.
estrange (*v.*) is-'trānj	turn (someone) from affection to dislike or enmity; make unfriendly; separate; alienate	A quarrel over an inheritance *estranged* the brothers for many years.
friction (*n.*) 'frik-shən	conflict of ideas between persons or parties of opposing views; disagreement	At the budget hearing, there was considerable *friction* between the supporters and the opponents of higher taxes.
irreconcilable (*adj.*) i-,re-kən-'sī-lə-bəl	unable to be brought into friendly accord or understanding; hostile beyond the possibility of reconciliation; not reconcilable; incompatible	It is doubtful whether anyone can make peace between the estranged partners; they have become *irreconcilable*.
litigation (*n.*) ,li-tə-'gā-shən	lawsuit; act or process of carrying on a lawsuit	Some business disputes can be settled out of court; others require *litigation*.
at variance ,at 'ver-ē-ən(t)s	in disagreement; at odds	Cynthia is an independent thinker. Her opinions are often *at variance* with those of the rest of our group.
wrangle (*v.*) 'raŋ-gəl	quarrel noisily; dispute angrily; brawl; bicker	When I left, two neighbors were quarreling noisily. When I returned an hour later, they were still *wrangling*.

EXERCISE 2.5: AGREEMENT AND DISAGREEMENT WORDS

Complete the partially spelled agreement or disagreement word.

1. We tried to __ __ con __ __ __ __ the two friends who had quarreled, but we failed.

2. If our bus and train schedules __ __ __ __ **tail**, we won't have to sit around in the waiting rooms.

3. Both sides must give in a little if there is to be a(n) __ __ __ __ **act**.

4. Our dog and cat are __ __ __ **pat** __ __ __ __; they get along well.

5. There is no reason for you to __ __ __ __ **oil** yourself in their altercation.

10. Eating

condiment (*n.*) 'kän-də-mənt	something (such as pepper or spices) added to or served with food to enhance its flavor; seasoning	There is a shelf in our kitchen for pepper, salt, mustard, catsup, and other *condiments*.
devour (*v.*) di-'vaủ(ə)r	eat up greedily; feast upon like an animal or a glutton; dispatch	The hikers were so hungry that they *devoured* the food as fast as it was served.
edible (*adj.*) 'e-də-bəl	fit for human consumption; eatable; comestible; nonpoisonous	Never eat wild mushrooms, even though they look *edible*. They may be poisonous.
glutton (*n.*) 'glə-tᵊn	1. greedy eater; person in the habit of eating too much	Andrea had a second helping and would have taken a third except that she didn't want to be considered a *glutton*.
	2. person with a great capacity for enduring or doing something	He is a *glutton* for punishment.
luscious (*adj.*) 'lə-shəs	delicious; juicy and sweet; delectable	Ripe watermelon is *luscious*. Everyone will want a second slice.
palatable (*adj.*) 'pa-lə-tə-bəl	agreeable to the taste; pleasing; savory	The main dish had little flavor, but I made it more *palatable* by adding condiments.
slake (*v.*) 'slāk	(with reference to thirst) bring to an end through refreshing drink; satisfy; quench	On a sultry afternoon, there is a long line of people at the drinking fountain, waiting to *slake* their thirst.
succulent (*adj.*) 'sə-kyə-lənt	full of juice; juicy	The steak will be dry if you leave it in the oven longer. Take it out now if you want it to be *succulent*.
voracious (*adj.*) vȯ-'rā-shəs	having a huge appetite; greedy in eating; gluttonous; ravenous	If Chester skips breakfast, he is *voracious* by lunchtime.

EXERCISE 2.6: EATING WORDS

Complete the partially spelled eating word.

1. There will be a choice of beverages for __ __ __ **king** your thirst.

2. Please leave some of that pie for us; don't be __ __ __ __ __ __ __ **ous**.

3. These oranges have too much pulp; they are not __ __ __ __ __ **lent**.

4. We have plenty of food on hand when our relatives come for dinner because they have __ **or** __ __ __ __ __ __ **appetites**.

5. Some prefer their food served unseasoned so that they themselves may add the __ __ __ **dim** __ __ __ **s**.

Review Exercises

 REVIEW 8: SENTENCE COMPLETION

Fill each blank with the word from the list below that best fits the context. Use each word only once.

accord	antagonize	apprise	at variance	clandestine
compatible	condiment	devour	divulge	elicit
embroil	enigma	estrange	glutton	litigation
palatable	reconcile	relent	slake	succulent

1. When the water in her canteen was consumed, the hiker _____d her thirst on some _____ berries that she found along the trail.

2. The reason for the treasurer's resignation was never _____d. To this day, it remains a(n) _____.

3. Gulliver was _____d of the king's plot to kill him by a daring friend who visited him _____ly.

4. Neither party could afford the high cost of _____, so they reached a(n) _____ out of court.

5. By intense questioning, the lawyer _____ed from the witness that her testimony was _____ with what she had told the police.

6. Though I sprinkled a heavy dose of _____s on the food I was served, I could not make it _____.

7. Several of us tried to _____ the two _____d cronies, but we succeeded only in making them more hostile to each other.

8. Mark _____d so many of his coworkers that the boss had to lecture him on the importance of being _____.

9. If she had not had to skip lunch, Sara would not have _____ed her dinner. Ordinarily, she is no _____.

10. The two neighboring countries have been _____ed with each other for centuries, and it is unlikely they will soon _____ in their hatreds.

REVIEW 9: SYNONYMS

Avoid repetition by replacing the boldfaced word or expression with a **synonym** from the list.

compact	correspond	covert	discrepancy	dovetail
edible	enlighten	luscious	manifest	wrangle

_____ 1. It was a delicious meal; the food was **delicious**.

_____ 2. Can you **inform** us about how the Johnsons are doing? We have had no information from them since they moved.

_____ 3. The truth is now **obvious** to everyone but Jack, who is obviously still confused.

_____ 4. It was no secret to our military experts that the ruthless dictator was making **secret** preparations for war.

_____ 5. Both sides agree to the truce and are ready to sign a(n) **agreement** to respect its conditions.

_____ 6. It takes an expert to distinguish poisonous mushrooms from those that are **nonpoisonous**.

_____ 7. They **quarrel noisily** all the time. They are unusually quarrelsome.

_____ 8. Here are two pieces of the picture puzzle that I cannot **fit together**. Can you help me make them fit?

_____ 9. We agree on most matters, but there are times when our views do not **agree**.

_____ 10. There is a difference between the price we paid and the price we should have paid, but fortunately it is only a slight **difference**.

REVIEW 10: ANTONYMS

Enter the word from the list below that is most nearly the **opposite** of the boldfaced word or words.

acquiesce	alienate	altercation	avoid	fit
inedible	latent	lurk	overt	unpalatable

1. Some of the catch was **fit for human consumption**; the rest was _____.

2. We had hoped for an **accord**, but the session ended in a(n) _____.

3. No sooner were they **reconciled** than they became _____d again.

4. Many now _____ fatty foods that they used to **devour**.

5. With condiments, this dish is **agreeable to my taste**; otherwise it is

_____.

6. Nobody **objected** to the proposal; all of us _____d.

7. Counterintelligence operations are **closed to public scrutiny**; they cannot be

_____.

8. Some details telephoned by civilians about strangers in their vicinity **dovetail** with the description of the escapee; others do not _____.

9. There is more to be feared from foes who _____ in the shadows than from those who **are in open view**.

10. Some of the child's talents are already **visible**; others are _____ and may emerge later.

 ## REVIEW 11: CONCISE WRITING

Express the thought of each sentence below in **no more than four words**.

1. The process of carrying on a lawsuit may cost a great deal of money.

_____

2. Lack of flexibility prevented a settlement from being reached in which each side would have yielded a little in its demands.

_____

3. The negotiations that had been carried on in secrecy failed to get anywhere.

_____

4. A conflict of ideas between parties of opposing views threatens to break up the alliance.

_____

5. The practice of lying can turn friends from affection to dislike for each other.

_____

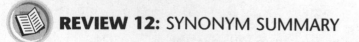 ## REVIEW 12: SYNONYM SUMMARY

Each line, when completed, should have three words similar in meaning. Enter the missing letters.

1. f __ t   m __ tch   __ __ __ __ __ __ pond

2. sep __ rate   al __ __ nate   __ __ __ range

3. sat __ __ fy

4. y __ __ ld

5. __ __ __ __ __ cover

6. sl __

7. inconsisten __ y

8. glut __ __ nous

9. dorm __ nt

10. str __ fe

11. sh __ w

12. delic __ __ __ s

13. sn __ __ k

14. agr __ __ __ ble

15. ass __ nt

16. extr __ __ t

17. seq __ __ ster

18. c __ mply

19. a __ c __ rd

20. spl __ t

q __ __ nch

sof __ en

c __ vert

f __ rtive

var __ __ tion

raven __ __ __

potent __ __ l

__ __ __ sension

__ __ __ play

__ __ lectable

__ __ ink

congen __ __ l

__ __ quiesce

__ voke

cl __ __ ster

ob __ y

coven __ nt

s __ hism

__ lake

__ __ lent

clan __ __ __ __ __ __ __

st __ __ lthy

__ __ __ crepancy

__ __ racious

late __ __

__ __ cord

m __ n __ fest

l __ s __ ious

l __ rk

comp __ t __ ble

a __ cede

el __ c __ t

__ __ clude

__ __ __ form

__ __ __ pact

cl __ __ v __ ge

REVIEW 13: ANALOGIES

Which lettered pair of words—*a, b, c, d,* or *e*—most nearly expresses the same relationship as the capitalized pair? Write the letter of your answer in the space provided.

___ 1. ENIGMA : BEWILDERMENT

    a. pain : swelling

    c. conservation : scarcity

    e. skid : icing

    b. irritability : fatigue

    d. blunder : embarrassment

___ 2. GLUTTON : FOOD

    a. alcoholic : beverages

    c. aggressor : restraint

    e. gossip : secrecy

    b. miser : hoarding

    d. workaholic : whiskey

___ 3. CLANDESTINE : SECRET

    a. gutless : dastardly   *b.* equitable : oppressive

    c. initial : terminal   *d.* evasive : frank

    e. atypical : customary

___ 4. STEALTHY : CAT

    a. gentle : mule   *b.* deliberate : hare

    c. timid : panther   *d.* lumbering : elephant

    e. blind : eagle

___ 5. COMESTIBLE : CONSUME

    a. unforgivable : condone   *b.* permissible : allow

    c. enigmatic : understand   *d.* transient : remain

    e. intolerable : endure

___ 6. MUSTARD : CONDIMENT

    a. cinnamon : appetite   *b.* bulb : socket

    c. oak : evergreen   *d.* saw : tool

    e. shrub : tree

___ 7. SLAKE : QUENCH

    a. acquiesce : object   *b.* deluge : inundate

    c. impede : expedite   *d.* ignite : extinguish

    e. squander : conserve

___ 8. SAVORY : TONGUE

    a. distinct : voice   *b.* wavy : hair

    c. melodious : ear   *d.* acute : vision

    e. desirous : fingers

___ 9. LATENT : INCONSPICUOUS

    a. manifest : invisible   *b.* toxic : nonpoisonous

    c. final : unalterable   *d.* rational : illogical

    e. tasty : unpalatable

___ 10. ALIAS : NAME

    a. wig : hair   *b.* arrow : direction

    c. razor : beard   *d.* detergent : dirt

    e. reply : inquiry

REVIEW 14: COMPOSITION

Answer in a sentence or two.

1. Why do people involved in clandestine activity often move in a stealthy way?

   _____

   _____

2. Is it necessary to divulge information that is already manifest? Why or why not?

   _____

   _____

3. Is a compromise more likely to lead to accord or discord? Explain.

   _____

   _____

4. Can you explain why people with irreconcilable differences often resort to litigation?

   _____

   _____

5. Describe a time you were embroiled in an altercation.

   _____

   _____

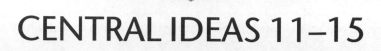

CENTRAL IDEAS 11–15

Pretest 3

Insert the *letter* of the best answer in the space provided.

1. A wait of _____ before being served is *inordinate.*
   (A) five minutes   (B) two hours   (C) thirty seconds

2. *Cogent* arguments are _____.
   (A) illogical   (B) preventable   (C) convincing

3. A *scrupulous* person has a high regard for _____.
   (A) what is right   (B) those in authority   (C) what is beautiful

4. If you feel *enervated,* you are not so _____ as usual.
   (A) bored   (B) nervous   (C) strong

5. A team that *defaults* _____ the game.
   (A) delays   (B) loses   (C) wins

> **THE ANSWERS ARE**
> **1.** B   **2.** C   **3.** A   **4.** C   **5.** B

How well did you do? Any questions that you may have missed or are uncertain about will be cleared up for you as you work through Central Ideas 11–15, which follow immediately.

11. Size, Quantity

colossal (*adj.*) kə-'lä-səl	huge; enormous; gigantic; mammoth; vast	The game was played in a *colossal* sports arena with a seating capacity of more than 60,000.
commodious (*adj.*) kə-'mō-dē-əs	spacious and comfortable; roomy; ample; not confining	It will be easy to move in the equipment because the halls and stairways are *commodious.*

gamut (*n.*) 'ga-mət	entire range of anything, as of musical notes, emotions, etc.	First I thought I had done very well, then well, and finally, poorly. I ran the *gamut* from confidence to despair.
infinite (*adj.*) 'in-fə-nət	without ends or limits; boundless; endless; inexhaustible	We do not know whether space is bounded or *infinite*.
infinitesimal (*adj.*) ,in-fi-nə-'te-sə-məl	so small as to be almost nothing; immeasurably small; very minute	If there is any salt in this soup, it must be *infinitesimal*. I can't taste it.
inflate (*v.*) in-'flāt	swell with air or gas; expand; puff up	Since one of the tires had lost air, we stopped at a gas station to *inflate* it.
inordinate (*adj.*) i-'nȯr-dᵊn-ət	much too great; not kept within reasonable bounds; excessive; immoderate	If you eat an *inordinate* amount of sweets, you are likely to gain weight.
iota (*n.*) ī-'ō-tə	(ninth and smallest letter of the Greek alphabet) very small quantity; infinitesimal amount; bit	If you make the same mistake again, despite all my warnings, I will not have one *iota* of sympathy for you.
magnitude (*n.*) 'mag-nə-,tüd	size; greatness; largeness; importance	To supervise eight hundred employees is a responsibility of considerable *magnitude*.
picayune (*adj.*) ,pi-kē-'yün	concerned with trifling matters; petty; small; of little value	In studying, don't spend too much time on *picayune* details. Concentrate on the really important matters.
pittance (*n.*) 'pi-tᵊn(t)s	small amount; meager wage or allowance	At those low wages, few will apply for the job. Who wants to work for a *pittance*?
puny (*adj.*) 'pyü-nē	slight or inferior in size, power, or importance; weak; insignificant	The skyscraper dwarfs the surrounding buildings. By comparison to it, they seem *puny*.
superabundance (*n.*) ,sü-pər-ə-'bən-dən(t)s	great abundance; surplus; excess	Ronald's committee doesn't need any more assistance. He has a *superabundance* of helpers.

EXERCISE 2.7: SIZE AND QUANTITY WORDS

Complete the partially spelled size or quantity word.

1. The homes from which students come run the __ **am** __ __ from affluence to indigence.

2. This __ __ __ **mod** __ __ __ __ sofa can accommodate four people comfortably.

3. There was a(n) __ __ __ **era** __ __ __ __ __ __ __ __ of food. We could have had several more guests for dinner.

4. The spare tire needs to be __ __ __ **late** __; it has too much air.

5. Management regards the demand for an immediate twenty percent increase in wages as __ __ __ __ **din** __ __ __.

12. Weakness

debilitate (*v.*) di-ˈbi-lə-ˌtāt	impair the strength of; enfeeble; weaken	The fever had so *debilitated* the patient that she lacked the strength to sit up.
decadent (*adj.*) ˈde-kə-dənt	marked by decay or decline; falling off; declining; deteriorating	When industry moves away, a flourishing town may quickly become *decadent*.
decrepit (*adj.*) di-ˈkre-pət	broken down or weakened by old age or use; worn out	Billy Dawes rode past the redcoats on a horse that looked *decrepit* and about to collapse.
dilapidated (*adj.*) də-ˈla-pə-ˌdā-təd	falling to pieces; decayed; partly ruined or decayed through neglect	Up the road was an abandoned farmhouse, partially in ruins, and near it a barn, even more *dilapidated*.
enervate (*v.*) ˈe-nər-ˌvāt	lessen the vigor or strength of; weaken; enfeeble	The extreme heat had *enervated* us. We had to rest under a shady tree until our strength was restored.
flimsy (*adj.*) ˈflim-zē	lacking strength or solidity; frail; unsubstantial	Judy understands algebra well, but I have only a *flimsy* grasp of the subject.
frail (*adj.*) ˈfrā(ə)l	not very strong; weak; fragile	Mountain climbing is for the robust, not the *frail*.
incapacitate (*v.*) ˌin-kə-ˈpa-sə-ˈtāt	render incapable or unfit; disable; paralyze	Ruth will be absent today. A sore throat has *incapacitated* her.
infirmity (*n.*) in-ˈfər-mə-tē	weakness; feebleness; frailty	On leaving the hospital, John felt almost too weak to walk, but he soon overcame this *infirmity*.

13. *Strength*

bulwark (*n.*)
ˈbu̇l-wərk

wall-like defensive structure; rampart; defense; protection; safeguard

For centuries the British regarded their navy as their principal *bulwark* against invasion.

citadel (*n.*)
ˈsi-tə-dᵊl

fortress; stronghold

The fortified city of Singapore was once considered unconquerable. In 1942, however, this *citadel* fell to the Japanese.

cogent (*adj.*)
ˈkō-jənt

forcible; compelling; powerful; convincing

A request for a raise is more likely to succeed if supported with *cogent* reasons.

dynamic (*adj.*)
dī-ˈna-mik

forceful; energetic; active

Audrey represents us forcefully and energetically. She is a *dynamic* speaker.

formidable (*adj.*)
ˈfȯr-mə-də-bəl

exciting fear by reason of strength, size, difficulty, etc.; hard to overcome; to be dreaded

The climbers gasped when they caught sight of the *formidable* peak.

forte (*n.*)
ˈfȯrt

strong point; that which one does with excellence

I am better than Jack in writing but not in math; that is his *forte*.

impregnable (*adj.*)
im-ˈpreg-nə-bəl

incapable of being taken by assault; unconquerable; invincible

Before World War II, the French regarded their Maginot Line fortifications as an *impregnable* bulwark against a German invasion.

invigorate (*v.*)
in-ˈvi-gə-ˌrāt

give vigor to; fill with life and energy; strengthen; enliven

If you feel enervated by the heat, try a swim in the cool ocean. It will *invigorate* you.

robust (*adj.*)
rō-ˈbəst

strong and healthy; vigorous; sturdy; sound

The lifeguard was in excellent physical condition. I had never seen anyone more *robust*.

tenacious (*adj.*)
tə-ˈnā-shəs

holding fast or tending to hold fast; unyielding; stubborn; strong

After the dog got the ball, I tried to dislodge it from her *tenacious* jaws, but I couldn't.

vehement (*adj.*)
ˈvē-ə-mənt

showing strong feeling; forceful; violent; furious

Your protest was too mild. If it had been more *vehement,* the supervisor might have paid attention to it.

vigor (*n.*)
ˈvi-gər

active strength or force; energy

The robust young pitcher performed with extraordinary *vigor* for seven innings, but weakened in the eighth and was removed from the game.

EXERCISE 2.8: WEAKNESS AND STRENGTH WORDS

Complete the partially spelled weakness or strength word.

1. It will be difficult to defeat the faculty players; they certainly do not look
— — — — — **pit**.

2. Ed was quite __ __ **ail** until the age of twelve, but then he developed into a robust youth.

3. I doubt you can beat Ann in tennis. It happens to be her __ **or** __ __.

4. A sprained ankle may sideline you for several weeks, but a fractured ankle will
— __ **cap** __ — — — — — — you for months.

5. Laziness, luxury, and a lack of initiative are some of the characteristics of a
— — **cad** — — — **society.**

14. Neglect

default (*n.*) di-'fȯlt	failure to do something required; neglect; negligence; failure to meet a financial obligation	The Royals must be on the playing field by 4 P.M. If they do not appear, they will lose the game by *default*.
default (*v.*)	fail to pay or appear when due	The finance company took away Mr. Lee's car when he *defaulted* on the payments.
heedless (*adj.*) 'hēd-ləs	not taking heed; inattentive; careless; thoughtless; unmindful; reckless	If you drive in a blizzard, *heedless* of the weather bureau's warnings, you may not reach your destination.
ignore (*v.*) ig-'nȯr	refuse to take notice of; disregard; overlook	Justin was given a ticket for *ignoring* a stop sign.
inadvertent (*adj.*) ‚i-nəd-'vər-tᵊnt	(used to describe blunders, mistakes, etc., rather than people) heedless; thoughtless; careless	Unfortunately, I made an *inadvertent* remark in Irma's presence about her losing the election.
neglect (*v.*) ni-'glekt	give little or no attention to; leave undone; disregard	Most members of the cast *neglected* their studies during rehearsals, but after the performance they caught up quickly.
neglect (*n.*)	lack of proper care or attention; disregard; negligence	For leaving his post, the guard was charged with *neglect* of duty.
remiss (*adj.*) ri-'mis	negligent; careless; lax	The owner of the stolen car was *remiss* in having left the keys in the vehicle.

sloven (*n.*) 'slə-vən	untidy person	Cleanup is easy at our lunch table if there are no *slovens*.
slovenly (*adj.*) 'slə-vən-lē	negligent of neatness or order in one's dress, habits, work, etc.; slipshod; sloppy	You would not expect anyone so neat in personal appearance to be *slovenly* in housekeeping.

15. Care

discreet (*adj.*) di-'skrēt	showing good judgment in speech and action; wisely cautious	You were *discreet* not to say anything about our plans when Harry was here. He can't keep a secret.
heed (*v.*) 'hēd	take notice of; give careful attention to; mind	I didn't *heed* the warning that the pavements were icy. That's why I slipped.
meticulous (*adj.*) mə-'ti-kyə-ləs	extremely or excessively careful about small details; fussy	Before signing a contract, read it carefully, including the fine print. This is one case where it pays to be *meticulous*.
scrupulous (*adj.*) 'skrü-pyə-ləs	having painstaking regard for what is right; conscientious; honest; strict; precise	My instructor refuses to be a judge because two of her former students are contestants. She is very *scrupulous*.
scrutinize (*v.*) 'skrü-tᵊn-ˌīz	examine closely; inspect	The gatekeeper *scrutinized* Harvey's pass before letting him in, but he just glanced at mine.
solicitude (*n.*) sə-'li-sə-ˌtüd	anxious or excessive care; concern; anxiety	My sister's *solicitude* over getting into college ended when she received word that she had been accepted.
vigilance (*n.*) 'vi-jə-lən(t)s	alert watchfulness to discover and avoid danger; alertness; caution; watchfulness	The security guard who apprehended the thief was praised for *vigilance*.
wary (*adj.*) 'war-ē	on one's guard against danger, deception, etc.; cautious; vigilant	General Braddock might not have been defeated if he had been *wary* of an ambush.

EXERCISE 2.9: NEGLECT AND CARE WORDS

Complete the partially spelled neglect or care word.

1. Before handing in my paper, I __ __ **rut** __ __ __ __ __ __ it to see if there were any errors.

2. When Mom scolded Jeffrey for the __ __ **oven** __ __ appearance of his room, he promised to make it more tidy.

3. If you __ __ **nor** __ the warning, you may have to suffer the consequences.

4. My aunt would have lost her case by __ __ **fault** if she had failed to appear in court.

5. Deborah is __ __ __ **up** __ __ __ __ __ about returning books to the library on time. She has never had to pay a fine.

Review Exercises

REVIEW 15: SENTENCE COMPLETION

Fill each blank with the word from the list below that best fits the context. Use each word only once.

colossal	debilitate	decrepit	default	discreet
formidable	forte	frail	heed	ignore
impregnable	inadvertent	invigorate	iota	puny
remiss	scrupulous	vehement	vigilance	vigor

1. Milly regrets that she _____d your directions. She could have saved a great deal of time and trouble if she had _____ed them.

2. Undercover detectives must be exceptionally _____. If they make one _____ remark, they may risk death.

3. Although Nathan, our _____ linebacker, is only of average size, he is so quick and strong that he has made our defense _____. Not one team has scored a touchdown against us.

4. In Lilliput, where people were six inches tall, Gulliver was _____, but in Brobdingnag, the land of the giants, he looked _____.

5. There is not one _____ of truth in the rumor that Barbara has misused club funds. She is the most _____ person I have ever met.

6. Her brother's _____ is carpentry. He can rebuild a(n) _____ house in a few weeks.

7. Despite their _____ protests, the farmer and his family were forced to vacate their property because they had _____ed on their mortgage.

8. Bart's long illness has left him so _____ that he has to postpone his return to the team to regain his _____.

9. The convict got away because his guards were _____. If they had exercised proper _____, he would not have escaped.

10. Pam felt _____d on Friday, after working fourteen hours at her office, but she hoped that the relaxation of the weekend would _____ her.

 **REVIEW 16:** SYNONYMS

Avoid repetition by replacing the boldfaced word or expression with a **synonym** from the following words.

bulwark	cogent	commodious	dynamic	flimsy
incapacitate	magnitude	robust	slovenly	solicitude

_____ 1. The Armed Forces protect our freedom. They are our principal **protection** against foreign aggression.

_____ 2. Arthritis is his most important ailment. He has other problems, too, but they are of lesser **importance**.

_____ 3. We are concerned about my sister's health, and when we don't hear from her our **concern** increases.

_____ 4. You seem to lack energy today. Usually, you are much more **energetic**.

_____ 5. The locker I was assigned to had been used by an untidy person; it was very **untidy**.

_____ 6. Injuries sustained in practice often **disable** athletes and put them on the disability list.

_____ 7. There is not too much room in this closet; that one is more **roomy**.

_____ 8. I am convinced you are in error, unless you can offer **convincing** proof to the contrary.

_____ 9. Eileen was not very strong before her appendectomy, but she will soon be **strong and healthy** again.

_____ 10. Most of the excuses that were given had almost no substance whatsoever; they were very **unsubstantial**.

REVIEW 17: ANTONYMS

Enter the word from the list below that is most nearly the **opposite** of the boldfaced word or words.

confining	heedless	ignore	infinite	inflate
meticulous	picayune	scrutinize	sloven	wary

1. Most of the salesclerks were **not fussy about small details**, but one was truly
   _____.

2. Thoughtless consumers behave as if our water supplies were _____, when in fact they are quite **limited**.

3. It is unlikely that a(n) _____ will quickly acquire the habits of a **neat person**.

4. The _____ driver slows down and looks in all directions before crossing an intersection; the **foolhardy** one speeds right through.

5. Hardly anyone **took notice of** the latecomers; most of the audience _____d them.

6. People used to **commodious** accommodations may find the ship's cabins too _____.

7. Customs officials do **not closely examine** every piece of a traveler's luggage, but they may select one suitcase and _____ its contents.

8. Smoking by visitors in a patient's room is a **major** violation of hospital rules; it is not a(n) _____ matter.

9. The driver was _____ of the altercation at the back of the bus because she had to be **attentive** to the road.

10. Try to have an even temper. Do not let one victory _____, or one defeat **deflate**, your self-esteem.

REVIEW 18: CONCISE WRITING

Express the thought of each sentence below in **no more than four words**.

1. The expenses that we had were so small that they came to almost nothing.

   _____

2. Addicts are subject to cravings that they are unable to keep within reasonable bounds.

   _____

3. Those who do proofreading have to be extremely careful about small details.

   _____

4. Many people pay little or no attention to the responsibilities that they are supposed to carry out.

_____

5. There is no fortress in the whole wide world that is not capable of being taken by assault.

_____

REVIEW 19: SYNONYM SUMMARY

Each line, when completed, should have three words similar in meaning. Enter the missing letters.

1. stren __ then	__ __ liven	invig __ r __ te
2. l __ x	car __ less	__ __ miss
3. con __ ern	__ __ xiety	soli __ itude
4. __ well	exp __ nd	__ __ flate
5. dis __ ble	paral __ ze	inca __ __ citate
6. f __ rceful	__ __ ergetic	__ __ namic
7. st __ rdy	__ __ gorous	__ __ bust
8. decl __ ning	__ __ teriorating	dec __ dent
9. __ __ __ regard	__ __ __ __ look	__ __ nore
10. __ __ gantic	mamm __ th	c __ l __ ss __ l
11. __ __ nest	consc __ __ nt __ ous	scr __ p __ lous
12. w __ __ k	insigni __ __ cant	p __ ny
13. __ __ fense	r __ mpart	bulw __ __ k
14. fr __ __ l	__ __ substantial	flim __ y
15. __ __ cessive	__ __ moderate	in __ rd __ nate
16. __ __ attentive	c __ __ __ less	heed __ __ __ __
17. s __ rpl __ s	__ __ cess	__ __ __ __ __ abundance
18. r __ __ my	__ mple	__ __ __ modious
19. strongh __ __ d	fort __ __ __ __	c __ t __ del
20. __ __ feeble	weak __ __	__ nervate

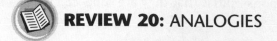

REVIEW 20: ANALOGIES

Which lettered pair of words—*a, b, c, d,* or *e*—most nearly expresses the same relationship as the capitalized pair? Write the letter of your answer in the space provided.

___ 1. DEBILITATE : VIGOR
   a. pauperize : penury
   b. jeopardize : danger
   c. incarcerate : liberty
   d. economize : conservation
   e. fortify : courage

___ 2. INFINITE : END
   a. vital : life
   b. significant : meaning
   c. immortal : existence
   d. commodious : room
   e. anonymous : name

___ 3. PITTANCE : ABUNDANCE
   a. sprinkle : deluge
   b. smidgen : trace
   c. conflagration : flame
   d. pity : compassion
   e. mountain : hill

___ 4. SLOVEN : IMMACULATE
   a. glutton : voracious
   b. despot : domineering
   c. craven : pusillanimous
   d. bigot : unprejudiced
   e. buffoon : ridiculous

___ 5. TENACIOUS : YIELD
   a. remorseful : repent
   b. unforgiving : relent
   c. wary : heed
   d. voracious : devour
   e. contentious : fight

___ 6. SCRUTINIZE : EXAMINE
   a. saunter : walk
   b. skim : read
   c. ape : copy
   d. mumble : talk
   e. doze : sleep

___ 7. IGNORE : OVERLOOK
   a. hoard : squander
   b. learn : instruct
   c. abate : intensify
   d. initiate : terminate
   e. acknowledge : avow

___ **8.** COLOSSAL : ELEPHANT

   a. puny : whale   *b.* gentle : lamb

   c. microscopic : ameba   *d.* extinct : dinosaur

   e. infectious : virus

   Hint: **Colossal** describes the size of an **elephant**.

___ **9.** DRUNKENNESS : FRAILTY

   a. tomato : vegetable   *b.* award : excellence

   c. diploma : document   *d.* gas : oxygen

   e. condiment : appetite

   Hint: Note that **tomato** is not a **vegetable**.

___ **10.** DECADENT : FLOURISHING

   a. picayune : invaluable   *b.* avaricious : greedy

   c. slipshod : untidy   *d.* lax : remiss

   e. scrupulous : precise

REVIEW 21: COMPOSITION

Answer in a sentence or two.

1. Tell why it is foolish to spend inordinate amounts of time on picayune matters.

_____

_____

2. Is a football team with puny players likely to beat a team with colossal players? Why or why not?

_____

_____

3. Why is an impregnable castle easier to defend than a dilapidated one?

_____

_____

4. Would you prefer to have a meticulous or slovenly appearance? Explain your answer.

_____

_____

5. What might a person, debilitated by disease, do to reinvigorate himself?

_____

_____

CENTRAL IDEAS 16–20

Pretest 4

Insert the *letter* of the best answer in the space provided.

1. When you *defer* to someone, you are _____.
   (A) wasting time   (B) being rude   (C) showing respect

2. Conditions were bad both _____ and *abroad*.
   (A) on land   (B) at home   (C) below deck

3. A *perennial* danger is one that is _____.
   (A) constant   (B) avoidable   (C) temporary

4. _____ is a serious *infraction*.
   (A) Losing your wallet   (B) Forgery   (C) Testifying under oath

5. Anything that is *incumbent* on you is _____.
   (A) unpleasant   (B) not your business   (C) your duty

THE ANSWERS ARE
1. C 2. B 3. A 4. B 5. C

Question 1 may have puzzled you, since *defer* was used in a way not yet studied. This is one of the vocabulary skills you will learn about in the final Central Ideas section, numbered 16-20.

16. Residence

abroad (*adv.*) ə-'brȯd	in or to a foreign land or lands	After living *abroad* for a time, Robert Browning became homesick for his native England.
commute (*v.*) kə-'myüt	travel back and forth daily, as from a home in the suburbs to a job in the city	Large numbers of suburban residents regularly *commute* to the city.
commuter (*n.*)	person who commutes	Many a *commuter* spends as much as three hours a day in getting to and from work.

denizen (*n.*) 'de-nə-zən	inhabitant; dweller; resident; occupant	On their safari, the tourists photographed lions, leopards, and other ferocious *denizens* of the jungle.
domicile (*n.*) 'dä-mə-ˌsīl	house; home; dwelling; residence; abode	Soon after they moved, the Coopers invited us to visit them at their new *domicile*.
inmate (*n.*) 'in-ˌmāt	person confined in an institution, prison, hospital, etc.	When the warden took charge, the prison had fewer than 100 *inmates*.
migrate (*v.*) 'mī-ˌgrāt	1. move from one place to settle in another	Because they were persecuted in England, the Puritans *migrated* to Holland.
	2. move from one place to another with the change of season	In winter, many European birds *migrate* to the British Isles in search of a more temperate climate.
native (*n.*) 'nā-tiv	person born in a particular place	His entire family are *natives* of New Jersey except the grandparents, who were born abroad.
native (*adj.*)	born or originating in a particular place	Tobacco, potatoes, and tomatoes are *native* American plants that were introduced into Europe by explorers returning from the New World.
nomad (*n.*) 'nō-ˌmad	member of a tribe that has no fixed abode but wanders from place to place; wanderer	*Nomads* have no fixed homes but move from region to region to secure their food supply.
nomadic (*adj.*) nō-'ma-dik	roaming from place to place; wandering; roving	Mobile homes appeal to people with *nomadic* inclinations.
sojourn (*n.*) 'sō-ˌjərn	temporary stay	On her trip home, Geraldine will stop in St. Louis for a two-day *sojourn* with relatives.

EXERCISE 2.10: RESIDENCE WORDS

Complete the partially spelled residence word.

1. Many Northerners __ __ **grate** to Florida in the winter.

2. Humans are vastly outnumbered by the other **den** __ __ __ __ __ of this earth.

3. Most people are not affluent enough to have a summer residence in the country and a permanent __ __ **mi** __ __ __ __ in the city.

4. These are not native melons; they are shipped from __ __ **road**.

5. The regulations permit __ __ **ma** __ __ __ to receive visitors on Sunday.

17. Disobedience

defiance (*n.*)
di-'fī-ən(t)s

refusal to obey authority; disposition to resist; state of opposition

The union showed *defiance* of the court order against a strike by calling the workers off their jobs.

infraction (*n.*)
in-'frak-shən

breaking (of a law, regulation, etc.); violation; breach

Unless the driver has a permit, parking in a handicapped space is an *infraction* of the law.

insubordinate (*adj.*)
,in(t)-sə-'bȯr-dᵊn-ət

not submitting to authority; disobedient; mutinous; rebellious

Had the cabinet officer ignored the President's instructions, he would have been *insubordinate* and would have been asked to resign.

insurgent (*n.*)
in-'sər-jənt

person who rises in revolt; rebel

When the revolt broke out, the government ordered its troops to arrest the *insurgents*.

insurrection (*n.*)
,in(t)-sə-'rek-shən

uprising against established authority; rebellion; revolt

Troops had to be used in 1794 to put down an *insurrection* in Pennsylvania known as the Whiskey Rebellion.

malcontent (*n.*)
'mal-kən-tent

discontented person; rebel

The work stoppage was caused by a few *malcontents* who felt they had been ignored when promotions were made.

perverse (*adj.*)
pər-'vərs

obstinate (in opposing what is right or reasonable); willful; wayward

Though I had carefully explained the shorter route to him, the *perverse* young man came by the longer way.

sedition (*n.*)
si-'di-shən

speech, writing, or action seeking to overthrow the government; treason

During World War I, about 1500 persons who spoke or wrote against our form of government or the war effort were arrested for *sedition*.

transgress (*v.*)
trans-'gres

go beyond set limits of; violate, break, or overstep a command or law

The coach imposed strict training rules on the soccer team, and he scolded any player who *transgressed*.

trespass (*v.*)
'tres-pəs

encroach on another's rights, privileges, property, etc.

The owner erected a "Keep Off" sign to discourage people from *trespassing* on her land.

18. *Obedience*

acquiesce (*v.*)
ˌa-kwē-ˈes

accept by keeping silent; submit quietly; comply

When Tom suggested that we go to the movies, I *acquiesced* because there seemed nothing else to do.

allegiance (*n.*)
ə-ˈlē-jən(t)s

loyalty; devotion; faithfulness; fidelity

When aliens become American citizens, they must pledge *allegiance* to the United States.

defer (*v.*)
di-ˈfər

yield to another out of respect, authority, or courtesy; submit politely

I thought my answer was correct, but I *deferred* to the teacher's opinion because of her superior knowledge.

discipline (*v.*)
ˈdi-sə-plən

train in obedience; bring under control

The Walkers should not complain that their son does not obey because they never tried to *discipline* him.

docile (*adj.*)
ˈdä-səl

easily taught; obedient; tractable; submissive

Diane listens when you explain something to her, but her sister is much less *docile*.

meek (*adj.*)
ˈmēk

submissive; yielding without resentment when ordered about or hurt by others; acquiescent

About a third of the commuters protested the fare hike. The rest were too *meek* to complain.

pliable (*adj.*)
ˈplī-ə-bəl

easily bent or influenced; yielding; adaptable

We tried to get Joe to change his mind, but he was not *pliable*. Perhaps you can influence him.

submit (*v.*)
səb-ˈmit

yield to another's will, authority, or power; yield; surrender

Though he had boasted he would never be taken alive, the fugitive *submitted* without a struggle when the police arrived.

tractable (*adj.*)
ˈtrak-tə-bəl

easily controlled, led, or taught; docile

George III wanted the thirteen colonies to be *tractable*.

EXERCISE 2.11: DISOBEDIENCE AND OBEDIENCE WORDS

Complete the partially spelled disobedience or obedience word.

1. Dictators want their subjects to be **me** __ __.

2. Mrs. Farrell often leaves her children in our care because they are very **do** __ __ __ __ with us.

3. The insurgents were ordered to yield, but they will never __ __ __ __ **it**.

4. When I asked my brother to turn down his radio, he made it even louder. I couldn't understand why he was so __ __ __ **verse.**

5. If the neighbors complain about your playing your saxophone after 10 P.M., you should, as a matter of courtesy, **de** __ __ __ to their wishes.

19. Time

chronic (*adj.*) 'krä-nik	1. marked by long duration or frequent recurrence	Carl's sore arm is not a new development but the return of a *chronic* ailment.
	2. having a characteristic, habit, disease, etc., for a long time; confirmed; habitual	Some people are *chronic* complainers. They are always dissatisfied.
concurrent (*adj.*) kən-'kər-ənt	occurring at the same time; simultaneous; contemporary	When the strike is settled, there will probably be an increase in wages and a *concurrent* increase in prices.
dawdle (*v.*) 'do̊-dəl	waste time; loiter; idle	Let's get going. If we *dawdle* we'll be late for dinner.
imminent (*adj.*) 'i-mə-nənt	about to happen; threatening to occur soon; near at hand	The sudden darkening of the skies and the thunder in the distance apprised us that rain was *imminent*.
incipient (*adj.*) in-'si-pē-ənt	beginning to show itself; commencing; in an early stage; initial	Certain serious diseases can be successfully treated if detected in an *incipient* stage.
intermittent (*adj.*) ,in-tər-'mi-tənt	coming and going at intervals; stopping and beginning again; recurrent; periodic	The showers were *intermittent*; there were intervals when the sun broke through the clouds.
perennial (*adj.*) pə-'re-nē-əl	1. lasting indefinitely; incessant; enduring; permanent; constant; perpetual; everlasting	Don't think that war has plagued only modern times. It has been a *perennial* curse.
	2. (of plants) continuing to live from year to year	Marigolds last only one season, but *perennial* plants such as lillies return year after year.
procrastinate (*v.*) prə-'kras-tə-'nāt	put off until later things that should be done now; defer; postpone	Most of the picnickers took cover when rain seemed imminent. The few that *procrastinated* got drenched.
protract (*v.*) prō-'trakt	draw out; lengthen in time; prolong; continue; extend	We had planned to stay only for lunch but, at our host's insistence, we *protracted* our visit until after dinner.

| sporadic (*adj.*) spə-'ra-dik | occurring occasionally or in scattered instances; isolated; infrequent | Though polio has been practically wiped out, there have been *sporadic* cases of the disease. |

EXERCISE 2.12: TIME WORDS

Complete the partially spelled time word.

1. My sister is perverse. If I ask her when she will be through with the phone, she will deliberately __ **rot** __ __ __ __ her conversation.

2. There are two excellent TV programs tonight but, unfortunately, they are __ __ __ **cur** __ __ __ __.

3. If public utilities provided __ __ **term** __ __ __ __ __ __ service, consumers would not stand for it.

4. Hay fever is a(n) __ __ __ **on** __ __ sickness that affects millions, particularly in the spring and fall.

5. The complaints, __ __ **or** __ __ __ __ at first, have become quite frequent.

20. Necessity

compulsory (*adj.*) kəm-'pəl-sə-rē	required by authority; obligatory	State law makes attendance at school *compulsory* for children of certain ages.
entail (*v.*) in-'tā(ə)l	involve as a necessary consequence; impose; require	A larger apartment will of course *entail* greater expense.
essence (*n.*) 'e-s³n(t)s	most necessary or significant part, aspect, or feature; fundamental nature; core	The union and management held a lengthy meeting without getting to the *essence* of the dispute—wages.
gratuitous (*adj.*) grə-'tü-ə-təs	uncalled for; unwarranted	Were it not for her *gratuitous* interference, the opposing sides would have quickly settled their dispute.
imperative (*adj.*) im-'per-ə-tiv	not to be avoided; urgent; necessary; obligatory; compulsory	To maintain a good credit rating, it is *imperative* that you pay your bills on time.
incumbent (*adj.*) in-'kəm-bənt	(with *on* or *upon*) imposed as a duty; obligatory	Arlo felt it *incumbent* on him to pay for the window, since he had hit the ball that broke it.

indispensable (*adj.*) ,in-di-'spen(t)-sə-bəl	absolutely necessary; essential	If we have to, we can do without luxuries and entertainment. However, food, shelter, and clothing are *indispensable*.
necessitate (*v.*) ni-'se-sə-,tāt	make necessary; require; demand	The sharp increase in the cost of fuel *necessitated* a rise in the bus fare.
oblige (*v.*) ə-'blīj	compel; force; put under a duty or obligation	The law *obliges* the police to secure a warrant before making a search.
obviate (*v.*) 'äb-vē-,āt	make unnecessary; preclude	Karen has agreed to lend me the book I need. This *obviates* my trip to the library.
prerequisite (*n.*) prē-'re-kwə-zət	something required beforehand	A satisfactory grade in Basic Art is a *prerequisite* for Advanced Art.
pressing (*adj.*) 'pre-siŋ	requiring immediate attention; urgent	Before rearranging my furniture, I have some more *pressing* matters to attend to, such as finishing my research paper.
superfluous (*adj.*) sü-'pər-flü-əs	more than what is enough or necessary; surplus; excessive; unnecessary	Our town already has enough gas stations; an additional one would be *superfluous*.

 EXERCISE 2.13: NECESSITY WORDS

Complete the partially spelled necessity word.

1. Since our trunk is rather small, we can take along only things that are
__ __ __ __ __ **pens** __ __ __ __.

2. Since they are your guests, isn't it __ __ __ __ **mbent** on you to make them feel at home?

3. Increased use of robots and computers in factories may __ __ **via** __ __ the hiring of additional employees.

4. The **ess** __ __ __ __ of the Bill of Rights is that it protects us against tyranny.

5. I was surprised to hear the team needs me because I had thought I was
super __ __ __ __ __ __.

Review Exercises

REVIEW 22: SENTENCE COMPLETION

Fill each blank with the word from the list below that best fits the context.
Use each word only once.

abroad	chronic	commute	defer	denizen
docile	domicile	entail	imperative	incumbent
insubordinate	insurrection	migrate	nomad	oblige
obviate	prerequisite	pressing	procrastinate	protract

1. If the _____s of this community want better street lighting, it is _____ on them to contribute to the expense of additional lampposts.

2. When her fans applauded so enthusiastically, the fatigued singer felt _____d to _____ her concert for an additional thirty minutes.

3. Because Andrea's job commands a high salary, she is willing to _____ three hours a day between her _____ and the company's headquarters.

4. Being a professional basketball player _____s living the life of a(n) _____, as pro teams have to travel from city to city across the country.

5. Unlike his predecessor, who was usually _____, Major obeys my every command. I am lucky to have such a(n) _____ dog.

6. Your research paper is due in three days, so it is _____ that you start working on it. Why do you always _____?

7. Renata has decided to _____ to a drier climate because of her _____ asthma.

8. A(n) _____ in his country required the president of the new democracy to end his travels _____ and return home immediately.

9. The reporter had to _____ her story on the museum exhibit when she was given a more _____ assignment.

10. Herman was told that his year of study in France will _____ his taking Introductory French, the _____ for Second-Year French.

REVIEW 23: SYNONYMS

Avoid repetition by replacing the boldfaced word or expression with a **synonym** from the following words.

acquiesce	allegiance	dawdle	discipline	indispensable
insurgent	pliable	perennial	sojourn	trespass

_____d 1. Some youngsters fail to obey regulations because they have never been **trained in obedience**.

_____s 2. The **rebels** refuse to end their rebellion unless their terms are met.

_____ 3. They stupidly took along unnecessary equipment, but forgot a few small items that were **absolutely necessary**.

_____ 4. Anyone who complains constantly about trivial matters is bound to be regarded as a **constant** nuisance.

_____ 5. We enjoyed our **temporary stay** with you; we regret we could not stay longer.

_____ 6. When unreasonable demands were made, we did not **submit quietly**. Why were you quiet?

_____ 7. The military leaders say they are loyal to the central government, but questions nevertheless remain about their **loyalty**.

_____ 8. We never encroached on their property. Why did they **encroach on ours**?

_____ 9. Let's not **waste time**. Time is precious.

_____ 10. The mayors have considerable influence with the governor, but sometimes he is not **easily influenced**.

REVIEW 24: ANTONYMS

Enter the word from the list below that is most nearly the **opposite** of the boldfaced word or words.

alien	indispensable	intermittent	meek	native
perennial	pliable	protract	submit	tractable

1. Some of the fruits and vegetables we buy are **imported**. Others are of _____ origin.

2. **Curtail** your introductory remarks. If you _____ them, you may bore the audience.

3. _____ individuals consider themselves dispensable; they would never be so **arrogant** as to say they are irreplaceable.

4. There would have been no room for compromise if the negotiators were **obstinate**; fortunately, they were _____.

5. Freedom-loving people would rather **resist** injustice than _____ to it.

6. The rain was **continuous**. If it were _____ I could have been outdoors briefly without getting drenched.

7. People whose **native** tongue is English may not understand conversations spoken in _____ languages.

8. With adequate security, a large crowd is _____; otherwise it may become **unruly**.

9. **Annual** plants die at the end of the growing season, but _____ ones flower year after year.

10. Americans consume some foods that are _____ for nutrition, and some that definitely are **not essential**.

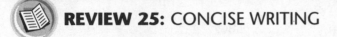 **REVIEW 25:** CONCISE WRITING

Express the thought of each sentence below in **no more than four words**.

1. Every workday, Beverly travels from her home in the suburbs to the city.

_____

2. The noise would stop for a while, and then it would start up all over again.

_____

3. Going to court either to sue someone or to resolve a dispute involves a great deal of expense as a necessary consequence.

_____

4. Tribes that used to roam from province to province were a threat to the continued existence of Rome.

_____

5. Europe was plagued by wars that went on and on for long periods of time.

_____

REVIEW 26: SYNONYM SUMMARY

Each line, when completed, should have three words similar in meaning.
Enter the missing letters.

1. pr __ l __ ng	__ __ tend	__ __ __ tract
2. w __ __ dering	__ __ ving	__ __ madic
3. f __ rce	c __ mp __ l	__ __ lige
4. y __ __ lding	ad __ pt __ ble	pl __ __ ble
5. rev __ lt	__ __ rising	in __ __ __ rection
6. __ weller	__ __ habitant	den __ __ __ __
7. nec __ __ __ ary	obl __ g __ tory	__ __ per __ tive
8. hab __ t __ al	__ __ __ firmed	__ __ ronic
9. v __ __ lation	br __ __ ch	__ __ fraction
10. __ __ frequent	is __ l __ ted	sp __ r __ dic
11. loyal __ __	__ __ votion	alleg __ __ nce
12. const __ nt	__ __ during	__ __ __ ennial
13. obst __ n __ te	w __ __ lful	p __ rv __ rse
14. __ __ __ ecessary	s __ rpl __ s	s __ p __ rfl __ ous
15. __ __ quiescent	s __ __ missive	m __ __ k
16. rebe __ __ ious	m __ t __ nous	__ __ sub __ rd __ nate
17. commen __ ing	in __ t __ __ l	incip __ __ nt
18. per __ __ dic	rec __ __ ring	in __ __ __ mittent
19. sim __ ltan __ ous	con __ __ mporary	__ __ __ current
20. ab __ de	__ __ sidence	__ __ __ icile

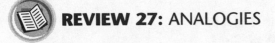

REVIEW 27: ANALOGIES

Which lettered pair of words—*a, b, c, d,* or *e*—most nearly expresses the same relationship as the capitalized pair? Write the letter of your answer in the space provided.

___ **1.** INDISPENSABLE : REPLACE

    a. insignificant : ignore   *b.* edible : devour

    c. foreseeable : avoid   *d.* incomprehensible : grasp

    e. inconsequential : disregard

    Hint: Something that is **indispensable** cannot be **replaced**.

___ **2.** NOMAD : ROVE

    a. nonconformist : acquiesce   *b.* hoarder : consume

    c. drudge : toil   *d.* obstructionist : cooperate

    e. transient : remain

___ **3.** JAYWALKING : INFRACTION

    a. opinion : fact   *b.* silk : fiber

    c. homicide : misdemeanor   *d.* sole : shoe

    e. moon : planet

___ **4.** DOCILE : DEFIANCE

    a. intelligent : curiosity   *b.* apprehensive : alarm

    c. discreet : caution   *d.* fair-minded : partiality

    e. appreciative : gratitude

    Hint: A **docile** person does not show **defiance**.

___ **5.** PROTRACT : CURTAIL

    a. obviate : preclude   *b.* extend : abbreviate

    c. lengthen : broaden   *d.* resist : withstand

    e. dawdle : procrastinate

___ **6.** SOJOURN : STAY

    a. lull : cessation   *b.* monument : reminder

    c. superabundance : supply   *d.* age : time

    e. odyssey : trip

___ **7.** SPORADIC : FREQUENT

    a. distant : remote   *b.* ordinary : commonplace

    c. frugal : economical   *d.* scrupulous : honest

    e. initial : terminal

___ **8.** INSUBORDINATE : OBEY

    a. cooperative : hinder   *b.* flexible : adapt

    c. shy : withdraw   *d.* meek : conform

    e. extravagant : waste

___ **9.** MALCONTENT : COMPLAINER

    a. acquaintance : crony   *b.* defendant : plaintiff

    c. competitor : rival   *d.* adversary : ally

    e. alien : citizen

___ **10.** MANSION : DOMICILE

    a. vehicle : limousine   *b.* cottage : castle

    c. banquet : meal   *d.* warehouse : storage

    e. hobby : vocation

 REVIEW 28: COMPOSITION

Answer in a sentence or two.

1. Why might it be difficult to send a package to the domicile of a nomad?

    _____

    _____

2. Are docile people likely to become insurgents? Explain.

    _____

    _____

3. Give an example of how society disciplines people who transgress its laws.

    _____

    _____

4. Is it incumbent on a student to show allegiance to his or her school? Why or why not?

    _____

    _____

5. Would you rather have sporadic or chronic headaches? Explain why.

    _____

    _____

3

Enlarging Vocabulary Through Anglo-Saxon Prefixes

What is a prefix?

A prefix is a sound (or combination of sounds) placed before and connected to a word or root to form a new word. Examples:

PREFIX		WORD OR ROOT		NEW WORD
FORE (Anglo-Saxon prefix meaning "beforehand")	+	SEE	=	FORESEE (meaning "see beforehand")
DIS (Latin prefix meaning "apart")	+	SECT (root meaning "cut")	=	DISSECT (meaning "cut apart")
HYPER (Greek prefix meaning "over")	+	CRITICAL	=	HYPERCRITICAL (meaning "overcritical")

Why study prefixes?

A knowledge of prefixes and their meanings can help you enlarge your vocabulary. The number of English words beginning with prefixes is considerable, and it keeps increasing. Once you know what a particular prefix means, you have a clue to the meaning of every word beginning with that prefix. For example, when you learn that the Latin prefix *bi* means "two," you will understand—and remember—the meaning of *bipartisan* ("representing two political parties"), *bilingual* ("speaking two languages"), *bisect* ("cut in two"), etc.

Our prefixes come mainly from Anglo-Saxon (Old English), Latin, and Ancient Greek.

Purpose of this chapter

This chapter has a double purpose: (1) to acquaint you with important Anglo-Saxon prefixes, and (2) to help you add to your vocabulary a number of useful words beginning with these prefixes.

ANGLO-SAXON PREFIXES 1–4

Pretest 1

Insert the *letter* of the best answer in the space provided.

1. An *outspoken* person is not likely to be _____.
   (A) bold
   (B) frank
   (C) shy

2. When you have a *foreboding,* you feel that something _____ is going to happen.
   (A) unimportant
   (B) unfortunate
   (C) good

3. *Misgivings* result from _____.
   (A) doubts and suspicions
   (B) selfishness
   (C) increased output

4. *Forebears* are associated mainly with the _____.
   (A) present
   (B) past
   (C) future

5. If you _____, you are being *overconfident.*
   (A) strike while the iron is hot
   (B) count your chickens before they are hatched
   (C) lock the barn after the horses are stolen

> **THE ANSWERS ARE**
> **1.** C **2.** B **3.** A **4.** B **5.** B

In the following pages you will learn many more words formed with the prefixes you have just met, namely, *fore-, mis-, out-,* and *over-.*

1. FORE-: "beforehand," "front," "before"

WORD	MEANING	TYPICAL USE
forearm (*n.*) 'for-,ärm	(literally, "front part of the arm") part of the arm from the wrist to the elbow	A weightlifter has well-developed *forearms.*
forebear (*n.*) 'for-,ber	(literally, "one who has been or existed before") ancestor; forefather	Do you know from whom you are descended? Who were your *forebears?*

foreboding (*n.*) fȯr-'bō-diŋ	feeling beforehand of coming trouble; misgiving; presentiment; omen	The day before the accident, I had a *foreboding* that something would go wrong.
forecast (*n.*) 'fȯr-,kast	estimate beforehand of a future happening; prediction; prophecy	Have you listened to the weather *forecast* for the weekend?
forefront (*n.*) 'fȯr-,frənt	(literally, "front part of the front") foremost place or part; vanguard	The mayor is at the *forefront* of the drive to attract new industry to the city.
foregoing (*adj.*) 'fȯr-,gō-iŋ	going before; preceding; previous	Carefully review the *foregoing* chapter before reading any further.
foremost (*adj.*) 'fȯr-,mōst	standing at the front; first; most advanced; leading; principal; chief	Marie Curie was one of the *foremost* scientists of the twentieth century.
foreshadow (*v.*) fȯr-'sha-,dō	indicate beforehand; augur; portend	Our defeat in the championship game was *foreshadowed* by injuries to two of our star players in a previous game.
foresight (*n.*) 'fȯr-,sīt	act of looking forward; prudence; power of seeing beforehand what is likely to happen	*Foresight* is better than hindsight.
foreword (*n.*) 'fȯr-,wərd	front matter preceding the text of a book; preface; introduction; prologue	Before Chapter 1, there is a brief *foreword* in which the author explains the aims of the book.

EXERCISE 3.1: *FORE-* WORDS

Fill each blank with the most appropriate *fore-* word.

1. When asked if she thought we would win, the coach refused to make a

   _____.

2. Instead of cramming for a test the night before, be sensible and spread your review over several of the _____ days.

3. These plastic gloves cover the hand, the wrist, and part of the _____.

4. I should have had the _____ to buy a sweater before it got too cold; now all the best ones have been sold.

5. As the spacecraft rose toward the sky, the astronaut had a _____ that he might not return.

2. MIS-: "bad," "badly," "wrongly"

misbelief (*n.*) ‚mis-bə-'lēf	wrong or erroneous belief	People generally believed the earth was flat until Columbus' momentous voyage corrected that *misbelief*.
misdeed (*n.*) ‚mis-'dēd	bad act; wicked deed; crime; offense	The criminals were punished for their *misdeeds* by fines and prison terms.
misfire (*v.*) ‚mis-'fīr	(literally, "fire wrongly") fail to fire or explode properly	The soldier's weapon *misfired* during target practice.
misgiving (*n.*) ‚mis-'gi-viŋ	uneasy feeling; feeling of doubt or suspicion; foreboding; lack of confidence	With excellent weather and a fine driver, we had no *misgivings* about the trip.
mishap (*n.*) 'mis-‚hap	bad happening; misfortune; unlucky accident; mischance	Right after the collision, each driver blamed the other for the *mishap*.
mislay (*v.*) ‚mis-'lā	put or lay in an unremembered place; lose	Yesterday I *mislaid* my keys, and it took me about a half hour to find them.
mislead (*v.*) ‚mis-'lēd	lead astray (in the wrong direction); deceive; delude; beguile	Some labels are so confusing that they *mislead* shoppers.
misstep (*n.*) ‚mis-'step	wrong step; slip in conduct or judgment; blunder	Quitting school is a *misstep* that you may regret for the rest of your life.

EXERCISE 3.2: *MIS-* WORDS

Fill each blank with the most appropriate *mis-* word.

1. Luckily, no one was seriously hurt in the _____.

2. Where is your pen? Did you lose it or _____ it?

3. I hated to lend Marie my notes because of a _____ that she might not return them in time.

4. There is always the likelihood that a rifle may _____.

5. Consumer groups have been attacking advertisements that _____ the public.

3. OUT-: "beyond," "out," "more than," "longer (faster, better) than"

outgrow (*v.*)
ˌaut-ʹgrō
grow beyond or too large for
The jacket I got last year is too small. I have *outgrown* it.

outlandish (*adj.*)
ˌaut-ʹlan-dish
looking or sounding as if it belongs to a (foreign) land beyond ours; strange; fantastic
Costume parties are amusing because people come in such *outlandish* costumes.

outlast (*v.*)
ˌaut-ʹlast
last longer than; outlive; survive
The table is more solidly constructed than the chairs and will probably *outlast* them.

outlook (*n.*)
ʹaut-ˌluk
looking ahead or beyond; prospect for the future
The *outlook* for unskilled laborers is not bright.

output (*n.*)
ʹaut-ˌput
(literally, what is "put out") yield or product; amount produced
The *output* of the average American factory increases as new equipment is introduced.

outrun (*v.*)
ˌaut-ʹrən
run faster than
The thief thought he could *outrun* his pursuers.

outspoken (*adj.*)
ˌaut-ʹspō-kən
speaking out freely or boldly; frank; vocal; not reserved
Alma sometimes hurts others when she criticizes their work because she is too *outspoken*.

outwit (*v.*)
ˌaut-ʹwit
get the better of by being more clever; outsmart; outfox
The fictional detective Sherlock Holmes manages to *outwit* the cleverest criminals.

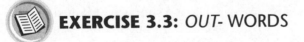

EXERCISE 3.3: *OUT-* WORDS

Fill each blank with the most appropriate *out-* word.

1. I know I shall get the truth when I ask Alice because she is very _____.

2. Where did you get that _____ hat? I never saw anything like it.

3. My little brother suffers from shyness, but Mom hopes he will _____ it.

4. These sneakers are the best I have ever had. They will _____ any other brand.

5. Our prospects of avoiding a deficit are good, but the _____ may change if we have unforeseen expenses.

4. OVER-: "too," "excessively," "over," "beyond"

overbearing (*adj.*)
,ō-vər-'ber-iŋ

domineering; bossy; inclined to dictate

Once Jason was given a little authority, he began to issue orders in an *overbearing* manner.

overburden (*v.*)
,ō-vər-'bər-dᵊn

place too heavy a load on; burden excessively; overtax; overload

It would *overburden* me to go shopping Thursday because I have so much homework that day.

overconfident (*adj.*)
,ō-vər-'kän-fə-dənt

too sure of oneself; excessively confident

I was so sure of passing that I wasn't going to study, but Dave advised me not to be *overconfident*.

overdose (*n.*)
'ō-vər-,dōs

quantity of medicine beyond what is to be taken at one time or in a given period; too big a dose

Do not take more of the medicine than the doctor ordered; an *overdose* may be dangerous.

overestimate (*v.*)
,ō-vər-'es-tə-māt

make too high an estimate (rough calculation) of the worth or size of something or someone; overvalue; overrate

Joe *overestimated* the capacity of the bus. He thought it could hold 60; it has room for only 48.

overgenerous (*adj.*)
,ō-vər-'jen-ə-rəs

too liberal in giving; excessively openhanded

Because the service was poor, Gina thought I was *overgenerous* in leaving a 15% tip.

overshadow (*v.*)
,ō-vər-'sha-dō

1. cast a shadow over; overcloud; obscure

Gary's errors in the field *overshadowed* his good work at the plate.

2. be more important than; outweigh

Don's game-saving catch *overshadowed* his previous errors in the outfield.

oversupply (*n.*)
,ō-vər-sə-'plī

too great a supply; an excessive supply

There is a shortage of skilled technicians but an *oversupply* of unskilled workers.

overwhelm (*v.*)
,ō-vər-'hwelm

cover over completely; overpower; overthrow; crush

The security guards were nearly *overwhelmed* by the crowds of shoppers waiting for the sale to begin.

 EXERCISE 3.4: *OVER-* WORDS

Fill each blank with the most appropriate *over-* word.

1. There will be much food left if you seriously _____ the number who will attend the party.

2. Frances would have been our first choice, but she already has too many responsibilities and we did not want to _____ her.

3. Why did you buy more Ping-Pong balls? Don't you know we have an _____?

4. I think my English teacher was _____ when he gave me 99 because I didn't deserve it.

5. At first the new supervisor was very domineering, but as she got to know the staff, she became less _____.

Review Exercises

REVIEW 1: WORD-BUILDING WITH *FORE-, MIS-, OUT-,* AND *OVER-*

Change each of the following expressions to a single word, as in 1, below.

foreseen _____	1. seen beforehand
_____	2. badly matched
_____	3. grown to excess
_____	4. use wrongly
_____	5. cooked too much
_____	6. person beyond the law
_____	7. wrong interpretation
_____	8. doom beforehand
_____	9. ride faster than
_____	10. inform incorrectly
_____	11. too cautious
_____	12. bad calculation
_____	13. front feet (of a four-legged animal)
_____	14. too simplified
_____	15. swim better than
_____	16. govern badly
_____	17. stay too long
_____	18. one who runs before
_____	19. wrong statement
_____	20. shout louder than

REVIEW 2: SENTENCE COMPLETION

Fill each blank with the word from the list below that best fits the context.

forearm	forecast	foremost	foreword	misgiving
mislaid	misled	misstep	outgrow	outlandish
output	outrun	outspoken	outwit	overbearing
overconfident	overdose	overestimate	oversupply	overwhelm

1. The _____ of "sunny with a high in the 70s" _____ me into scheduling the picnic for today. How was I to know it would rain?

2. Many of us, no matter how old we get, will never _____ our love for circus clowns and their _____ costumes.

3. Jim didn't practice because he thought he could easily _____ his competitors. After the race, he realized he had been _____.

4. The master criminal _____d his own cleverness when he thought he could _____ Sherlock Holmes.

5. After the interview, Frank had few, if any, _____s. He thought he had said all the correct things and could not recall a single _____.

6. One reason our representative was reelected by a(n) _____ing margin is that she has always been _____ in her defense of the environment.

7. One thing that impressed me as I watched the _____ tennis player in the world win his third straight championship was the huge size of his right _____.

8. Ed did not read the book. He couldn't get beyond the first paragraph of the _____ because he disliked the writer's _____ attitude.

9. When she realized there was a(n) _____ of shoes on the market, the company president ordered _____ to be cut back at all her plants.

10. Andy wondered if he had lost his watch or just _____ it. He had been sleepy all day, perhaps because of a(n) _____ of his flu medicine.

 REVIEW 3: SYNONYMS

Avoid repetition by replacing the boldfaced word or expression with a **synonym** from the following words.

forebear	foreboding	forecast	misbelief	misdeed
mishap	outlast	overburden	overgenerous	overshadow

_____ 1. When it comes to tipping for exceptional service, some people are **inclined to be exceptionally liberal**.

_____ 2. I had a **feeling beforehand** that we would lose. What did you feel the outcome would be?

_____   3. Your recent successes are important. They **are more important than** your earlier mistakes.

_____s   4. Some criminals show no remorse for their **crimes**.

_____ed   5. I thought the replacement soles would not last long, but they **lasted longer than** the original ones.

_____   6. Unfortunately, they had one **misfortune** after another.

_____ed   7. You are already **bearing too heavy a load**. We must not add to your load.

_____s   8. A visit to the land of our **ancestors** can teach us much about our ancestry.

_____   9. The pollsters are predicting that the governor will be reelected. Do you agree with that **prediction**?

_____   10. I awoke on a holiday in the **mistaken belief** that it was a school day and was halfway to the bus stop before realizing my mistake.

REVIEW 4: ANTONYMS

Enter the word from the list below that is most nearly the **opposite** of the boldfaced word or words.

forebear	foregoing	foremost	foresight	foreword
misdeed	mislead	overcautious	overestimate	undercook

1. Most of us are pretty good in **hindsight** but deficient in _____.

2. Some works have not only a(n) _____, or prologue, but also a(n) **afterword**, or epilogue.

3. People who lack self-confidence **underestimate** themselves and _____ their opponents.

4. If Adam and Eve were our _____s, then all of us are their **descendants**.

5. In a eulogy, the speaker dwells on the **positive achievements**, rather than the _____s, of the departed person.

6. Why is it that protection of the environment, which should be one of our _____ concerns, so often gets the **least** attention?

7. In matters where your own judgment may _____ you, seek out someone who can **enlighten** you.

8. Certain foods must not be served unless they have been **thoroughly cooked**; if _____ed, they may cause food poisoning.

9. The character who appeared briefly in the _____ scene will be seen again in one of the **subsequent** episodes.

10. After realizing that I had been **too careless**, I went to the extreme of becoming _____.

REVIEW 5: CONCISE WRITING

Express the thought of each sentence below in **no more than four words**.

1. Most people do not have the power of seeing beforehand what is likely to happen.

_____

2. Doses of medicine that exceed the prescribed amount are capable of killing people.

_____

3. Which spark plug is it that failed to fire in a proper way?

_____

4. Grandma broke the part of her arm from her wrist to her elbow.

_____

5. Percy managed to get the better of his enemies by being more clever than they were.

_____

 REVIEW 6: SYNONYM SUMMARY

Each line, when completed, should have three words similar in meaning.
Enter the missing letters.

1. ch __ __ f   princip __ __   __ __ __ __ most
2. __ __ fense   cr __ me   __ __ __ deed
3. __ __ __ __ father __ __ cestor   __ __ __ __ b __ __ r
4. __ __ __ fortune   __ __ __ chance   mish __ __
5. str __ nge   __ __ __ tastic   __ __ __ land __ __ __
6. fr __ nk   v __ c __ l   __ __ __ spoke __
7. __ __ under   __ lip   __ __ __ step
8. boss __   __ __ mineering   __ __ __ __ bear __ __ __
9. cr __ sh   __ __ __ __ throw   __ __ __ __ __ helm
10. __ __ __ diction   prophe __ y   __ __ __ __ cast
11. overval __ __   __ __ __ __ rate   __ __ __ __ es __ __ mate
12. __ men   __ __ __ sentiment   __ __ __ __ boding
13. __ __ __ __ mart   __ __ __ fox   __ __ twit
14. overt __ __   __ __ __ __ load   __ __ __ __ b __ __ den

15. __ __ __ face   in __ __ __ duction   __ __ __ __ word

16. pre __ eding   prev __ __ __ __   fore __ __ __ __ __

17. __ __ __ vive   __ __ __ live   __ __ __ last

18. overcl __ __ d   __ __ __ cure   __ __ __ __ shad __ __

19. dec __ __ ve   beg __ __ le   __ __ __ lead

20. a __ g __ r   p __ rtend   __ __ __ __ __ __ ado __

REVIEW 7: ANALOGIES

Which lettered pair of words—*a, b, c, d,* or *e*—most nearly expresses the same relationship as the capitalized pair? Write the letter of your answer in the space provided.

___   **1.** OVERBEARING : DOMINEER

      a. meek : complain   *b.* nomadic : rove

      c. immaculate : litter   *d.* submissive : defy

      e. scrupulous : deceive

___   **2.** GRANDPARENT : FOREBEAR

      a. bowl : vessel   *b.* officer : lieutenant

      c. civilian : combatant   *d.* ship : frigate

      e. native : alien

___   **3.** FOREWORD : TEXT

      a. dessert : dinner   *b.* book : encyclopedia

      c. climax : play   *d.* dawn : sunrise

      e. toll : tax

___   **4.** MISDEED : PENALIZE

      a. infraction : overlook   *b.* offense : tolerate

      c. obligation : forget   *d.* promise : break

      e. feat : acclaim

___   **5.** FOREBODING : APPREHENSION

      a. truce : hostility   *b.* confession : guilt

      c. recovery : ecstasy   *d.* rumor : confidence

      e. impasse : settlement

___   **6.** HOAX : MISLEAD

      a. threat : intimidate   *b.* definition : confuse

      c. duty : perform   *d.* enigma : resolve

      e. fine : pay

___ **7.** OVERGENEROSITY : BANKRUPTCY

    a. illiteracy : enlightenment   *b.* gluttony : indigestion

    c. penury : riches   *d.* avarice : pity

    e. impetuosity : patience

___ **8.** FOREARM : ELBOW

    a. ankle : wrist   *b.* muscle : nerve

    c. leg : knee   *d.* lip: mouth

    e. knuckle : hand

___ **9.** OVERDOSE : FATALITY

    a. mishap : blunder   *b.* covenant : disagreement

    c. famine : drought   *d.* surplus : scarcity

    e. thaw : avalanche

 REVIEW 8: COMPOSITION

Answer in a sentence or two.

1. Describe a time when you had a foreboding that a mishap might occur.

_____

_____

2. What misgivings would you have about making friends with an overbearing person?

_____

_____

3. What might a writer foreshadow with a description of an army that was far too confident of victory?

_____

_____

4. What is one way in which the police try to outwit those who would do misdeeds?

_____

_____

5. If you were to meet your forebears today, might they seem outlandish in some way? Explain.

_____

_____

ANGLO-SAXON PREFIXES 5–8

Pretest 2

Insert the *letter* of the best answer in the space provided.

1. An *understudy* is not a _____ performer.
   (A) prepared   (B) substitute   (C) regular

2. Cars with a high *upkeep* _____.
   (A) use less costly fuels   (B) are often in the repair shop   (C) pick up speed rapidly

3. A *withdrawal* is the same as _____.
   (A) a retreat   (B) a deposit   (C) an attack

4. When you wish to _____ something in a sentence, *underscore* it.
   (A) stress   (B) correct   (C) erase

5. An *unabridged* dictionary _____.
   (A) is not complete   (B) has no illustrations   (C) has not been shortened

THE ANSWERS ARE
1. C **2.** B **3.** A **4.** A **5.** C

The material that follows will introduce you to many additional words formed with the prefixes *un-*, *under-*, *up-*, and *with-*.

5. UN-: "not," "lack of," "do the opposite of," "remove or release from"

unabridged (*adj.*) ˌən-ə-ˈbrijd	not abridged; not made shorter; uncut; complete	Though an abridged dictionary is convenient to use, it contains far fewer definitions than an *unabridged* dictionary.
unbiased (*adj.*) ˌən-ˈbī-əst	not biased; not prejudiced in favor of or against; fair	Don't ask the mother of a contestant to serve as a judge because it may be hard for her to remain *unbiased*.

unconcern (*n.*)
‚ən-kən-'sərn
lack of concern, anxiety, or interest; indifference; apathy
The audience was breathless with anxiety during the daring tightrope act, though the acrobats themselves performed with seeming *unconcern* for their own safety.

undeceive (*v.*)
‚ən-di-'sēv
free from deception or mistaken ideas; set straight; disabuse
If you think I can get Mrs. Owens to hire you because she is my cousin, let me *undeceive* you. I have no influence with her.

ungag (*v.*)
‚ən-'gag
remove a gag from; release from censorship
With the dictator's downfall, the censorship decrees were abolished, and the press was *ungagged*.

unnerve (*v.*)
‚ən-'nərv
deprive of nerve or courage; cause to lose self-control; upset; enervate
The harassing noises of hostile fans so *unnerved* our star player that he missed two foul shots in a row.

unquenchable (*adj.*)
‚ən-'kwen-chə-bəl
not quenchable; not capable of being satisfied; insatiable; inextinguishable
As a teenager, Jules had an *unquenchable* thirst for adventure stories; he read one after another.

unscramble (*v.*)
‚ən-'skram-bəl
do the opposite of scramble; restore to intelligible form
The previous secretary had mixed up the files so badly that it took me a week to *unscramble* them.

unshackle (*v.*)
‚ən-'shak-əl
release from a shackle (anything that confines the legs or arms); set free; liberate
When a captain put mutinous sailors in irons in the olden days, nobody was allowed to *unshackle* them.

unwary (*adj.*)
‚ən-'war-ē
not wary; not alert; heedless; rash
An *unwary* pedestrian is much more likely to be struck by a car than one who looks both ways and crosses with the light.

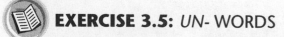 **EXERCISE 3.5:** *UN-* WORDS

Fill each blank with the most appropriate *un-* word.

1. Some baseball fans never miss a home game; they have an _____ appetite for the sport.

2. The guards were warned that their prisoner was desperate and would try to escape if they were the least bit _____.

3. I visited Grandma every day she was in the hospital. I can't understand why you accuse me of _____ about her health.

4. For a reliable definition of a technical word, consult an _____ dictionary.

5. Both the strikers and their employers want the mayor to arbitrate their dispute because they consider him _____.

6. UNDER-: "beneath," "lower," "insufficient(ly)"

underbrush (n.)
'ən-dər-ˌbrəsh

shrubs, bushes, etc., growing beneath large trees in a wood; undergrowth

On its way through the dense jungle, the patrol had to be constantly wary of enemy soldiers who might be lurking in the *underbrush*.

underdeveloped (*adj.*)
ˌən-dər-di-'ve-ləpt

insufficiently developed because of a lack of capital and trained personnel for exploiting natural resources; backward; behindhand

The United States has spent billions to help the *underdeveloped* nations improve their standard of living.

undergraduate (*n.*)
ˌən-dər-'gra-jə-wət

(literally, "lower than a graduate") a student in a college or university who has not yet earned a bachelor's degree

Full-time *undergraduates* can earn a bachelor's degree in four years.

underpayment (*n.*)
ˌən-dər-'pā-mənt

insufficient payment

If too little is deducted from your weekly wages for income tax, the result is an *underpayment* at the end of the year.

underprivileged (*adj.*)
ˌən-dər-'priv-lijd

insufficiently privileged; deprived through social or economic oppression of some fundamental rights supposed to belong to all; disadvantaged; deprived

The goal of the fund is to give as many *underprivileged* children as possible an opportunity for a vacation away from the city next summer.

underscore (*v.*)
'ən-dər-skȯr

draw a line beneath; emphasize; stress

When you take notes, *underscore* items that are especially important.

undersell (*v.*)
ˌən-dər-'sel

sell at a lower price than

The expression "You can't get it anywhere else for less" means about the same as "We will not be *undersold*."

undersigned (*n.*)
'ən-dər-ˌsīnd

person or persons who sign at the end of (literally, "under") a letter or document

Among the *undersigned* in the petition to the governor were some of the most prominent persons in the state.

understatement (*n.*)
'ən-dər-ˌstāt-mənt

a statement below the truth; a restrained statement in mocking contrast to what might be said

Frank's remark that he was "slightly bruised" in the accident is an *understatement*; he suffered two fractured ribs.

| **understudy** (*n.*)
ˈən-dər-ˌstə-dē | one who "studies under" and learns the part of a regular performer so as to be a substitute if necessary | While Madeline is recuperating from her illness, her role will be played by an *understudy*. |

EXERCISE 3.6: *UNDER-* WORDS

Fill each blank with the most appropriate *under-* word.

1. The advanced course is for students with a bachelor's degree, but a qualified _____ may enroll if the instructor approves.

2. An _____ must master long and difficult roles, yet has no assurance of ever being called on to perform.

3. Arline told me she "passed," but that's an _____; she got the highest mark in the class.

4. Mike's tee shot disappeared after hitting one of the trees, and he had to hunt for the ball in the _____.

5. Because they buy in larger quantities at lower prices, chain-store operators are usually able to _____ small merchants.

7. UP-: "up," "upward"

upcoming (*adj.*) ˈəp-ˌkə-miŋ	coming up; being in the near future; forthcoming; approaching	A monthly bulletin mailed to each customer gives news of *upcoming* sales.
update (*v.*) ˈəp-ˌdāt	bring up to date; modernize; renovate	New highway construction requires auto clubs to *update* their road maps annually.
upgrade (*v.*) ˈəp-ˌgrād	raise the grade or quality of; improve	Many employees attend evening courses to *upgrade* their skills and improve their chances for promotion.
upheaval (*n.*) ˌəp-ˈhē-vəl	violent heaving up, as of the earth's crust; commotion; violent disturbance; outcry	The prime minister's proposal for new taxes created such an *upheaval* that his government fell.
upkeep (*n.*) ˈəp-ˌkēp	maintenance ("keeping up"); cost of operating and repairing	Susan traded in her old car because the *upkeep* had become too high.
uplift (*v.*) əp-ˈlift	lift up; elevate; raise	The news that employers are rehiring has *uplifted* the hopes of many of the unemployed.

upright (*adj.*) ˈəp-ˌrīt	standing up straight on the feet; erect; honest; scrupulous	When knocked to the canvas, the boxer waited till the count of nine before resuming an *upright* position.
uproot (*v.*) ˌəp-ˈrüt	pull up by the roots; remove completely; eradicate; annihilate	The love of liberty is so firmly embedded in people's hearts that no tyrant can hope to *uproot* it.
upstart (*n.*) ˈəp-ˌstärt	person who has suddenly risen to wealth and power, especially if he or she is conceited and unpleasant	When the new representative entered the legislature, some older members regarded her as an *upstart*.
upturn (*n.*) ˈəp-ˈtərn	upward turn toward better conditions	Most merchants report a slowdown in sales for October, but confidently expect an *upturn* with the approach of Christmas.

 EXERCISE 3.7: *UP-* WORDS

Fill each blank with the most appropriate *up-* word.

1. Perhaps today's victory, the first in four weeks, marks an _____ in the team's fortunes.

2. To improve her book, the author will have to _____ the last chapter to include the events of the past ten years.

3. If practicable, _____ weeds by hand, instead of destroying them with chemicals that might damage the environment.

4. What is the name of the city agency responsible for the _____ of our roads?

5. To stay in business, manufacturers must improve the quality of their products whenever their competitors _____ theirs.

8. WITH-: "back," "away," "against"

withdraw (*v.*) with-ˈdrȯ	1. take or draw back or away; take out from a place of deposit	The community association is her principal backer; if it *withdraws* its support, I don't see how she can be elected.
	2. leave; retreat	The invaders were ordered to *withdraw*.
withdrawal (*n.*) with-ˈdrȯ-əl	1. act of taking back or drawing out from a place of deposit	When I am short of cash, I make a *withdrawal* from my bank account.
	2. retreat; exit; departure	The invaders made a hasty *withdrawal*.

withdrawn (*adj.*) wi<u>th</u>-'drȯn	drawn back or removed from easy approach; socially detached; unresponsive, introverted	Lola's brother keeps to himself and hardly says anything, though we try to be friendly; he seems *withdrawn*.
withhold (*v.*) wi<u>th</u>-'hōld	hold back; keep from giving; restrain; curb	I would appreciate it if you would please *withhold* your comment until I have finished speaking.
withholding tax (*n.*) wi<u>th</u>-'hōl-diŋ 'taks	sum withheld or deducted from wages for tax purposes	Your employer is required to deduct a certain amount from your salary as a *withholding tax* payable to the federal government.
withstand (*v.*) wi<u>th</u>-'stand	stand up against; hold out; resist; endure	The walls of a dam must be strong enough to *withstand* tremendous water pressure.
notwithstanding (*prep.*) ˌnät-wi<u>th</u>-'stan-diŋ	(literally, "not standing against") in spite of; despite	*Notwithstanding* their advantage of height, the visitors were unable to beat our basketball team.

EXERCISE 3.8: *WITH-* WORDS

Fill each blank with the most appropriate *with-* word.

1. Electronic banking lets you make a deposit or a _____ at any time.

2. Whenever you get a raise, your _____ goes up.

3. Construction of the new roadway has been approved, _____ the protests from residents of the area.

4. Because of a disagreement with her partners, the lawyer announced that she would _____ from the firm and open an office of her own.

5. The training that astronauts receive equips them to _____ the hazards of space exploration.

Review Exercises

REVIEW 9: WORD-BUILDING WITH *UN-, UNDER-, UP-,* AND *WITH-*

Change each of the following expressions to a single word, as in 1, below.

__underlying__   1. lying beneath

_____   2. not able to be avoided

_____   3. holds back

_____ 4. insufficiently paid

_____ 5. act or instance of rising up

_____ 6. do the opposite of lock

_____ 7. lower (criminal) part of the world

_____ 8. standing up against

_____ 9. one who holds up, supports, or defends

_____ 10. sum taken (drawn) back from a bank account

_____ 11. not sociable

_____ 12. upward stroke

_____ 13. charged lower than the proper price

_____ 14. drew back or away

_____ 15. lack of reality

_____ 16. lifted upward

_____ 17. one who holds back

_____ 18. released from a leash

_____ 19. beneath the surface of the sea

_____ 20. upward thrust

REVIEW 10: SENTENCE COMPLETION

Fill each blank with the word from the list below that best fits the context.

notwithstanding	unabridged	unbiased	unconcern	undeceive
underbrush	underscore	undersell	undersigned	understudy
unnerve	unquenchable	unshackle	unwary	upcoming
upgrade	uplift	upright	withdrawn	withhold

1. The parents of the _____ boy took him to the circus, hoping that it might help to _____ his spirits.

2. If you expect to find this extremely technical word in that little dictionary of yours, let me _____ you. Only a(n) _____ dictionary will have it.

3. A(n) _____ camper, walking barefoot in the _____, was bitten by a snake.

4. The new electronics store is using heavy TV advertising to _____ its claim that it will _____ all competitors.

5. Spurred by their _____ desire for freedom, the prisoners managed to _____ their wrists.

6. Maxine's _____ about the _____ test contrasts sharply with my own anxiety over it.

7. The prospect of suddenly being called upon to be the star does not _____ an experienced _____ familiar with the role.

8. The petition reads: "We, the _____ XYZ Club members, are willing to pay higher dues to _____ the refreshments served after meetings."

9. _____ rumors to the contrary, the candidate insists that she is _____, and she pledges that she will be fair to everyone.

10. The dealer who sold us the used car was a(n) _____ person. He did not _____ information from us about the true condition of the vehicle.

 REVIEW 11: ANTONYMS

Enter the word from the list below that is most nearly the **opposite** of the boldfaced word.

unabridged	unbiased	unconcern	underdeveloped	undergraduate
underpayment	understatement	unscrambled	unwary	upgraded

1. Be **cautious** this morning. You may slip on the ice if you are _____.

2. Once you receive your bachelor's degree, you are no longer an _____ but a **graduate.**

3. Only _____ persons should be on the jury. No one **prejudiced** in favor of or against the defendant should be chosen to serve.

4. Be accurate in describing your injuries when you file an accident report. Avoid both **exaggeration** and _____.

5. It is a fact that **industrial** nations enjoy a higher standard of living than those that are _____.

6. Someone **jumbled** up the pieces of the picture puzzle after I had finally _____ them.

7. If you have made an **overpayment**, you will receive a refund; but if you have made an _____, you still owe some money.

8. People who look with _____ on the proposed legislation might show some **anxiety** if they knew how it might affect them.

9. An advantage an **abridged** dictionary has over one that is _____ is that it is much less cumbersome.

10. If the winds diminish, the storm will be **downgraded** to a gale, but if they increase to 74 miles an hour, it will be _____ to a hurricane.

REVIEW 12: SYNONYMS

Avoid repetition by replacing the boldfaced word or expression with a **synonym** from the following words.

eradicate	understudy	ungag	update	upheaval
upkeep	upturn	withdraw	withdrawal	withstand

_____ 1. What caused the **disturbance**? Why were the people disturbed?

_____ 2. Though the new ruler has promised to **free** the press **from censorship**, he is now tightening censorship controls.

_____ 3. Jackie is learning the dispatcher's duties to qualify as his **substitute**, should substitution ever be necessary.

_____ 4. It is hard to **uproot** a weed that is deeply rooted.

_____ 5. The invaders were supposed to retreat to their own lines. What is delaying their **retreat**?

_____ 6. It cost $1400 to maintain our old car last year, and next year the **maintenance** may be even more expensive.

_____d 7. Our neighbors have **modernized** their kitchen. It now has a decidedly modern look.

_____ 8. Parents can hold their own against most complaints from children, but they cannot **hold out against** continual nagging.

_____ 9. It takes just a few seconds to **take out** money from your savings account when you use an automated teller machine.

_____ 10. Business is improving. There has been an encouraging **improvement** in retail sales.

REVIEW 13: CONCISE WRITING

Express the thought of each sentence below in **no more than four words**.

1. Houdini succeeded in getting out of the shackles that were restraining his arms and legs.

_____

2. There are people who through no fault of their own are deprived of some of the fundamental rights that all human beings are supposed to have.

_____

3. Conceited individuals who have suddenly come into wealth and power can be bossy and domineering over others.

_____

4. Those who referee games must not show any favoritism to one side or the other.

_____

5. Sally has learned the ins and outs of my job and can take over my duties in the event of an emergency.

_____

REVIEW 14: SYNONYM SUMMARY

Each line, when completed, should have three words similar in meaning. Enter the missing letters.

1. end __ re	res __ st	__ __ __ __ stand
2. r __ sh	heed __ __ __ __	__ __ wary
3. h __ nest	scrup __ lous	up __ __ __ __ __
4. st __ ess	__ __ phasize	under __ __ __ __ __
5. retr __ __ t	l __ __ ve	with __ __ __ __
6. f __ __ r	unpre __ __ diced	__ __ biased
7. l __ berate	fr __ __	__ __ shack __ __
8. comm __ tion	__ __ __ cry	__ __ heav __ __
9. inextin __ __ ishable	__ __ satiable	__ __ quench __ ble
10. ex __ t	depart __ re	__ __ __ __ draw __ __
11. compl __ te	__ __ cut	__ __ __ bridged
12. m __ dernize	__ __ novate	__ __ date
13. erad __ cate	annihil __ __ __	__ __ root
14. __ __ __ advantaged	__ __ prived	underpr __ v __ l __ ged
15. __ __ difference	ap __ thy	__ __ concern
16. appr __ __ ching	f __ rthcoming	up __ __ __ __ __ __
17. backw __ rd	b __ hindhand	__ __ __ __ __ developed
18. restr __ __ n	c __ __ b	__ __ __ __ hold
19. r __ __ se	impr __ ve	__ __ grade
20. __ __ set	en __ rvate	__ __ nerve

REVIEW 15: ANALOGIES

Which lettered pair of words—*a, b, c, d,* or *e*—most nearly expresses the same relationship as the capitalized pair? Write the letter of your answer in the space provided.

___ 1. UNGAG : CENSOR
    a. overlook : neglect   *b.* liberate : unshackle
    c. abandon : retain   *d.* inform : undeceive
    e. hesitate : waver

___ 2. WARY : HEED
    a. acquiescent : rebel   *b.* infallible : err
    c. lavish : economize   *d.* voracious : devour
    e. opinionated : compromise

___ 3. UNDERSTUDY : INSURANCE
    a. exercise : circulation   *b.* privacy : door
    c. guest : hospitality   *d.* bodyguard : security
    e. bore : excitement

___ 4. SHACKLES : HANDCUFFS
    a. tree : birch   *b.* legs : limbs
    c. measles : disease   *d.* fence : barrier
    e. flavor : condiments
    Hint: **Shackles** is the category to which **handcuffs** belongs.

___ 5. WITHDRAWN : SOCIABILITY
    a. arrogant : humility   *b.* unassertive : timidity
    c. outgoing : warmth   *d.* intrepid : valor
    e. immaculate : tidiness

___ 6. UPDATE : MODERNIZE
    a. soothe : infuriate   *b.* invalidate : approve
    c. yield : defer   *d.* expedite : procrastinate
    e. bury : disinter

___ 7. UPRIGHT : TRUST
    a. corrupt : contempt   *b.* domineering : obedience
    c. indolent : promotion   *d.* inhumane : sympathy
    e. gossipy : credence
    Hint: An **upright** person is worthy of **trust.**

___ 8. UNDERSCORE : EMPHATIC

    a. simplify : complex   *b.* overshadow : inconspicuous

    c. rectify : inequitable   *d.* decontaminate : impure

    e. legalize : unlawful

___ 9. UNCONCERN : INTEREST

    a. cordiality : friendliness   *b.* perseverance : ambition

    c. fervor : enthusiasm   *d.* honesty : virtue

    e. mediocrity : excellence

___ 10. INTREPID : UNNERVE

    a. pliable : influence   *b.* audible : hear

    c. timorous : scare   *d.* outspoken : silence

    e. avaricious : share

    Hint: An **intrepid** person cannot be **unnerved**.

REVIEW 16: WORD-BUILDING WITH EIGHT ANGLO-SAXON PREFIXES

Replace the italicized words with one word beginning with *fore-, mis-, out-, over-, un-, under-, up-,* or *with-*. See 1, below.

foretell   1. If you study your opponent's habits, you may be able to *tell beforehand* what his or her next move will be.

_____ 2. We won because we *played better than* our opponents.

_____ 3. After the hike, we rested because we were *excessively tired.*

_____ 4. It is a mistake to exaggerate your abilities and talents, but it is just as bad *to set too low an estimate on* them.

_____ 5. The dispute has been *wrongly handled* from the very beginning.

_____ 6. Harry is usually *too critical* when he judges somebody else's work.

_____ 7. You will not get a good picture if the film is *exposed for less than the time needed.*

_____ 8. The will provided that all of the property was to go to the wife if she *lived longer than* her husband.

_____ 9. As a courteous guest, you should know when to leave; do not *stay beyond* your welcome.

_____ 10. The district attorney promised to *remove the mask of* the criminals posing as respectable citizens.

_____ 11. By stressing scholarship, our principal has succeeded in *lifting* the reputation of our school *up to a higher level.*

_____ 12. The early snowfall gave us a *taste beforehand* of the bitter winter to come.

_____ **13.** A captain *has a higher rank than* a lieutenant.

_____ **14.** We spoke in *lower tones* so as not to be overheard.

_____ **15.** As I passed the kitchen, I caught a *glimpse beforehand* of what we are having for dinner.

_____ **16.** Abe Lincoln had the *bad fortune* to lose his mother when he was only nine.

_____ **17.** The hospital has beds for 90 patients; in addition, it provides daily treatment for hundreds of *patients who live beyond the hospital grounds.*

_____ **18.** I have never heard you utter a single *statement lacking in accuracy.*

_____ **19.** From the prisoners' outward appearance, it did not seem that they had been mistreated or *insufficiently fed.*

_____ **20.** Lauren wanted to go on the overnight camping trip, but her father *held back* his consent, saying she was still too young.

 **REVIEW 17:** COMPOSITION

Answer in a sentence or two.

1. What is one way society tries to upgrade the lives of the underprivileged?

_____

_____

2. Describe an upcoming event in your life that could prove to be unnerving.

_____

_____

3. Why is it hard for a tree to withstand uprooting?

_____

_____

4. Would an upright business owner withhold money owed to his employees? Explain.

_____

_____

5. What might an underdeveloped nation do to gain an upturn in its economy?

_____

_____

Chapter 4

Enlarging Vocabulary Through Latin Prefixes

LATIN PREFIXES 1–6

Pretest 1

Insert the *letter* of the best answer in the space provided.

1. *Postscripts* are especially helpful to the letter writer who _____.
   - (A) forgets to answer
   - (B) answers too late
   - (C) makes omissions

2. *Bicameral* legislatures _____.
   - (A) serve for two years
   - (B) consist of two houses
   - (C) meet twice a year

3. There is more excitement over the *advent* of spring than over its _____.
   - (A) departure
   - (B) onset
   - (C) arrival

4. You *antedate* me as a member because you joined the club _____ me.
   - (A) after
   - (B) with
   - (C) before

5. A *semidetached* building touches _____ other building(s).
   - (A) one
   - (B) no
   - (C) two

6. Was the story *absorbing* or _____?

    (A) true to life   (B) interesting   (C) boring

THE ANSWERS ARE

1. C 2. B 3. A 4. C 5. A 6. C

In the following pages you will learn additional words formed with the six Latin prefixes involved in the pretest: *ab-, ad-, ante-, post-, bi-,* and *semi-*.

1. AB-, A-, ABS-: *"from," "away," "off"*

The prefix *ab* (sometimes written *a* or *abs*) means "from," "away," or "off." Examples:

PREFIX		ROOT		NEW WORD
AB ("off")	+	RUPT ("broken")	=	ABRUPT ("broken off"; "sudden")
A ("away")	+	VERT ("turn")	=	AVERT ("turn away")
ABS ("from")	+	TAIN ("hold")	=	ABSTAIN ("hold from"; "refrain")

WORD	MEANING	TYPICAL USE
abdicate (*v.*) ˈab-di-ˌkāt	formally remove oneself from; give up; relinquish; renounce; resign	The aging monarch *abdicated* the throne and went into retirement.
abduct (*v.*) ab-ˈdəkt	carry off or lead away by force; kidnap	The Greeks attacked Troy to recover Helen, who had been *abducted* by the Trojan prince Paris.
abhor (*v.*) ab-ˈhȯr	shrink from; detest; loathe; hate	Janet is doing her best to pass the course because she *abhors* the thought of having to repeat it in summer school.
abnormal (*adj.*) ab-ˈnȯr-məl	deviating from the normal; unusual; irregular	We had three absences today, which is *abnormal*. Usually, everyone is present.
abrasion (*n.*) ə-ˈbrā-zhən	scraping or wearing away of the skin by friction; irritation	The automobile was a total wreck, but the driver, luckily, escaped with minor cuts and *abrasions*.
abrupt (*adj.*) ə-ˈbrəpt	broken off; sudden; unexpected	Today's art lesson came to an *abrupt* end when the gongs sounded for a fire drill.
abscond (*v.*) ab-ˈskänd	steal off and hide; depart secretly; flee; escape	A wide search is under way for the manager who *absconded* with the company's funds.

absolve (*v.*) əb-'zälv	1. set free from some duty or responsibility; exempt; excuse	Ignorance of the law does not *absolve* a person from obeying it.
	2. declare free from guilt or blame; exculpate; exonerate	Of the three suspects, two were found guilty, and the third was *absolved*.
absorbing (*adj.*) əb-'sȯr-biŋ	fully taking away one's attention; extremely interesting; engrossing	That was an *absorbing* book. It held my interest from beginning to end.
abstain (*v.*) əb-'stān	withhold oneself deliberately from doing something; refrain; desist	My dentist said I would have fewer cavities if I *abstained* from sweets.
averse (*adj.*) ə-'vərs	(literally, "turned from") opposed; disinclined; unwilling	I am in favor of the dance, but I am *averse* to holding it on May 25.
avert (*v.*) ə-'vərt	turn away; ward off; prevent; forestall	The mayor tried to *avert* a strike by municipal employees.
avocation (*n.*) ‚a-və-'kā-shən	occupation away from one's customary occupation; hobby	My aunt, a pediatrician, composes music as an *avocation*.

EXERCISE 4.1: *AB-, A-,* AND *ABS-* WORDS

Fill each blank with the most appropriate word from group 1.

1. Some love spinach; others _____ it.

2. A snowstorm in late May is _____ for Chicago.

3. My father plays golf. What is your father's _____?

4. The dictator refused to _____ and was eventually overthrown.

5. Gene said the movie was interesting, but I didn't find it too _____.

6. It was very decent of Marge to _____ me of blame by admitting she was at fault.

7. The kidnapper was arrested when he tried to _____ the executive.

8. I nominate Harriet for treasurer. She knows how to keep records and can be trusted not to _____ with our dues.

9. The owner must raise $20,000 in cash at once if she is to _____ bankruptcy.

10. We are _____ to further increases in the sales tax. It is too high already.

2. AD-: "to," "toward," "near"

adapt (*v.*) ə-'dapt	1. (literally, "fit to") adjust; suit; fit	People who work at night have to *adapt* themselves to sleeping in the daytime.
	2. make suitable for a different use; modify	Lorraine Hansberry's hit Broadway play, A Raisin in the Sun, was later *adapted* for the screen.
addicted (*adj.*) ə-'dik-təd	given over (to a habit); habituated; devoted	You will not become *addicted* to smoking if you refuse cigarettes when they are offered.
adequate (*adj.*) 'a-di-kwət	equal to, or sufficient for, a specific need; enough; sufficient	The student who arrived ten minutes late did not have *adequate* time to finish the test.
adherent (*n.*) ad-'hir-ənt	one who sticks to a leader, party, etc.; follower; faithful supporter	You can count on Martha's support in your campaign for reelection. She is one of your most loyal *adherents*.
adjacent (*adj.*) ə-'jā-sᵊnt	lying near; nearby; neighboring; bordering	The island of Cuba is *adjacent* to Florida.
adjoin (*v.*) ə-'jȯin	be next to; be in contact with; border; abut	Mexico *adjoins* the United States.
adjourn (*v.*) ə-'jərn	put off to another day; suspend a meeting to resume at a future time; defer; recess	The judge *adjourned* the court to the following Monday.
advent (*n.*) 'ad-,vent	a "coming to"; arrival; approach	The weather bureau gave adequate warning of the *advent* of the hurricane.
adversary (*n.*) 'ad-vər-,ser-ē	person "turned toward" or facing another as an opponent; foe; antagonist	Before the contest began, the champion and her *adversary* shook hands.
adverse (*adj.*) ad-'vərs	in opposition to one's interests; hostile; unfavorable	Because of *adverse* reviews, the producer announced that the play will close with tonight's performance.

EXERCISE 4.2: *AD-* WORDS

Fill each blank with the most appropriate word from group 2.

1. With the _____ of autumn, the days become shorter.

2. England was our _____ in the War of 1812.

3. Is it very expensive to _____ a summer home for year-round living?

4. We have sweets, but only occasionally. We are not _____ to them.

5. The candidate has few supporters in the rural areas; most of his _____s are in the cities.

---

3. ANTE-: "before"
4. POST-: "after"

antecedents (*n. pl.*) ˌan-tə-ˈsē-dənts	ancestors; forebears; predecessors	Ronald's *antecedents* came to this country more than a hundred years ago.
antedate (*v.*) ˈan-ti-ˌdāt	1. assign a date before the true date	If you used yesterday's date on a check written today, you have *antedated* the check.
	2. come before in date; predate; precede	Alaska *antedates* Hawaii as a state, having gained statehood on January 3, 1959, seven months before Hawaii.
postdate (*v.*) ˈpōst-ˌdāt	assign a date after the true date	I *postdated* the check; it has tomorrow's date on it.
ante meridiem (*adj.*) ˌan-ti mə-ˈri-dē-əm	before noon	In 9 A.M., A.M. stands for *ante meridiem,* meaning "before noon."
post meridiem (*adj.*) ˌpōst mə-ˈri-dē-əm	after noon	In 9 P.M., P.M. stands for *post meridiem,* meaning "afternoon."
anteroom (*n.*) ˈan-ti-ˌrüm	room placed before and forming an entrance to another; antechamber; waiting room	If the physician is busy when patients arrive, the nurse asks them to wait in the *anteroom.*
postgraduate (*adj.*) ˌpōst-ˈgra-jə-wət	having to do with study after graduation, especially after graduation from college	After college, Nina hopes to do *postgraduate* work in law school.

postmortem (*n.*) 'pōst-'mòr-təm	1. thorough examination of a body after death; autopsy	The purpose of a *postmortem* is to discover the cause of death.
	2. detailed analysis or discussion of an event just ended	In a *postmortem* after a defeat, we discuss what went wrong and what we can do to improve.
postscript (*n.*) 'pōst-,skript	note added to a letter after it has been written	After signing the letter, I noticed I had omitted an important fact, and I had to add a *postscript*.

 ## EXERCISE 4.3: *ANTE-* AND *POST-* WORDS

Fill each blank with the most appropriate word from groups 3 and 4.

1. After graduating from the College of the City of New York, Jonas Salk did _____ study at New York University to earn an M.D. degree.

2. Mr. Sims told me to put tomorrow's date on the letter, but I forgot to _____ it.

3. The _____ showed that the patient had died of natural causes.

4. In some areas, the peasants still use the same methods of farming as their _____ did centuries ago.

5. You will not need a(n) _____ if you plan your letter carefully.

5. BI-: "two"
6. SEMI-: "half," "partly"

bicameral (*adj.*) bī-'kam-rəl	consisting of two chambers or legislative houses	Our legislature is *bicameral*; it consists of the House of Representatives and the Senate.
bicentennial (*n.*) ,bī-sen-'te-nē- əl	two-hundredth anniversary	Our nation's *bicentennial* was celebrated in 1976.
biennial (*adj.*) bī-'e-nē-əl	occurring every two years	A defeated candidate for the House of Representatives can run again in two years because the elections are *biennial*.
semiannual (adi.) ,se-mē-'an-yə-wəl	occurring every half year, or twice a year; semiyearly	Promotion in our school is *semiannual*, occurring in January and June.

bimonthly (*adj.*)
bī-'mənth-lē

occurring every two months

We receive only six utility bills a year because we are billed on a *bimonthly* basis.

semimonthly (*adj.*)
,se-mē-'mənth-lē

occurring every half month, or twice a month

Employees paid on a *semimonthly* basis receive two salary checks per month.

bilateral (*adj.*)
bī-'la-t(ə)-rəl

having two sides

French forces joined the Americans in a *bilateral* action against the British at the Battle of Yorktown in 1781.

bilingual (*adj.*)
bī-'liŋ-gwəl

1. speaking two languages equally well

New York has a large number of *bilingual* citizens who speak English and a foreign language.

2. written in two languages

The instructions on the voting machine are *bilingual;* they are in English and Spanish.

bipartisan (*adj.*)
bī-'pär-tə-zən

representing two political parties

Congressional committees are *bipartisan;* they include Democratic and Republican members.

bisect (*v.*)
'bī-,sekt

divide into two equal parts

A diameter is a line that *bisects* a circle.

semicircle (*n.*)
'se-mē-,sər-kəl

half of a circle

At the end of the lesson, students gathered about the teacher in a *semicircle* to ask additional questions.

semiconscious (*adj.*)
,se-mē-'kän(t)-shəs

half conscious; not fully conscious

In the morning, as you begin to awaken, you are in a *semiconscious* state.

semidetached (*adj.*)
,se-mē-di-'tacht

partly detached; sharing a wall with an adjoining building on one side, but detached on the other

All the houses on the block are attached, except the corner ones, which are *semidetached.*

semiskilled (*adj.*)
,se-mē-'skild

partly skilled

Workers in a *semiskilled* job usually do not require a long period of training.

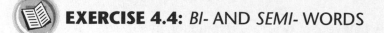

EXERCISE 4.4: *BI-* AND *SEMI-* WORDS

Fill each blank with the most appropriate word from groups 5 and 6.

1. Everyone will benefit from the warmth of the fireplace if you arrange the chairs around it in a _____ .

2. The inspections are _____; there is one every six months.

3. A state that has both an assembly and a senate has a _____ legislature.

4. America's foreign policy is _____; it represents the views of both major political parties.

5. A _____ house shares a common wall.

Review Exercises

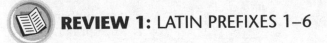

REVIEW 1: LATIN PREFIXES 1–6

In the space before each Latin prefix in column I, write the *letter* of its meaning from column II.

COLUMN I	COLUMN II
___ 1. ab-, a-, or abs-	*a.* half or partly
___ 2. semi-	*b.* two
___ 3. ante-	*c.* from, away, or off
___ 4. ad-	*d.* after
___ 5. post-	*e.* to, toward, or near
___ 6. bi-	*f.* before

REVIEW 2: WORD-BUILDING

Fill in the prefix in column I and the complete word in column III. (The answer to question 1 has been inserted as an example.)

COLUMN I	COLUMN II	COLUMN III
1. __AD__ *to*	+ HERENT *one who sticks*	= __ADHERENT__ *one who sticks to; follower*
2. _____ *two*	+ LINGUAL *pertaining to a tongue*	= _____ *speaking two languages*
3. _____ *after*	+ DATED	= _____ *dated after (the true date)*
4. _____ *away*	+ RASION *scraping*	= _____ *scraping away (of the skin)*

5. _____ + CHAMBER = _____
   before   room   *room before another; waiting room*

6. _____ + SKILLED = _____
   partly   *partly skilled*

7. _____ + HORS = _____
   from   shrinks   *shrinks from; loathes; detests*

8. _____ + LATERAL = _____
   two   pertaining to a side   *having two sides*

9. _____ + CIRCLE = _____
   half   *half circle*

10. _____ + JACENT = _____
    near   lying   *lying near; neighboring*

11. _____ + RUPT = _____
    off   broken   *broken off; sudden; unexpected*

12. _____ + VERSE = _____
    away   turned   *turned away; opposed; unwilling*

13. _____ + PONING = _____
    after   putting   *putting after; deferring; delaying*

14. _____ + EQUATE = _____
    to   equal   *equal to; sufficient; enough*

15. _____ + CAMERAL = _____
    two   pertaining to a chamber   *consisting of two chambers*

16. _____ + CENTENNIAL = _____
    two   hundredth anniversary   *two-hundredth anniversary*

17. _____ + APTED = _____
    to   fitted   *fitted to; adjusted*

18. _____ + TAINING = _____
    from   holding   *holding oneself from doing something; refraining*

19. _____ + SCRIPT = _____
    after   written   *note added after signature of a letter*

20. _____ + VERT = _____
    off   turn; ward   *ward off; turn away; prevent*

REVIEW 3: SENTENCE COMPLETION

Fill each blank with the word from the list below that best fits the context.

abdicate	abhor	abrupt	abscond	absorbing
adapt	addicted	adequate	adjourn	advent
adversary	antecedents	anteroom	averse	avocation
bilingual	bipartisan	postmortem	postscript	semidetached

1. Ken, who plays golf eight hours a day, claims it is just his _____, but he is quite obviously _____ to it.

2. Though it is true that our _____ were hunters, many of us _____ the practice.

3. In the _____ to her letter, Lucille indicated that she would not be _____ to a phone call from her former friend.

4. Surprisingly enough, the _____ committee reached agreement quickly and was able to _____ in less than an hour.

5. Used to rural life, the family could not _____ to their _____ city home, where noises from their neighbor penetrated the common wall.

6. The book Alice was reading was so _____ that she did not notice the _____ of the storm.

7. In the coroner's _____, the detective waited patiently for the results of the _____ on the murder victim.

8. The game came to a(n) _____ halt when a stranger dashed onto the court and _____ed with the only basketball we had.

9. Believing his health was no longer _____ for him to rule, the ailing monarch decided to _____ his throne.

10. _____ American officers who knew the language of our _____ helped to negotiate the truce.

REVIEW 4: SYNONYMS

Avoid repetition by replacing the boldfaced word or expression with a **synonym** from the following words.

abnormal	absolve	adjoin	adversary	adverse
avert	bicentennial	bilateral	bisect	semiconscious

_____d 1. Two of the suspects were found guilty, and one was **declared free of guilt**.

_____ 2. **Cut** this six-foot board **in two** to give us two three-foot lengths.

_____ 3. It would be **unusual** if traffic were light at 5 P.M. because that is usually a busy hour.

_____ 4. Often, for the first minute or two after I awake, I am only **half awake**.

_____ 5. Was the accident unpreventable, or could you have done something to **prevent** it?

_____ 6. The weather yesterday was **unfavorable** for sailing, but today it is supposed to be favorable.

_____ 7. Who else is opposing you in the election? Is Olga your only **opponent**?

_____ 8. Both sides have joined in a **two-sided** effort to improve working conditions.

_____s 9. The post office is next to the railroad station, and the hardware store **is next to** the bakery.

_____ 10. The United States celebrated its one-hundredth anniversary as a nation in 1876 and its **two-hundredth anniversary** in 1976.

REVIEW 5: ANTONYMS

Enter the word from the list below that is most nearly the **opposite** of the boldfaced word or words.

abhor	abrupt	adequate	adherent	adjacent
adversary	adverse	antecedents	avocation	postgraduate

1. We _____ villains but **admire** heroes and heroines.

2. Many a nation that was our _____ in World War II is now our **ally**.

3. General Benedict Arnold was a loyal and courageous _____ of the Revolutionary cause until 1780, when he turned **renegade**.

4. Though we were promised _____ school funding, the money voted by the legislature is **insufficient**.

5. There was no parking space in the field _____ to the building; we had to park in a **distant** lot.

6. The _____ comments of the judges outweighed their **favorable** ones.

7. As _____ of future generations, we must protect the resources of this planet. Otherwise, our **descendants** may not forgive us.

8. Growth in childhood is **gradual**; there are usually no _____ changes.

9. The grades students earn in their _____ courses are usually better than those they achieved in their **undergraduate** work.

10. From the knowledge Sarah has about gardening, one might think it is her **profession**, but it is just her _____.

REVIEW 6: CONCISE WRITING

Express the thought of each sentence below in **no more than four words.**

1. Wasn't Antony the one who stood in opposition to Brutus?

   _____

2. Skating is what she enjoys doing when she is not at work in her regular occupation.

   _____

3. The legislature that France has is made up of two houses.

   _____

4. What is the reason that made them depart in secret?

   _____

5. We met with circumstances that were not favorable to our interests.

   _____

REVIEW 7: SYNONYM SUMMARY

Each line, when completed, should have three words similar in meaning.
Enter the missing letters.

1. n __ __ ghboring   n __ __ rby   __ __ jacent

2. int __ r __ sting   __ __ grossing   __ __ sorbing

3. l __ __ the   __ __ test   abh __ r

4. an __ estors   foreb __ __ rs   __ __ __ __ cedents

5. f __ t   su __ t   __ __ apt

6. host __ le   __ __ favorable   __ __ verse

7. follow __ __   supp __ __ ter   adh __ r __ nt

8. __ __ expected   sudd __ __   __ __ rupt

9. appr __ __ ch   arriv __ l   __ __ vent

10. __ __ nounce   resi __ n   abdi __ __ __ __

11. d __ f __ r   r __ cess   adj __ __ rn

12. __ scape   fl __ __   __ __ scond

13. unus __ __ l   __ __ regular   __ __ normal

14. b __ rd __ r   __ but   __ __ join

15. __ __ topsy   anal __ sis   post __ __ __ tem

16. habit __ ated   __ __ voted   __ __ dicted

17. prec __ d __   __ __ __ date   ante __ __ __ __

18. enou __ __   suffi __ __ ent   __ __ __ quate

19. opp __ n __ nt   __ __ tagonist   __ __ versary

20. ex __ nerate   exc __ lp __ te   __ __ solve

 ## REVIEW 8: ANALOGIES

Which lettered pair of words—*a, b, c, d,* or *e*—most nearly expresses the same relationship as the capitalized pair? Write the letter of your answer in the space provided.

___ 1. AVERSE : OPPOSE
  a. devious : elucidate   *b.* convinced : doubt
  c. cordial : alienate   *d.* frank : disclose
  e. original : imitate

___ 2. POSTSCRIPT : LETTER
  a. postmark : envelope   *b.* headline : article
  c. caboose : train   *d.* rain : rainbow
  e. bookmark : place

___ 3. UNPLIABLE : ADAPT
  a. law-abiding : trespass   *b.* rational : think
  c. literate : write   *d.* docile : heed
  e. perceptive : foresee

  Hint: An **unpliable** person does not **adapt**.

___ 4. ADHERENT : LOYALTY
  a. beggar : resources   *b.* perjurer : credibility
  c. fugitive : pursuit   *d.* bigot : tolerance
  e. prodigy : talent

___ 5. BILINGUAL : LANGUAGE
  a. versatile : skill   *b.* outspoken : tongue
  c. nimble : agility   *d.* observant : vision
  e. ambidextrous : hand

___ **6.** ABSOLVE : GUILT

     a. implicate : suspicion   *b.* enlighten : ignorance

     c. incarcerate : penitentiary   *d.* upgrade : rank

     e. illuminate : light

___ **7.** ADVERSARY : ALLY

     a. fan : addict   *b.* spy : informer

     c. radical : conservative   *d.* poltroon : craven

     e. monarch : despot

___ **8.** SEMIANNUAL : YEARLY

     a. half : whole   *b.* fragment : piece

     c. month : year   *d.* core : exterior

     e. crescent : moon

___ **9.** ABRASION : SKIN

     a. fertility : soil   *b.* drought : precipitation

     c. erosion : stone   *d.* propulsion : wind

     e. conflagration : fire

___ **10.** ABSCOND : DEPART

     a. state : proclaim   *b.* grant : withhold

     c. conceal : reveal   *d.* conspire : agree

     e. declare : announce

REVIEW 9: COMPOSITION

Answer in a sentence or two.

1. Would you rather be paid on a bimonthly or semimonthly basis? Give reasons for your choice.

2. Do you think it is abnormal for people to abhor their adversaries? Why or why not?

3. Why might a doctor at a postmortem take note of any unusual abrasions?

4. Would most people be adverse to riding with a semiconscious driver? Why?

_____

_____

5. Tell how one of your antecedents adapted to life in the United States.

_____

_____

LATIN PREFIXES 7–12

Pretest 2

Insert the *letter* of the best answer in the space provided.

1. To take part in a school's *intramural* program, you must _____.
   (A) be on the school team
   (B) have approval for competing with students of other schools
   (C) be a student at the school

2. A *countermanded* order should _____.
   (A) be ignored
   (B) receive preference
   (C) be obeyed

3. When there is an *exclusive* showing of a film at a theater, _____.
   (A) no other theater in town has it
   (B) all seats are reserved
   (C) children unaccompanied by adults are excluded

4. People who *inhibit* their curiosity usually _____.
   (A) open packages as soon as received
   (B) mind their own business
   (C) have little patience

5. The chairperson said Phil's suggestion was *extraneous,* but I thought it was _____.
   (A) original
   (B) relevant
   (C) off the topic

6. A friend who *intercedes* for you _____.
   (A) takes the blame for you
   (B) takes your place
   (C) pleads for you

THE ANSWERS ARE
1. C 2. A 3. A 4. B 5. B 6. C

The following pages will acquaint you with additional words formed with the six Latin prefixes involved in the pretest: *ex-*, *in-*, *extra-*, *intra-*, *contra-*, and *inter-*.

7. E-, EX-: *"out," "from," "away"*
8. IN-, IM-: *"in," "into," "on," "against," "over"*

WORD	MEANING	TYPICAL USE
emigrate (*v.*) ʹe-mə-ˌgrāt	move out of a country or region to settle in another	At thirteen, Maria Callas *emigrated* from the United States.
immigrate (*v.*) ʹi-mə-ˌgrāt	move into a foreign country or region as a permanent resident	At thirteen, Maria Callas *immigrated* to Greece.
eminent (*adj.*) ʹe-mə-nənt	standing or jutting out; conspicuous; famous; distinguished; noteworthy	Maria Callas became an *eminent* opera singer.
imminent (*adj.*) ʹi-mə-nənt	hanging over one's head; threatening; about to occur; impending	At the first flash of lightning, the beach crowd scurried for shelter from the *imminent* storm.
enervate (*v.*) ʹe-nər-ˌvāt	(literally, "take out the nerves or strength") lessen the strength of; enfeeble; weaken	I was so *enervated* by the broiling sun that I had to sit down.
erosion (*n.*) i-ʹrō-zhən	gradual wearing away; deterioration; depletion	Running water is one of the principal causes of soil *erosion*.
evoke (*v.*) i-ʹvōk	bring out; call forth; elicit; produce	The suggestion to lengthen the school year has *evoked* considerable opposition.
invoke (*v.*) in-ʹvōk	call on for help or protection; appeal to for support	Refusing to answer the question, the witness *invoked* the Fifth Amendment, which protects persons from being compelled to testify against themselves.
excise (*v.*) ek-ʹsīz	cut out; remove by cutting out	With a penknife, he peeled the apple and *excised* the wormy part.
incise (*v.*) in-ʹsīz	cut into; carve; engrave	The letters on the cornerstone had been *incised* with a power drill.

exclusive (*adj.*) iks-'klü-siv	1. shutting out, or tending to shut out, others	An *exclusive* club does not readily accept newcomers.
	2. not shared with others; single; sole	Before the game, each team had *exclusive* use of the field for a ten-minute practice period.
inclusive (*adj.*) in-'klü-siv	1. (literally, "shutting in") including the limits (dates, numbers, etc.) mentioned	The film will be shown from August 22 to 24, *inclusive,* for a total of three days.
	2. broad in scope; comprehensive	An unabridged dictionary is much more *inclusive* than an ordinary desk dictionary.
exhibit (*v.*) ig-'zi-bət	(literally, "hold out") show; display	The museum is now *exhibiting* the art of the Inuit people of northern Canada.
inhibit (*v.*) in-'hi-bət	(literally, "hold in") hold in check; restrain; repress	Many could not *inhibit* their tears; they cried openly.
expel (*v.*) ik-'spel	drive out; force out; compel to leave; banish; eject	The student who was *expelled* from the university because of poor grades applied for readmission the following term.
impel (*v.*) im-'pel	drive on; force; compel	We do not know what *impelled* the secretary to resign.
implicate (*v.*) 'im-plə-‚kāt	(literally, "fold in or involve") show to be part of or connected with; involve; entangle	One of the accused persons confessed and *implicated* two others in the crime.
impugn (*v.*) im-'pyün	(literally, "fight against") call in question; assail by words or arguments; attack as false; contradict; attack; malign	The treasurer should not have been offended when asked for a financial report. No one was *impugning* his honesty.
incarcerate (*v.*) in-'kär-sə-‚rāt	put in prison; imprison; confine	After their escape and recapture, the convicts were *incarcerated* in a more secure prison.
inscribe (*v.*) in-'skrīb	(literally, "write on") write, engrave, or print to create a lasting record; imprint; autograph	The name of the winner will be *inscribed* on the medal.
insurgent (*n.*) in-'sər-jənt	one who rises in revolt against established authority; rebel; mutineer	The ruler promised to pardon any *insurgents* who would lay down their arms.
insurgent (*adj.*)	rebellious; insubordinate; mutinous	General Washington led the *insurgent* forces in the Revolutionary War.

📖 **EXERCISE 4.5:** *E-, EX-, IN-,* AND *IM-* WORDS

Fill each blank with the most appropriate word from groups 7 and 8.

1. This afternoon the swimming team has _____ use of the pool. No one else will be admitted.

2. No one can _____ the settler's claim to the property, since he holds the deed to the land.

3. Over the centuries, the Colorado River has carved its bed out of solid rock by the process of _____.

4. A lack of opportunity compelled thousands to _____ from their native land.

5. Proposals to increase taxes usually _____ strong resistance.

6. The famine-stricken nation is expected to _____ the help of its more fortunate neighbors.

7. On the front page, I am going to _____ these words: "To Dad on his fortieth birthday. Love, Ruth."

8. Learning that their arrest was _____, the insurgent leaders went into hiding.

9. The judge asked the guards to _____ the spectators who were creating a disturbance.

10. We just had to see what was in the package. We could not _____ our curiosity.

9. EXTRA-: "outside"
10. INTRA-: "within"

extracurricular (*adj.*) ,ek-strə-kə-'ri-kyə-lər	outside the regular curriculum or course of study	Why don't you join an *extracurricular* activity, such as a club, the school newspaper, or a team?
extraneous (*adj.*) ek-'strā-nē-əs	coming from or existing outside; foreign; not essential; not pertinent; irrelevant	You said you would stick to the topic, but you keep introducing *extraneous* issues.
extravagant (*adj.*) ik-'stra-vi-gənt	1. outside or beyond the bounds of reason; excessive	Reliable manufacturers do not make *extravagant* claims for their products.
	2. spending lavishly; wasteful	In a few months, the *extravagant* heir spent the fortune of a lifetime.

intramural (*adj.*) ,in-trə-'myür-əl	within the walls or boundaries (of a school, college, etc.); confined to members (of a school, college, etc.)	At most schools, the students participating in *intramural* athletics vastly outnumber the students involved in interscholastic sports.
intraparty (*adj.*) ,in-trə-'pär-tē	within a party	The Democrats are trying to heal *intraparty* strife so as to present a united front in the coming election.
intrastate (*adj.*) ,in-trə-'stāt	within a state	Commerce between the states is regulated by the Interstate Commerce Commission, but *intrastate* commerce is supervised by the states themselves.
intravenous (*adj.*) ,in-trə-'vē-nəs	within or by way of the veins	Patients are nourished by *intravenous* feeding when too ill to take food by mouth.

EXERCISE 4.6: *EXTRA-* AND *INTRA-* WORDS

Fill each blank with the most appropriate word from groups 9 and 10.

1. Your claim that you would win by a landslide was certainly _____, as you were nearly defeated.

2. An air conditioner cools a room and helps to shut out _____ noises.

3. The theft must be regarded as an _____ matter, unless the stolen goods have been transported across state lines.

4. Some educators want to concentrate on _____ athletics and do away with interscholastic competition.

5. Though fencing is not in the curriculum, it is offered as an _____ activity.

11. CONTRA-, CONTRO-, COUNTER-: *"against," "contrary"*

con (*adv.*) 'kän	(short for *contra*) against; on the negative side	I abstained from casting my ballot because I could not decide whether to vote *pro* or *con*.
con (*n.*)	(used mainly in the plural) opposing argument; reason against	Before taking an important step, carefully study the *pros* and *cons* of the matter.

contraband (*n.*) ʹkän-trə-‚band	merchandise imported or exported contrary to law; smuggled goods	Customs officials examined the luggage of the suspected smuggler but found no *contraband*.
contravene (*v.*) ‚kän-trə-ʹvēn	go or act contrary to; violate; disregard; infringe	By invading the neutral nation, the dictator *contravened* an earlier pledge to guarantee its independence.
controversy (*n.*) ʹkän-trə-‚vər-sē	(literally, "a turning against") dispute; debate; quarrel	Our *controversy* with Great Britain over the Oregon Territory nearly led to war.
counter (*adv.*) ʹkaůn-tər	(followed by *to*) contrary; in the opposite direction	The student's plan to drop out of school runs *counter* to his parents' wishes.
countermand (*v.*) ʹkaůn-tər-‚mand	cancel (an order) by issuing a contrary order; revoke	The health commissioner ordered the plant to close, but a judge *countermanded* the order.
incontrovertible (*adj.*) ‚in-kän-trə-ʹvər-tə-bəl	not able to be "turned against" or disputed; unquestionable; certain; indisputable	The suspect's fingerprints on the safe were considered *incontrovertible* evidence of participation in the robbery.

EXERCISE 4.7: *CONTRA-, CONTRO-,* AND *COUNTER-* WORDS

Fill each blank with the most appropriate word from group 11.

1. Until we became embroiled in _____, Peggy and I were the best of friends.

2. A birth certificate is _____ proof of age.

3. Vessels carrying _____ are subject to seizure.

4. A superior officer has the power to _____ the orders of a subordinate.

5. I cannot support you in an activity that you undertook _____ to my advice.

12. INTER-: *"between"*

intercede (*v.*) ‚in-tər-ʹsēd	(literally, "go between") interfere to reconcile differences; mediate; plead in another's behalf; intervene	I would have lost my place on line if you hadn't *interceded* for me.
intercept (*v.*) ‚in-tər-ʹsept	(literally, "catch between") stop or seize on the way from one place to another; interrupt; catch	We gained possession of the ball when Russ *intercepted* a forward pass.

interlinear (*adj.*)
,in-tər-'li-nē-ər

inserted between lines already printed or written

It is difficult to make *interlinear* notes if the space between the lines is very small.

interlude (*n.*)
'in-tər-,lüd

anything filling the time between two events; interval; break; intermission

Between World War I and II, there was a twenty-one-year *interlude* of peace.

intermediary (*n.*)
,in-tər-'mē-dē-,er-ē

go-between; mediator

For his role as *intermediary* in helping to end the Russo-Japanese War, Theodore Roosevelt won the Nobel Peace Prize.

intermission (*n.*)
,in-tər-'mi-shən

pause between periods of activity; interval; interruption

During the *intermission* between the first and second acts, you will have a chance to purchase refreshments.

intersect (*v.*)
,in-tər-'sekt

(literally, "cut between") cut by passing through or across; divide; cross

Broadway *intersects* Seventh Avenue at Times Square.

interurban (*adj.*)
,in-tər-'ər-bən

between cities or towns

The only way to get to the next town is by automobile or taxi; there is no *interurban* bus.

intervene (*v.*)
,in-tər-'vēn

1. come between

The summer vacation *intervenes* between the close of one school year and the beginning of the next.

2. come in to settle a quarrel; intercede; mediate

Let the opponents settle the dispute by themselves; don't *intervene*.

 ## EXERCISE 4.8: *INTER-* WORDS

Fill each blank with the most appropriate word from group 12.

1. A conspicuous warning signal must be posted wherever railroad tracks _____ a highway.

2. Though asked repeatedly to be an _____ in the labor dispute, the mayor so far has refused to intercede.

3. Radio stations sometimes offer a brief _____ of music between the end of one program and the start of another.

4. A special task force is trying to _____ the invaders.

5. Construction funds have been voted for a four-lane _____ highway linking the three cities.

Review Exercises

REVIEW 10: LATIN PREFIXES 7–12

In the space before each Latin prefix in column I, write the *letter* of its meaning from column II.

COLUMN I	COLUMN II
___ 1. *intra-*	*a.* out, from, away
___ 2. *inter-*	*b.* against, contrary
___ 3. *extra-*	*c.* in, into, on, against, over
___ 4. *e-, ex-*	*d.* within
___ 5. *contra-, contro-, counter-*	*e.* between
___ 6. *in-, im-*	*f.* outside

REVIEW 11: WORD-BUILDING

Fill in the prefix in column I and the complete word in column III.

COLUMN I	COLUMN II	COLUMN III
1. _____ *between*	+ VENE *come*	= _____ *come between*
2. _____ *in*	+ HIBIT *hold*	= _____ *hold in; restrain*
3. _____ *away*	+ ROSION *wearing*	= _____ *gradual wearing away*
4. _____ *against*	+ VERSY *turning*	= _____ *a turning against; dispute*
5. _____ *against*	+ SURGENT *rising*	= _____ *rising against; rebellious*
6. _____ *within*	+ VENOUS *pertaining to the veins*	= _____ *within the veins*
7. _____ *between*	+ LINEAR *pertaining to lines*	= _____ *inserted between the lines*
8. _____ *outside*	+ CURRICULAR *pertaining to the curriculum*	= _____ *outside the curriculum*

9. _____ + MIGRATE = _____
   into   *move*   *move into a foreign country*

10. _____ + CISE = _____
    out   *cut*   *cut out*

11. _____ + MURAL = _____
    within   *pertaining to walls*   *within the walls or boundaries*

12. _____ + MAND = _____
    against   *command*   *cancel by issuing a contrary order*

13. _____ + URBAN = _____
    between   *pertaining to cities*   *between cities or towns*

14. _____ + CISE = _____
    into   *cut*   *cut into; engrave*

15. _____ + VAGANT = _____
    outside   *wandering*   *outside the bounds of reason; excessive*

16. _____ + BAND = _____
    against   *ban; decree*   *goods imported contrary to law*

17. _____ + PEL = _____
    on   *drive*   *drive on; force*

18. _____ + HIBIT = _____
    out   *hold*   *hold out; show; display*

19. _____ + CEDE = _____
    between   *go*   *go between to reconcile differences; mediate*

20. _____ + MINENT = _____
    out   *projecting*   *projecting out; distinguished*

 REVIEW 12: SENTENCE COMPLETION

Fill each blank with the word from the list below that best fits the context.

contraband	controversy	countermand	eminent	evoke
excise	exclusive	exhibit	extravagant	immigrate
imminent	impel	incarcerate	incontrovertible	inscribe
insurgent	intercept	intermission	intervene	intravenous

1. Acting on a tip from an informer, customs agents were able to _____ a shipment of _____.

2. The heir's spending has been so _____ that his financial ruin is _____.

3. When details of the proposed six-lane highway through the center of town are disclosed, they will surely _____ considerable _____.

4. Few had ever heard of Lynn until the Philadelphia Museum of Art _____ed her work and transformed her into a(n) _____ painter.

5. The thief would have been _____d for ten years if a higher court had not _____ed the sentence.

6. If the civil strife in that country continues much longer, it may _____ many more of its inhabitants to _____ to America.

7. The suit charges that the company has been unfairly _____ in its hiring practices, and it asks the court to _____.

8. After the tumor was _____d, the patient required _____ feeding for three days.

9. During the ten-minute _____, several admirers approached the playwright and asked him to _____ their programs.

10. The dictator's claim that the rebellion has failed is contradicted by _____ evidence that the _____s are gaining the upper hand.

REVIEW 13: SYNONYMS

Avoid repetition by replacing the boldfaced word or expression with a **synonym**.

contravene	extracurricular	extraneous	extravagant	implicate
impugn	intercede	intermediary	intersect	invoke

_____ed **1.** Not only did they call his ability into question, but they also **questioned** his character.

_____ **2.** The law protects everyone. Even criminals **call upon** the Constitution **for protection**.

_____ **3.** Sports are not a part of the curriculum; they are **outside the curriculum**.

_____ **4.** Let us stick to the topic. We will get nowhere if we keep introducing matters that are **outside the topic of our discussion**.

_____ **5.** The point where two roads **cross** is a dangerous crossing.

_____d **6.** The accused falsely **involved** others who had no involvement whatsoever with the plot.

_____s **7.** We have little regard for anyone who **disregards** regulations that he or she wants others to observe.

_____ **8.** How can you ask us to be reasonable when you yourself are making demands that are so **beyond the bounds of reason**?

_____ **9.** Please do not **interfere**; we do not want any interference.

_____ **10.** Communication between the two adversaries is being conducted through a(n) **go-between**.

REVIEW 14: ANTONYMS

Enter the word from the list below that is most nearly the **opposite** of the boldfaced word or words.

con	enervate	erosion	expel	extracurricular
extravagant	inhibit	interlinear	intraparty	intrastate

1. The tiresome shopping trip had _____d my sister, but a short nap and a shower **reinvigorated** her.

2. Traffic usually moves faster on **interstate** highways than on _____ roads.

3. After the severe beach _____ caused by the storm, the town promised speedy **restoration** of the shoreline.

4. You made so many _____ corrections that it was hard to read what you had written **on the lines**.

5. Why did he _____ his resentment for so long before deciding to **express** it?

6. The club voted to _____ a member for nonpayment of dues and to **admit** two new applicants.

7. Do they realize that they may have to be **frugal** later if they are _____ now?

8. So far you have told us the **pros** of your plan, but how about the _____s?

9. If the Independents continue their self-destructive _____ sniping, they will be ill-equipped for the **interparty** contests that lie ahead.

10. Anyone who excels both in **curricular** work and _____ activities is indeed an exceptional person.

REVIEW 15: CONCISE WRITING

Express the thought of each sentence below in **no more than four words**.

1. Who are the ones who have risen in revolt against established authority?

_____

2. You made claims that are beyond the bounds of reason.

_____

3. Shouldn't those who commit the crime of burglary be put behind prison bars?

_____

4. Schools encourage sports activities that involve participation by their own students.

_____

5. Rains are a cause of the gradual wearing away of the soil.

_____

REVIEW 16: SYNONYM SUMMARY

Each line, when completed, should have three words similar in meaning. Enter the missing letters.

1. f __ rce	comp __ l	imp __ __
2. interv __ l	__ __ __ __ __ lude	inter __ __ ssion
3. disting __ __ shed	not __ worthy	__ minent
4. can __ el	rev __ ke	counter __ __ nd
5. elic __ t	prod __ ce	__ voke
6. q __ __ rrel	__ __ __ pute	contro __ __ __ rsy
7. thr __ __ tening	__ __ pending	__ __ minent
8. __ __ prison	__ __ __ fine	incar __ __ rate
9. interf __ r __	__ __ __ __ __ vene	inter __ __ __ de
10. compreh __ __ sive	br __ __ d	__ __ clusive
11. restr __ __ n	__ __ press	__ __ hibit
12. inv __ lve	__ __ tangle	__ __ plicate
13. unsh __ red	s __ le	__ __ clusive
14. weak __ __	__ __ feeble	__ nervate
15. cont __ __ dict	mal __ gn	imp __ gn
16. v __ olate	__ __ __ regard	__ __ __ travene
17. impr __ nt	__ __ grave	__ __ scribe
18. __ __ essential	irrel __ v __ nt	extran __ ous
19. deter __ __ ration	depl __ tion	__ r __ sion
20. ej __ ct	b __ n __ sh	__ __ pel

REVIEW 17: ANALOGIES

Which lettered pair of words—*a, b, c, d,* or *e*—most nearly expresses the same relationship as the capitalized pair? Write the letter of your answer in the space provided.

___ 1. IMMINENT : ANXIETY
    a. reasonable : controversy   *b.* uncomplicated : confusion
    c. abrupt : surprise   *d.* objective : indignation
    e. commonplace: attention
    Hint: Something that is **imminent** causes **anxiety.**

___ 2. INHIBIT : REPRESS
    a. grasp : release   *b.* withhold : grant
    c. oblige : refuse   *d.* conceal : display
    e. withstand : resist

___ 3. INCONTROVERTIBLE : DISPUTE
    a. unimportant : ignore   *b.* unique : replace
    c. accessible : approach   *d.* vulnerable : injure
    e. excusable : forgive

___ 4. INTERMEDIARY : UNBIASED
    a. interpreter : bilingual   *b.* despot : glorified
    c. umpire : partisan   *d.* infant : unsupervised
    e. ignoramus : heeded

___ 5. CLIQUE : EXCLUSIVE
    a. benefactor : uncharitable   *b.* mob : docile
    c. accomplice : irreproachable   *d.* recluse : sociable
    e. conspiracy : clandestine

___ 6. EMINENT : NOTE
    a. corrupt : trust   *b.* admirable : contempt
    c. indolent : promotion   *d.* culpable : blame
    e. helpless : ridicule

___ 7. ENERVATE : FEEBLE
    a. misinform : knowledgeable   *b.* pacify : tractable
    c. intimidate : intrepid   *d.* accommodate : hostile
    e. convince : uncertain

___ **8.** EXTRANEOUS : PERTINENT

    a. outdated : fashionable   *b.* rigid : inflexible

    c. foreign : alien   *d.* enigmatic : mysterious

    e. improbable : unlikely

___ **9.** INTERMISSION : PAUSE

    a. curtain : window   *b.* commission : service

    c. parsley : herb   *d.* truce : combat

    e. recess : energy

___ **10.** MINUTE : INTERLUDE

    a. seed : plant   *b.* whale : mammal

    c. skyscraper : edifice   *d.* tanker : vessel

    e. pittance : amount

REVIEW 18: COMPOSITION

Answer in a sentence or two.

1. Why might a king incarcerate insurgent soldiers?

2. Are eminent citizens likely to be members of an exclusive club? Explain.

3. Give an example of government inhibiting the movement of contraband.

4. Why might a leader's extravagant spending cause a controversy during hard economic times?

5. Describe a time you were impelled to argue against a rule that ran counter to your interests.

LATIN PREFIXES 13–18

Pretest 3

Insert the *letter* of the best answer in the space provided.

1. Inhabitants of a *secluded* dwelling have few_____.
   (A) windows   (B) expenses   (C) neighbors

2. *Malice* cannot exist between _____.
   (A) old rivals   (B) true friends   (C) close relatives

3. An *illegible* mark cannot be _____.
   (A) raised   (B) erased   (C) read

4. The opposite of a *benediction* is a _____.
   (A) curse   (B) contradiction   (C) blessing

5. A *dispassionate* witness is likely to be _____.
   (A) prejudiced   (B) calm   (C) easily upset

6. *Deciduous* trees _____.
   (A) shed their leaves   (B) resist disease   (C) are green all year

THE ANSWERS ARE
1. C   **2.** B   **3.** C   **4.** A   **5.** B   **6.** A

The following pages will introduce you to many more words formed with the six Latin prefixes involved in the pretest: *in-, bene-, mal-, de-, dis-,* and *se-*.

13. IN-, IL-, IM-, IR-: "not," "un"

WORD	MEANING	TYPICAL USE
illegible (*adj.*) ‚i(l)-'le-jə-bəl	not legible; impossible or hard to read; undecipherable	I could read most of the signatures, but a few were *illegible*.
illiterate (*adj.*) ‚i(l)-'li-tə-rət	not literate; unable to read or write; uneducated	The new nation undertook to teach its *illiterate* citizens to read and write.

illogical (*adj.*)
‚i(l)-ˈlä-ji-kəl

not logical; not observing the rules of logic (correct reasoning); irrational; fallacious

It is *illogical* to vote for a candidate whom you have no faith in.

immaculate (*adj.*)
i-ˈma-kyə-lət

not spotted; absolutely clean; stainless

Before dinner, the tablecloth was *immaculate*.

immature (*adj.*)
‚i-mə-ˈtür

not mature; not fully grown or developed; young; childish

Seniors often consider sophomores too *immature*.

impunity (*n.*)
im-ˈpyü-nə-tē

state of being not punished; freedom from punishment, harm, loss, etc.; immunity

As a result of stricter enforcement, speeders are no longer able to break the law with *impunity*.

inaccessible (*adj.*)
‚i-nik-ˈse-sə-bəl

not accessible; unreachable; hard to get to; unapproachable

For most of the year, the Inuit settlements in northern Quebec are *inaccessible,* except by air.

incessant (*adj.*)
(‚)in-ˈse-sᵊnt

not ceasing; continuing without interruption; interminable; ceaseless

It is almost impossible to cross the street during the rush hour because of the *incessant* flow of traffic.

inflexible (*adj.*)
(‚)in-ˈflek-sə-bəl

not flexible; not easily bent; firm; unyielding

No compromise is possible when both sides remain *inflexible*.

ingratitude (*n.*)
in-ˈgra-tə-‚tüd

state of being not grateful; ungratefulness; lack of gratitude

Valerie refuses to let me see her notes, though I have always lent her mine. What *ingratitude*!

inhospitable (*adj.*)
‚in-(‚)hä-ˈspi-tə-bəl

not hospitable; not showing kindness to guests and strangers; unfriendly

When the visitors come to our school, we should make them feel at home; otherwise they will think we are *inhospitable*.

insoluble (*adj.*)
(‚)in-ˈsäl-yə-bəl

1. not soluble; incapable of being solved; unsolvable; irresolvable

Scientists are finding solutions to many problems that formerly seemed *insoluble*.

2. not capable of being dissolved

Salt dissolves in water, but sand is *insoluble*.

irreconcilable (*adj.*)
i-‚re-kən-ˈsī-lə-bəl

not reconcilable; not able to be brought into friendly accord or compromise; incompatible

After Romeo and Juliet died, their families, who had been *irreconcilable* enemies, became friends.

irrelevant (*adj.*)
i-ˈre-lə-vənt

not relevant; inapplicable; off the topic; extraneous

Stick to the topic; don't make *irrelevant* remarks.

irrevocable (*adj.*)
i-ˈre-və-kə-bəl

not revocable; incapable of being recalled or revoked; unalterable; irreversible

As an umpire's decision is *irrevocable,* it is useless to argue over a call.

EXERCISE 4.9: *IN-, IL-, IM-,* AND *IR-* WORDS

Fill each blank with the most appropriate word from group 13.

1. Half frozen, the traveler knocked at a strange door, hoping the inhabitants would not be so _____ as to turn him away from their fire.

2. Prior to their arrest, the gang had committed a number of thefts with _____.

3. The detective finally succeeded in clearing up the seemingly _____ mystery by tracking down every clue.

4. On some of the very old tombstones in Boston's Granary Burying Ground, the inscriptions are almost _____.

5. Before the bridge was built, the island had been _____ from the mainland, except by ferry.

14. BENE-: "good," well"
15. MAL-, MALE-: "evil," "ill," "bad," "badly"

benediction (*n.*) ,be-nə-'dik-shən	(literally, "good saying") blessing; good wishes; approbation	Robinson Crusoe ran off to sea against his parents' wishes and without their *benediction*.
malediction (*n.*) ,ma-lə-'dik-shən	(literally, "evil saying") curse	With her dying breath, Queen Dido pronounced a *malediction* on Aeneas and all his descendants.
benefactor (*n.*) 'be-nə-,fak-tər	(literally, "one who does good") person who gives kindly aid, money, or a similar benefit	The museum could not have been built without the gift of ten million dollars by a wealthy *benefactor*.
malefactor (*n.*) 'ma-lə-,fak-tər	(literally, "one who does evil") offender; evildoer; criminal	Shortly after the crime, the *malefactor* was apprehended and brought to trial.
beneficial (*adj.*) ,be-nə-'fi-shəl	productive of good; helpful; advantageous	Rest is usually *beneficial* to a person suffering from a bad cold.
beneficiary (*n.*) ,be-nə-'fi-shē-,er-ē	person receiving some good, advantage, or benefit	The sick and the needy will be the *beneficiaries* of your gift to the community fund.
benevolent (*adj.*) bə-'ne-və-lənt	(literally, "wishing well") disposed to promote the welfare of others; kind; charitable	*Benevolent* employers have a sincere concern for the welfare of their employees.

malevolent (*adj.*) mə-'le-və-lənt	(literally, "wishing ill") showing ill will; spiteful; malicious; vicious	In Robert Louis Stevenson's novel KIDNAPPED, David Balfour visits a *malevolent* uncle who tries to kill him.
maladjusted (*adj.*) ,ma-lə-'jəs-təd	badly adjusted; out of harmony with one's environment	Having grown up in a quiet small town, Jesse was now a *maladjusted* city dweller who complained about noise and crowds.
malice (*n.*) 'ma-ləs	ill will; intention or desire to harm another; enmity; malevolence	My tire did not have a leak; someone had deflated it out of *malice*.
malnutrition (*n.*) ,mal-nü-'tri-shən	bad or faulty nutrition; poor nourishment	The lack of fresh fruit and vegetables in a person's diet may cause *malnutrition*.
maltreat (*v.*) ,mal-'trēt	treat badly or roughly; mistreat; abuse	Jen felt *maltreated* when the teacher scolded her for something that was not her fault.

EXERCISE 4.10: *BENE-, MAL-,* AND *MALE-* WORDS

Fill each blank with the most appropriate word from groups 14 and 15.

1. Polar bears are at home in cold climates, but their thick fur would leave them _____ in a warmer environment.

2. The hero of Charles Dickens' novel *Great Expectations* received considerable financial aid from an unknown _____.

3. Mrs. Adams will inherit a fortune, since she is named as the exclusive _____ in her wealthy aunt's will.

4. Paula couldn't understand why anyone should bear her so much _____ as to tear her notebook to bits.

5. Philip Nolan, in Edward Everett Hale's short story "The Man Without a Country," is punished for uttering a _____ on the United States.

16. DE-: *"down," "down from," "opposite of"*

decadent (*adj.*) 'de-kə-dənt	(literally, "falling down") deteriorating; growing worse; declining	The *decadent* rooming house was once a flourishing hotel.
deciduous (*adj.*) di-'si-jə-wəs	having leaves that fall off at the end of the growing season; shedding leaves	Maple, elm, birch, and other *deciduous* trees lose their leaves in the fall.

demented (*adj.*) di-'men-təd — out of (down from) one's mind; mad; insane; deranged — Whoever did this must have been *demented*; no sane person would have acted in such a way.

demolish (*v.*) di-'mä-lish — pull or tear down; destroy; raze; wreck — A wrecking crew is *demolishing* the old building.

demote (*v.*) di-'mōt — move down in grade or rank; degrade; downgrade — For being absent without leave, the corporal was *demoted* to private.

dependent (*adj.*) di-'pen-dənt — (literally, "hanging down from") unable to exist without the support of another — Children are *dependent* on their parents until they are able to earn their own living.

depreciate (*v.*) di-'prē-shē-,āt — 1. go down in price or value — New automobiles *depreciate* rapidly, but antiques tend to go up in value.

2. speak slightingly of; belittle; disparage — The store manager would feel you are *depreciating* him if you refer to him as the "head clerk."

despise (*v.*) di-'spīz — look down on; scorn; feel contempt for; abhor; disdain — Benedict Arnold was *despised* by his fellow Americans for betraying his country.

deviate (*v.*) 'dē-vē-,āt — turn aside, or down (from a route or rule); stray; wander; digress — Dr. Parker does not see a patient without an appointment, except in an emergency, and she does not *deviate* from this policy.

devour (*v.*) di-'vaů(-ər) — (literally, "gulp down") eat greedily; eat like an animal — Wendy must have been starved; she *devoured* her food.

EXERCISE 4.11: *DE-* WORDS

Fill each blank with the most appropriate word from group 16.

1. The bus driver cannot take you to your door because he is not permitted to _____ from his route.

2. Streets lined with _____ trees are strewn with fallen leaves each autumn.

3. The patient's speech was not rational but like that of a _____ person.

4. Retired people like to have an income of their own so as not to be _____ on others.

5. By A.D. 400, the Romans were well past the peak of their glory and had become a _____ people.

17. DIS-: "opposite of," "differently," "apart," "away"

discontent (*adj.*)
,dis-kən-'tent
(usually followed by *with*) opposite of "content"; dissatisfied; discontented; disgruntled
Dan was *discontent* with the mark on his Spanish exam; he had expected at least 10 points more.

discredit (*v.*)
(,)dis-'kre-dət
disbelieve; refuse to trust
The parents *discredited* the child's story, since he was in the habit of telling falsehoods.

discrepancy (*n.*)
dis-'kre-pən-sē
disagreement; difference; inconsistency; variation
The first witness said the incident had occurred at 10:00 A.M., but the second witness insisted the time was 10:45. This *discrepancy* puzzled the police.

disintegrate (*v.*)
di-'sin-tə-,grāt
do the opposite of "integrate" (make into a whole); break into bits; crumble; decay
The driveway needs to be resurfaced; it is beginning to *disintegrate*.

dispassionate (*adj.*)
,dis-'pa-shə-nət
opposite of "passionate" (showing strong feeling); calm; composed; impartial
For a *dispassionate* account of how the fight started, ask a neutral observer, not a participant.

disrepair (*n.*)
dis-ri-'par
opposite of good condition or repair; bad condition
The new owner did not take proper care of the building, and it soon fell into *disrepair*.

dissent (*v.*)
di-'sent
feel differently; differ in opinion; disagree
When the matter was put to a vote, 29 agreed and 4 *dissented*.

dissident (*adj.*)
'di-sə-dənt
(literally, "sitting apart") not agreeing; dissenting; nonconformist
The compromise was welcomed by all the strikers except a small *dissident* group who felt that the raises were too small.

distract (*v.*)
di-'strakt
draw away, or divert the attention of; confuse; bewilder
When the bus is in motion, passengers should do nothing to *distract* the driver.

EXERCISE 4.12: *DIS-* WORDS

Fill each blank with the most appropriate word from group 17.

1. The leader conferred with several _____ members of his party in an attempt to win them over to his views.

2. Add your marks for the different parts of the test to see if they equal your total mark. If there is a _____, notify the teacher.

3. The negligent owner allowed her equipment to fall into _____.

4. I had no reason to _____ the information, since it came from a reliable source.

5. Turn off the television set while you are trying to concentrate, or it will _____ your attention.

18. SE-: "apart"

secede (*v.*) si-'sēd	(literally, "go apart") withdraw from an organization or federation	When Lincoln was elected President in 1860, South Carolina *seceded* from the Union.
secession (*n.*) si-'se-shən	(literally, "a going apart") withdrawal from an organization or federation	South Carolina's *secession* was followed by that of ten other states and led to the formation of the Confederacy.
seclude (*v.*) si-'klüd	keep apart from others; place in solitude; isolate; sequester	Monica was so upset over losing her job that she *secluded* herself and refused to see anyone.
secure (*adj.*) si-'kyùr	1. apart, or free, from care, fear, or worry; confident; assured	Are you worried about passing, or do you feel *secure*?
	2. safe against loss, attack, or danger	Guests who want their valuables to be *secure* are urged to deposit them in the hotel vault.
sedition (*n.*) si-'di-shən	going apart from, or against, an established government; action, speech, or writing to overthrow the government; insurrection; treason	The signers of the Declaration of Independence, if captured by the enemy, would probably have been tried for *sedition*.
segregate (*v.*) 'se-gri-,gāt	(literally, "set apart from the herd") separate from the main body; isolate	During the swim period, the nonswimmers are *segregated* from the rest of our group to receive special instruction.

EXERCISE 4.13: *SE-* WORDS

Fill each blank with the most appropriate word from group 18.

1. The law forbids public institutions to _____ people by race, sex, or religion.

2. In a dictatorship, anyone who criticizes the head of state may be charged with _____.

3. Three of the teams have threatened to _____ from the league unless at least two umpires are assigned to each game.

4. As the storm approached, coastal residents were evacuated to more _____ quarters in the interior.

5. Some prefer to study for a test with friends; others like to _____ themselves with their books.

Review Exercises

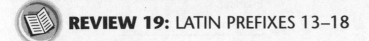

REVIEW 19: LATIN PREFIXES 13–18

In the space before each Latin prefix in column I, write the *letter* of its correct meaning from column II.

COLUMN I	COLUMN II
___ 1. mal-, male-	*a.* opposite of, differently, apart, away
___ 2. se-	*b.* not, un
___ 3. bene-	*c.* down, down from, opposite of
___ 4. dis-	*d.* apart
___ 5. de-	*e.* good, well
___ 6. in-, il-, im-, ir-	*f.* evil, ill, bad, badly

REVIEW 20: WORD-BUILDING

Fill in the prefix in column I and the complete word in column III.

COLUMN I	COLUMN II	COLUMN III
1. _____ *ill*	+ VOLENT *wishing*	= _____ *wishing ill; spiteful*
2. _____ *not*	+ LITERATE *able to read and write*	= _____ *unable to read and write*
3. _____ *down*	+ VOUR *gulp*	= _____ *eat greedily*
4. _____ *apart*	+ CURE *care*	= _____ *apart (free) from care*
5. _____ *not*	+ SOLUBLE *capable of being solved*	= _____ *incapable of being solved*

6. _____ + SPISE = _____
   down   look   look down on; scorn

7. _____ + DICTION = _____
   good   saying   blessing

8. _____ + LEGIBLE = _____
   not   able to read   not able to be read

9. _____ + INTEGRATE = _____
   opposite of make into a whole break into bits

10. _____ + FACTOR = _____
    evil   one who does   evildoer

11. _____ + MACULATE = _____
    not   spotted   unspotted; absolutely clean

12. _____ + CREDIT = _____
    opposite of believe   do opposite of believe; refuse to trust

13. _____ + MOTE = _____
    down   move   move down in rank

14. _____ + PUNITY = _____
    not   punishment   freedom from punishment

15. _____ + SENT = _____
    differently feel   feel differently; disagree

16. _____ + NUTRITION = _____
    bad   nourishment   poor nourishment

17. _____ + RELEVANT = _____
    not   applicable   not applicable; extraneous

18. _____ + CEDE = _____
    apart   go   go apart; withdraw from an organization

19. _____ + CADENT = _____
    down   falling   falling down; deteriorating

20. _____ + MATURE = _____
    not   fully grown   not fully grown

REVIEW 21: SENTENCE COMPLETION

Fill each blank with the word from the list below that best fits the context.

benefactor	demented	demote	depreciate	discontent
discredit	disrepair	dissident	distract	illiterate
illogical	incessant	ingratitude	inhospitable	insoluble
malice	malnutrition	secede	seclude	secure

1. Worried that the daily events of the city would _____ her from her work, the novelist _____ d herself in a mountain cabin.

2. The Southern states _____ d from the Union because they were _____ with the policies of the federal government.

3. The aunt never gets a visit from the nephews and nieces whom she put through college. Such _____ to a(n) _____ is indeed shocking.

4. When he said, "Madam, this is not a meal to ask a man to," Samuel Johnson _____ d the food his hostess had served. He considered her _____ .

5. By her _____ stress on the importance of reading, the superintendent hopes to ensure that no one in her district will remain _____ .

6. The colonel has been a model officer. I can only guess that his superior was acting out of _____ when he tried to _____ him.

7. Those detectives who termed the case "_____" did not adhere strictly to the principles of rational thinking. Their approach was _____ .

8. The children felt perfectly _____ in a tree house that was in such _____ that its collapse was clearly imminent.

9. The survivor had scarcely slept or eaten for several days. His seemingly _____ state of mind was the result of fatigue and _____ .

10. A group of _____ stockholders tried to _____ the company president by calling attention to his huge annual salary.

REVIEW 22: SYNONYMS

Avoid repetition by replacing the boldfaced word or expression with a **synonym** from the following words.

dependent	demolish	despise	deviate	discrepancy
dissent	immaculate	immature	inaccessible	inflexible

_____   1. You deserve a medal for cleanliness; your room is **absolutely clean**.

_____   2. They won't yield an inch. How can we reach a compromise if they are so **unyielding**?

_____   3. We **feel contempt for** the vandals who did this contemptible thing.

_____ ed   4. Almost everyone agreed. I was one of the very few who **disagreed**.

_____   5. You're acting like a child. Stop being **childish**.

_____ 6. The crash site is very **hard to get to**, but helicopters may be able to get there.

_____ 7. Now, they are **unable to exist without support from others**, but someday they will be able to support themselves.

_____ 8. The account of the first eyewitness differs slightly from that of the second. Did you notice the **difference**?

_____ing 9. One destructive child kept **destroying** what the others were trying to build.

_____ 10. Did the plane strictly adhere to its course, or did it **go off course** at any time?

 ## REVIEW 23: ANTONYMS

Enter the word from the list below that is most nearly the **opposite** of the boldfaced word or words.

beneficial	decadent	deciduous	dispassionate	illegible
irrelevant	maladjusted	malediction	malevolent	maltreat

1. It is hard to believe that this _____ place was once a **flourishing** mining town.

2. Most of the shrubs here are **evergreen**; only the azaleas are _____.

3. A **biased** observer may be unable to give a(n) _____ account of what happened.

4. The medication is not entirely _____; it has some **detrimental** side effects.

5. Some who are now **in harmony with their environment** might become _____ if they were to find themselves in other surroundings.

6. Prisoners of war are to be **humanely treated**; they must not be _____ed.

7. We tried to stay **on the topic**; little was said that was _____.

8. Did you get a **readable** copy? Mine is _____.

9. They came for a **blessing** but were sent off with a(n) _____.

10. Relatives could not understand how someone so **benevolent** to strangers could have been _____ to his own family.

REVIEW 24: CONCISE WRITING

Express the thought of each sentence below in **no more than four words.**

1. The question that Terry is asking has nothing to do with the topic that we are discussing.

   _____

2. Maple trees lose their leaves at the end of the growing season.

   _____

3. The postcard that came in the mail from Bill is impossible to read.

   _____

4. Some did not tell the truth and were able to get away with it.

   _____

5. The destination that they are heading for seems hard to get to.

   _____

REVIEW 25: SYNONYM SUMMARY

Each line, when completed, should have three words similar in meaning. Enter the missing letters.

1. cr __ m __ nal	ev __ ldoer	m __ l __ factor
2. diff __ r __ nce	inconsisten __ y	__ __ __ crepancy
3. charit __ ble	k __ nd	__ __ __ __ volent
4. sc __ rn	__ __ hor	__ __ spise
5. tr __ __ son	ins __ __ rection	__ __ dition
6. __ __ sane	__ __ ranged	__ __ mented
7. cr __ mble	__ __ cay	dis __ __ tegrate
8. enm __ ty	mal __ volence	__ __ __ ice
9. w __ nder	d __ gress	dev __ __ te
10. __ __ reversible	__ __ alterable	irre __ __ cable
11. advantag __ __ us	help __ __ __	benefi __ __ al
12. sep __ rate	is __ late	se __ __ egate
13. inapplic __ ble	extran __ ous	irr __ l __ v __ nt

14. __ __ terminable   cease __ __ __ __   inces __ __ nt

15. __ __ rational   fallac __ __ us   __ __ logical

16. disp __ r __ ge   __ __ little   __ __ preciate

17. __ __ __ fident   ass __ red   sec __ re

18. dis __ __ tisfied   disgr __ ntled   __ __ __ content

19. r __ ze   d __ stroy   __ __ molish

20. i __ __ late   se __ __ ester   __ __ clude

 ## REVIEW 26: ANALOGIES

Which lettered pair of words—*a, b, c, d,* or *e*—most nearly expresses the same relationship as the capitalized pair? Write the letter of your answer in the space provided.

___ 1. IRREVOCABLE : ALTER

    a. unique : match   *b.* feasible : do

    c. disputable : question   *d.* inconsequential : defer

    e. tractable : manage

___ 2. BENEFACTOR : MALICE

    a. perpetrator : offense   *b.* tutor : instruction

    c. fledgling : experience   *d.* curator : museum

    e. beneficiary : assistance

___ 3. IMPUNITY : PUNISHMENT

    a. merit : reward   *b.* frailty : injury

    c. insecurity : anxiety   *d.* infallibility : error

    e. susceptibility : disease

___ 4. SWINDLER : MALEFACTOR

    a. reader : subscriber   *b.* infant : dependent

    c. consumer : manufacturer   *d.* columnist : publisher

    e. physician : pediatrician

___ 5. GLUTTONOUS : DEVOUR

    a. lavish : conserve   *b.* withdrawn : socialize

    c. dissident : agree   *d.* avaricious : hoard

    e. determined : waver

___ 6. DISPASSIONATE : PARTIALITY

    a. merciless : cruelty   *b.* indecisive : hesitation

    c. maltreated : resentment   *d.* indifferent : interest

    e. malevolent : spite

___ 7. MALNUTRITION : HEALTH

    a. scandal : reputation   *b.* exercise : appetite

    c. misinformation : inconvenience   *d.* commendation : promotion

    e. enlightenment : knowledge

___ 8. IRRATIONAL : LOGIC

    a. loyal : allegiance   *b.* facetious : laughter

    c. corrupt : ethics   *d.* sturdy : stamina

    e. contentious : controversy

___ 9. INCESSANT : INTERMITTENT

    a. slovenly : untidy   *b.* dormant : sluggish

    c. robust : strong   *d.* meek : acquiescent

    e. permanent : transient

___ 10. IMMACULATE : SPOT

    a. airtight : weakness   *b.* imperfect : flaw

    c. noxious : harm   *d.* priceless : worth

    e. versatile : use

REVIEW 27: COMPOSITION

Answer in a sentence or two.

1. Would you rather be shipwrecked on a desert island with a benefactor or a malefactor?

_____

_____

2. Does it make sense to demolish all buildings in disrepair? Why or why not?

_____

_____

3. Why might the leaders of a country claim a dissident group was irrelevant?

_____

_____

4. Should a government treat acts of sedition with impunity? Explain.

_____

_____

5. Would you be surprised if a benevolent organization treated you inhospitably? Why or why not?

_____

_____

LATIN PREFIXES 19–24

Pretest 4

Insert the *letter* of the best answer in the space provided.

1. A *protracted* illness is not _____.

   (A) curable   (B) contagious   (C) brief

2. The term *circumlocution* in the margin of your composition paper indicates you have _____.

   (A) used too many words   (B) wandered off the topic   (C) used a slang expression
       to express an idea

3. Thoughts that *obsess* you _____ your mind.

   (A) bypass   (B) trouble   (C) relax

4. Those who work in *collusion* are seeking to _____.

   (A) escape noise   (B) assist others   (C) commit fraud

5. A snowfall in Virginia in _____ is *premature*.

   (A) December   (B) September   (C) March

6. If you make a *pertinent* comment, you are _____.

   (A) being rude   (B) delaying the discussion   (C) advancing the discussion

THE ANSWERS ARE

1. C 2. A 3. B 4. C 5. B 6. C

The following pages will introduce several additional words formed with the prefixes involved in the pretest: *circum-, con-, ob-, per-, pre-,* and *pro-.*

19. CIRCUM-: "around," "round"

WORD	MEANING	TYPICAL USE
circumference (*n.*) sər-ʹkəm-fə-rəns	distance around a circle or rounded body; perimeter	The *circumference* of the earth is greatest at the equator and diminishes as we go toward the North or South Pole.
circumlocution (*n.*) ˌsər-kəm-lō-ʹkyü-shən	roundabout way of speaking; use of excessive number of words to express an idea; verbiage; tautology	The *circumlocution* "the game ended with a score that was not in our favor" should be replaced by "we lost the game."
circumnavigate (*v.*) ˌsər-kəm-ʹna-və-ˌgāt	sail around	Ferdinand Magellan's expedition was the first to *circumnavigate* the globe.
circumscribe (*v.*) ʹsər-kᵊm-ˌskrīb	1. draw a line around	On the composition I got back, the teacher had *circumscribed* a misspelled word to call it to my attention.
	2. limit; restrict	The patient was placed on a very *circumscribed* diet; there are very few foods she is permitted to eat.
circumspect (*adj.*) ʹsər-kᵊm-ˌspekt	looking around and paying attention to all possible consequences before acting; cautious; prudent	Don't jump to a conclusion before considering all the facts. Be *circumspect.*
circumvent (*v.*) ˌsər-kᵊm-ʹvent	go around; get the better of; frustrate; skirt; bypass	To *circumvent* local sales taxes, shoppers buy in neighboring communities that do not have such taxes.

EXERCISE 4.14: *CIRCUM-* WORDS

Fill each blank with the most appropriate word from group 19.

1. A physician may decide to _____ the physical activities and diet of a heart-disease patient.

2. Obey the regulations; don't try to _____ them.

3. If you had been _____ you would have tested the used camera before buying it.

4. The _____ of the earth at the equator is nearly 25,000 miles.

5. The rowers had expected to _____ the island in a couple of hours, but by evening they were less than halfway around.

20. CON-, CO-, COL-, COR-: "together," "with"

coalesce (*v.*) ˌkō-ə-ˈles	grow together; unite into one; join; combine	During the Revolutionary War, the thirteen colonies *coalesced* into one nation.
coherent (*adj.*) kō-ˈhir-ənt	sticking together; logically connected; consistent; logical	In *coherent* writing, every sentence is connected in thought to the previous sentence.
collaborate (*v.*) kə-ˈla-bə-ˌrāt	work together with another or others, especially as a coauthor	George and Helen Papashvily *collaborated* on ANYTHING CAN HAPPEN and several other books.
collusion (*n.*) kə-ˈlü-zhən	(literally, "playing together") secret agreement for a fraudulent purpose; conspiracy; plot	The federal agency claimed the price increases were due to *collusion* among the producers.
concord (*n.*) ˈkän-ˌkȯrd	state of being together in heart or mind; agreement; harmony	Neighbors cannot live in *concord* if their children keep fighting with one another.
congenital (*adj.*) kən-ˈje-nə-tᵊl	(literally, "born with") existing at birth; inborn; innate	Helen Keller's deafness and blindness were not *congenital* defects; she was normal at birth.
convene (*v.*) kən-ˈvēn	come together in a body; meet; assemble	The House and the Senate will *convene* at noon to hear an address by the President.
correspond (*v.*) ˌkȯr-ə-ˈspänd	1. (literally, "answer together") agree; be in harmony; match; tally	Helene's account of how the argument started does not *correspond* with Sam's version.
	2. communicate by exchange of letters	Bill and I *correspond* regularly.

📖 **EXERCISE 4.15:** *CON-, CO-, COL-,* AND *COR-* WORDS

Fill each blank with the most appropriate word from group 20.

1. Though elected in November of even-numbered years, the new Congress does not _____ until the following January.

2. If your seat number does not _____ to your ticket number, the usher may ask you to move.

3. When Billy Budd, the peacemaker, was aboard, there was perfect _____ among the sailors.

4. Do you want to _____ with me, or do you prefer to work alone?

5. Just above St. Louis, the Missouri and Mississippi rivers _____ into a single waterway.

21. OB-: "against," "in the way," "over"

obliterate (*v.*) ə-'bli-tə-ˌrāt	(literally, "cover over letters") erase; blot out; destroy; remove all traces of	Today's rain has completely *obliterated* yesterday's snow; not a trace remains.
obsess (*v.*) əb-'ses	(literally, "sit over") trouble the mind of; haunt; preoccupy	Ian is *obsessed* with the idea of becoming a professional ballplayer.
obstacle (*n.*) 'äb-sti-kəl	something standing in the way; hindrance; obstruction; impediment	If Albert were to visit Rome, the language would be no *obstacle*; he knows Italian.
obstruct (*v.*) əb-'strəkt	be in the way of; hinder; impede; block	The disabled vehicles *obstructed* traffic until removed by a tow truck.
obtrude (*v.*) əb-'trüd	(literally, "thrust against") thrust forward without being asked; intrude; impose	It is unwise for outsiders to *obtrude* their opinions into a family quarrel.
obviate (*v.*) 'äb-vē-ˌāt	(literally, "get in the way of") meet and dispose of; make unnecessary; forestall; avert	By removing her hat, the woman in front *obviated* the need for me to change my seat.

EXERCISE 4.16: *OB-* WORDS

Fill each blank with the most appropriate word from group 21.

1. A dropout will discover that the lack of a high school diploma is a serious
   _____ to employment.

2. The pickets sat on the front steps in an attempt to _____ the entrance.

3. To _____ waiting on line at the box office, order your tickets by mail.

4. Though Harry is a very careful driver, the possibility of his having a serious accident
   continues to _____ his parents.

5. Claire tried to forget the incident, but she couldn't _____ it from her
   mind.

22. PER-: "through," "to the end," "thoroughly"

perennial (*adj.*)
pə-'re-nē-əl
continuing through the years; enduring; unceasing
Authors have come and gone, but Shakespeare has remained a *perennial* favorite.

perennial (*n.*)
plant that lives through the years
Perennials like the azalea and forsythia bloom year after year.

perforate (*v.*)
'pər-fə-,rāt
(literally, "bore through") make a hole or holes through; pierce; puncture
The tack I stepped on went through the sole of my shoe, but luckily did not *perforate* my skin.

permeate (*v.*)
'pər-mē-,āt
pass through; penetrate; spread through; pervade
The aroma of freshly brewed coffee *permeated* the cafeteria.

perplex (*v.*)
pər-'pleks
confuse thoroughly; puzzle; bewilder
I need help with the fourth problem; it *perplexes* me.

persist (*v.*)
pər-'sist
(literally, "stand to the end")
1. continue in spite of opposition; refuse to stop; persevere
Dr. Brown warned Janet of the consequences if she *persisted* in smoking despite his warnings.

2. continue to exist; last; endure
The rain was supposed to end in the morning, but it *persisted* through the afternoon and evening.

pertinent (*adj.*)
'pər-tᵊn-ənt
(literally, "reaching through to") connected with the matter under consideration; to the point; related; relevant
Stick to the point; don't give information that is not *pertinent*.

perturb (*v.*)
pər-'tərb
disturb thoroughly or considerably; make uneasy; agitate; upset
Sandra's folks were *perturbed* when they learned she had failed two subjects.

EXERCISE 4.17: *PER-* WORDS

Fill each blank with the most appropriate word from group 22.

1. The claim of wage earners that they are being overtaxed is by no means new; it has been their _____ complaint.

2. Why do you _____ in asking to see my notes when I have told you I don't have any?

3. Train conductors use hole punchers to _____ passenger tickets.

4. We thought the news would upset Jane, but it didn't seem to _____ her.

5. Road signs that _____ residents of this community are even more confusing to out-of-town visitors.

23. PRE-: "before," "beforehand," "fore-"

precede (*v.*) pri-'sēd	go before; come before	Did your complaint follow or *precede* Jane's?
preclude (*v.*) pri-'klüd	put a barrier before; impede; prevent; make impossible	A prior engagement *precludes* my coming to your party.
precocious (*adj.*) pri-'kō-shəs	(literally, "cooked or ripened before its time") showing mature characteristics at an early age	If Nancy's three-year-old sister can read, she must be a *precocious* child.
preconceive (*v.*) ‚prē-kən-'sēv	form an opinion of beforehand, without adequate evidence	The dislike I had *preconceived* for the book disappeared when I read a few chapters.
prefabricated (*adj.*) prē-'fa-bri-‚kā-təd	constructed beforehand	*Prefabricated* homes are quickly erected by putting together large sections previously constructed at a factory.
preface (*n.*) 'pre-fəs	foreword; preliminary remarks; author's introduction to a book	The *preface* usually provides information that the reader should know before beginning the book.
premature (*adj.*) ‚prē-mə-'tyu̇r	before the proper or usual time; early; untimely	Since less than half of the votes have been counted, my opponent's claims of victory are *premature*.
premeditate (*v.*) prē-'me-də-‚tāt	consider beforehand	The jury decided that the blow was struck in a moment of panic and had not been *premeditated*.

presume (*v.*) pri-'züm	(literally, "take beforehand") take for granted without proof; assume; suppose	Nineteen of the sailors have been rescued. One is missing and *presumed* dead.
preview (*n.*) 'prē-,vyü	view of something before it is shown to the public	Last night Carole and Bob attended a *preview* of a play scheduled to open next Tuesday.

 EXERCISE 4.18: *PRE-* WORDS

Fill each blank with the most appropriate word from group 23.

1. Mozart, who began composing at the age of five, was definitely _____.

2. The bills they have to pay do not _____ their making further purchases; they can use their credit.

3. I _____ the directions to Barbara's house are correct, since she gave them to me herself.

4. A group of distinguished specialists saw a _____ of the exhibit before it was opened to the public.

5. The report that the President was in town was _____ because his plane had not yet landed.

24. PRO-: "forward," "forth"

procrastinate (*v.*) prə-'kras-tə-nāt	(literally, "move forward to tomorrow") put things off from day to day; delay; dawdle	Start working on the assignment without delay. It doesn't pay to *procrastinate*.
proficient (*adj.*) prə-'fi-shənt	(literally, "going forward") well advanced in any subject or occupation; skilled; adept; expert	When I fell behind, the teacher asked one of the more *proficient* students to help me.
profuse (*adj.*) prə-'fyüs	pouring forth freely; exceedingly generous; extravagant; lavish	Despite a large income, the actor has saved very little because he is a *profuse* spender.
project (*v.*) prə-'jekt	throw or cast forward	The fireboat's powerful engines *projected* huge streams of water on the blazing pier.
prominent (*adj.*) 'prä-mə-nənt	(literally, "jutting forward") standing out; notable; important; conspicuous	The mayor, the governor, and several other *prominent* citizens attended the preview.

propel (*v.*) prə-'pel	impel forward; drive onward; force ahead; push; thrust	High winds *propelled* the flames, and they spread rapidly.
proponent (*n.*) prə-'pō-nənt	person who puts forth a proposal or argues in favor of something; advocate; supporter	At the budget hearing, both *proponents* and opponents of the tax increase will be able to present their views.
prospect (*n.*) 'prä-,spekt	thing looked forward to; expectation; vision	To a first-year student, graduation is a distant but pleasant *prospect*.
prospects (*n. pl.*) 'prä-,spekts	chances	The *prospects* of our winning are slim.
protract (*v.*) prō-'trakt	(literally, "drag forward") draw out; lengthen; extend; prolong	Our cousins stayed with us only for the day, though we urged them to *protract* their visit.
protrude (*v.*) prō-'trüd	thrust forth; stick out; bulge; jut	Keep your feet under your desk; if they *protrude* into the aisle, someone may trip over them.
provoke (*v.*) prə-'vōk	1. call forth; bring on; cause	Maria's account of her experiences as a babysitter *provoked* much laughter.
	2. make angry; annoy; incense; irritate	There would have been no quarrel if Lisa hadn't *provoked* you by calling you a liar.

EXERCISE 4.19: *PRO-* WORDS

Fill each blank with the most appropriate word from group 24.

1. The _____ of a sizable raise impelled the new employee to do her best.

2. Your enthusiastic supporters are _____ in their praise of your merits.

3. George Stephenson was the first to use steam power to _____ a locomotive.

4. You must not expect an apprentice to be as _____ as an experienced worker.

5. The proposal to demolish the historic building is sure to _____ a storm of protest.

Review Exercises

 REVIEW 28: LATIN PREFIXES 19–24

In the space before each Latin prefix in column I, write the *letter* of its correct meaning from column II.

COLUMN I

___ 1. *per-*

___ 2. *ob-*

___ 3. *circum-*

___ 4. *pro-*

___ 5. *con-, co-, col-, cor-*

___ 6. *pre-*

COLUMN II

a. together, with

b. through, to the end, thoroughly

c. forward, forth

d. before, beforehand, fore

e. around, round

f. against, in the way, over

 REVIEW 29: WORD-BUILDING

Fill in the prefix in column I and the complete word in column III.

COLUMN I

1. _____
   together

2. _____
   beforehand

3. _____
   around

4. _____
   forward

5. _____
   together

6. _____
   through

7. _____
   in the way

8. _____
   beforehand

COLUMN II

+ HERENT
  sticking

+ CONCEIVE
  form an opinion

+ NAVIGATE
  sail

+ JECT
  throw

+ LABORATE
  work

+ MEATE
  pass

+ STACLE
  something standing

+ FACE
  something said

COLUMN III

= _____
  sticking together; logically connected

= _____
  form an opinion beforehand

= _____
  sail around

= _____
  throw or cast forward

= _____
  work together

= _____
  pass through; penetrate

= _____
  something standing in the way; obstruction

= _____
  something said beforehand; foreword

9. _____ + VENE = _____
together *come* *come together; assemble*

10. _____ + FORATE = _____
through *bore* *bore through; pierce*

11. _____ + TRUDE = _____
against *thrust* *thrust forward without being asked*

12. _____ + VOKE = _____
forth *call* *call forth; cause*

13. _____ + LOCUTION = _____
round *speaking* *roundabout way of speaking*

14. _____ + CLUDE = _____
before *put a barrier* *put a barrier before; prevent*

15. _____ + RESPOND = _____
together *answer* *match; agree*

16. _____ + TURB = _____
thoroughly *disturb* *disturb thoroughly; upset*

17. _____ + CEDE = _____
before *go* *go before; come before*

18. _____ + PONENT = _____
forth *one who puts* *one who puts forth a proposal*

19. _____ + FABRICATED = _____
beforehand *constructed* *constructed beforehand*

20. _____ + SESS = _____
over *sit* *trouble the mind of; haunt*

REVIEW 30: SENTENCE COMPLETION

Fill each blank with the word from the list below that best fits the context.

circumlocution	circumspect	coalesce	collaborate	correspond
obliterate	obstruct	perplex	persist	preclude
preconceive	prefabricate	preface	premature	premeditate
presume	preview	prominent	prospect	provoke

1. The speaker's ineptitude, particularly his fondness for _____,
_____d some in the audience to leave early.

2. The arrival of spring keeps _____ing the experts. Sometimes it is late, and
sometimes _____.

3. Many of the people who plan to buy a home have the _____d notion
that _____d houses are necessarily of low quality.

4. In the _____ to their book, the authors describe how a chance meeting at a writers' conference led them to _____.

5. The perpetrator was _____ enough to _____ all shreds of incriminating evidence.

6. When the noted reviewer began to get fewer invitations to _____s, she _____d it was because of her low ratings of many recent movies.

7. She is determined, nevertheless, to _____ in writing honest reviews. After all, it was her candor that made her _____.

8. A longer prison sentence was _____d when the jury determined that the crime had not been _____d.

9. So much political support has _____d around the candidate that the _____ of his being elected is much stronger.

10. The defense witness's testimony did not at all _____ with that of the prosecution witness. Was it possibly an attempt to _____ justice?

REVIEW 31: SYNONYMS

Avoid repetition by replacing the boldfaced word or expression with a **synonym** from the following words.

circumnavigate	circumvent	congenital	convene	perturb
precede	procrastinate	proficient	proponent	protract

_____ 1. We have delayed too long; we must not **delay** any further.

_____ 2. Next month the board will **meet** in a new meeting place.

_____ 3. When you went sailing, did you **sail around** any of the islands in the sound?

_____ 4. I don't know who comes after me in the batting order, but I am sure that I **come before** you.

_____s 5. Drew did not support my proposal at first, but now he is one of its chief **supporters**.

_____ 6. Prejudice is not **inborn**; no one is born with it.

_____ed 7. Someone must have said something to upset Amy; she is very **upset**.

_____ 8. A few wanted to **prolong** the discussion, but the majority refused to stay longer.

_____ 9. Those who try to **get around** the law may get into trouble.

_____ 10. Though Joyce had no computer skills when she was hired, she has become a highly **skilled** programmer.

REVIEW 32: ANTONYMS

Enter the word from the list below that is most nearly the **opposite** of the boldfaced word.

circumscribe   congenital   correspond   obstacle   persist
pertinent   proficient   prominent   proponent   protract

1. The poster, unfortunately, was **inconspicuous**. It should have been in a more
_____ place.

2. I was criticized for omitting some _____ details and including some that were quite **irrelevant**.

3. The scars on my arm were **acquired** through injuries. The birthmarks, of course, are
_____.

4. The patient _____ed in smoking, though his physician had warned him to **desist**.

5. I am neither an **opponent** nor a(n) _____ of the proposed changes.

6. The mediators seek to **curtail** the walkout, saying there is little to be gained by
_____ing it.

7. Some graceful and _____ dancers were once awkward and **inept**.

8. Sometimes, what we perceive as a(n) _____ turns out to be an **advantage**.

9. The conclusions reached by two independent investigators should have
_____ed, but they **disagreed**.

10. To allow him a greater variety of foods, the patient's strictly _____d diet has been somewhat **expanded**.

REVIEW 33: CONCISE WRITING

Express the thought of each sentence below in **no more than four words**.

1. Carefully consider all the possible consequences of what you intend to do before you do it.

_____

2. It is obvious that a secret agreement was in existence for fraudulent purposes.

_____

3. Those who are in favor of the proposal please say "aye."

_____

4. The practice of using an excessive number of words to express an idea interferes with communication.

_____

5. Does the question you are asking have anything to do with the matter that we are discussing?

_____

REVIEW 34: SYNONYM SUMMARY

Each line, when completed, should have three words similar in meaning. Enter the missing letters.

1. p __ sh	thr __ st	pr __ p __ l
2. not __ ble	__ __ __ spicuous	__ __ __ minent
3. agr __ __ ment	h __ rm __ ny	c __ nc __ rd
4. p __ __ rce	p __ nct __ re	p __ rf __ rate
5. comb __ ne	j __ __ n	__ __ alesce
6. h __ __ nt	__ __ __ occupy	__ __ sess
7. s __ ppose	__ __ sume	pr __ s __ me
8. l __ st	__ __ dure	pers __ st
9. m __ tch	__ ally	__ __ __ respond
10. ann __ y	ir __ __ tate	pr __ v __ ke
11. in __ orn	__ __ nate	__ __ __ genital
12. ag __ tate	__ __ set	pert __ rb
13. l __ gical	cons __ stent	co __ __ rent
14. e __ rly	__ __ timely	pre __ __ ture
15. sk __ rt	b __ pass	__ __ __ __ __ __ vent
16. __ vert	f __ restall	__ __ viate
17. pen __ trate	perv __ de	__ __ __ meate
18. b __ lge	j __ t	__ __ __ trude
19. end __ ring	unc __ __ sing	per __ __ nial
20. verb __ age	tautol __ gy	__ __ __ __ __ __ locution

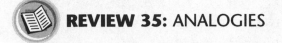

REVIEW 35: ANALOGIES

Which lettered pair of words—*a, b, c, d,* or *e*—most nearly expresses the same relationship as the capitalized pair? Write the letter of your answer in the space provided.

___ 1. CORRESPOND : LETTERS
    a. obliterate : traces   *b.* converse : words
    c. proofread : errors   *d.* soundproof : noises
    e. economize : expenses

___ 1. CURTAIL : PROTRACT
    a. attack : impugn   *b.* inflate : expand
    c. separate : coalesce   *d.* violate : contravene
    e. bicker : wrangle

___ 3. COLLUSION : DEFRAUD
    a. prosecution : exonerate   *b.* conservation : deplete
    c. condemnation : laud   *d.* revolution : change
    e. recuperation : weaken

___ 4. PREFACE : BOOK
    a. dawn : night   *b.* footnote : page
    c. dessert : repast   *d.* threshold : door
    e. overture : opera

___ 5. CIRCUMSPECT : CAUTION
    a. objective : facts   *b.* tolerant : bigotry
    c. gluttonous : restraint   *d.* impulsive : patience
    e. hypocritical : sincerity

___ 6. ADEPT : PROFICIENT
    a. manifest : evident   *b.* clandestine : overt
    c. thrifty : wasteful   *d.* compatible : uncongenial
    e. domesticated : wild

___ 7. FATIGUE : PROFICIENCY
    a. intimidation : tension   *b.* poverty : crime
    c. automation : drudgery   *d.* exercise : longevity
    e. repetition : boredom

___ 8. PROVOKE : ANGRY

    a. impoverish : indigent   *b.* convince : suspicious

    c. placate : hostile   *d.* absolve : blameworthy

    e. educate : ignorant

___ 9. ENIGMA : PERPLEX

    a. license : prohibit   *b.* forecast : guarantee

    c. rumor : reassure   *d.* relapse : accelerate

    e. impediment : obstruct

___ 10. PROFUSE : EXTRAVAGANCE

    a. frank : evasion   *b.* nonconformist : compliance

    c. outgoing : seclusion   *d.* indolent : procrastination

    e. uncharitable : benevolence

REVIEW 36: COMPOSITION

Answer in a sentence or two.

1. Why might circumlocutions be an obstacle to communication?

_____

_____

2. Are you perturbed about the prospects of your favorite sports team this year?

_____

_____

3. Would you rather collaborate on a school project with a perplexing student or a precocious student? Explain.

_____

_____

4. Would you be happy if your performance provoked profuse praise? Why or why not?

_____

_____

5. How is obstructing justice similar to circumventing the law?

_____

_____

5

Enlarging Vocabulary Through Latin Roots

What is a root?

A *root* is a word or basic element from which other words are derived. For example, *kind* is the root of *unkind, kindest, kindly,* and *unkindness.* As you can see, the *root* is the part of a word that is left after an addition, such as a prefix or a suffix, has been removed.

Sometimes a root has more than one form, as in the words *enjoy, rejoice, joyous,* and *enjoyable.* Here, the root is *joy* or *joi.*

Why study roots?

Once you know what a particular root means, you have a clue to the meaning of words derived from that root. For example, when you have learned that the root *MAN* means "hand," you are better able to understand—and remember—that *manacles* are *"handcuffs"*; that to *manipulate* is to *"handle"* or "manage skillfully"; and that a *manual* operation is "something done by *hand.*"

Purpose of this chapter

This chapter aims to enlarge your vocabulary by acquainting you with twenty Latin roots and some English words derived from them. Be sure to memorize the roots; they will help you unlock the meaning of numerous words beyond those discussed in this chapter.

LATIN ROOTS 1–10

Pretest 1

Insert the *letter* of the best answer in the space provided.

1. Some people are *gregarious*; others _____.
   (A) arrive late   (B) keep to themselves   (C) are ready to help

2. An *enamored* individual is _____.
   (A) well rounded   (B) armed   (C) captivated

3. The *literal* meaning of a word is its _____.
   (A) original meaning   (B) hidden meaning   (C) meaning in literature

4. A person with an *affinity* for sports is not _____ them.
   (A) repelled by   (B) absorbed in   (C) talented in

5. Prices in *flux* _____.
   (A) keep changing   (B) rise sharply   (C) drop rapidly

6. Don't be _____. Give them a *lucid* answer.
   (A) frank   (B) misled   (C) vague

7. There can be no *animus* in a person of _____ will.
   (A) good   (B) ill   (C) strong

8. There was _____, instead of *cohesion*.
   (A) ignorance   (B) disunity   (C) uncertainty

9. Any *unilateral* action is a _____ undertaking.
   (A) worldwide   (B) cooperative   (C) one-sided

10. A *regenerated* community _____.
    (A) shows new life   (B) resists changes   (C) grows steadily worse

THE ANSWERS ARE
1. B   2. C   3. A   4. A   5. A
6. C   7. A   8. B   9. C   10. A

In doing the pretest, you would have found it helpful to know the meaning of the roots *greg, amor, litera, fin, flux, luc, anim, hes, lateral,* and *gen.* You will learn how to use these roots in the pages that follow.

1. AM, AMOR: *"love," "liking," "friendliness"*

WORD	MEANING	TYPICAL USE
amateur (*n.*) 'a-mə-(,)tər	(literally, "lover") 1. person who follows a particular pursuit as a pastime, rather than as a profession 2. one who performs rather poorly; inexperienced person	The performance was staged by a group of *amateurs* who have been studying dramatics as a hobby. When it comes to baking a cake, you are the expert; I'm only an *amateur*.
amiable (*adj.*) 'ā-mē-ə-bəl	likable; good-natured; pleasant and agreeable; obliging	Charlotte is an *amiable* person; everybody likes her.
amicable (*adj.*) 'a-mi-kə-bəl	characterized by friendliness rather than antagonism; friendly; neighborly; not quarrelsome	Let us try to settle our differences in an *amicable* manner.
amity (*n.*) 'a-mə-tē	friendship; goodwill; friendly relations	We must look ahead to the time when the dispute is over and *amity* is restored.
amorous (*adj.*) 'a-mə-rəs	strongly moved by love; loving; inclined to love; enamored	In the famous balcony scene, *amorous* Romeo expresses undying love for Juliet.
enamored (*adj.*) i-'na-mərd	(usually followed by *of*) inflamed with love; charmed; captivated	Jason became *enamored* of the young woman and asked her to marry him.

2. ANIM: *"mind," "will," "spirit"*

animosity (*n.*) ,a-nə-'mä-sə-tē	ill will (usually leading to active opposition); violent hatred; enmity; antagonism	Someday the *animosity* that led to the war will be replaced by amity.
animus (*n.*) 'a-nə-məs	ill will (usually controlled)	Though Howard defeated me in the election, I bear no *animus* toward him; we are good friends.
equanimity (*n.*) ,ē-kwə-'ni-mə-tē	evenness of mind or temper under stress; emotional balance; composure; calmness; equilibrium	If you become extremely upset when you lose a game, it is a sign that you lack *equanimity*.
magnanimous (*adj.*) mag-'na-nə-məs	showing greatness or nobility of mind; chivalrous; forgiving; generous in overlooking injury or insult	The first time I was late for practice, Ms. O'Neill excused me with the warning that she would not be so *magnanimous* the next time.

unanimity (*n.*) ,yü-nə-'ni-mə-tē	oneness of mind; complete agreement	In almost every discussion there is bound to be some disagreement. Don't expect *unanimity*.
unanimous (*adj.*) yü-'na-nə-məs	of one mind; in complete accord	Except for one student, who voted "no," the class was *unanimous* in wanting the party.

EXERCISE 5.1: *AM, AMOR,* AND *ANIM* WORDS

Fill each blank with the most appropriate word from groups 1 and 2.

1. After his first success as a screen lover, the actor was cast only in _____ roles.

2. The prospect of financial reward has induced many a(n) _____ to turn professional.

3. Don't brood over your defeat. Accept it with _____.

4. Narcissus was too conceited to like anyone else; he was _____ of himself.

5. The 9–0 verdict shows that the judges were _____.

3. *FIN: "end," "boundary," "limit"*

affinity (*n.*) ə-'fi-nə-tē	(literally, condition of being "near the boundary" or "a neighbor") kinship; sympathy; liking; attraction	Because they share the same language and ideals, the Americans and the English have an *affinity* for one another.
confine (*v.*) kən-'fīn	keep within limits; restrict; limit	I will *confine* my remarks to the causes of inflation; the next speaker will discuss its effects.
definitive (*adj.*) di-'fi-nə-tiv	serving to end an unsettled matter; conclusive; final	The officials accused of bribery confessed when the district attorney presented *definitive* evidence of their guilt.
finale (*n.*) fə-'na-lē	end or final part of a musical composition, opera, play, etc.; conclusion	The acting was superb from the opening scene to the *finale*.
finis (*n.*) 'fi-nəs	end; conclusion	The word *finis* on the screen indicated that the film had ended.

4. FLU, FLUC, FLUX: "flow"

fluctuate (*v.*) 'flək-chə-,wāt	flow like a wave; move up and down; change often and irregularly; be unsteady	Last week the stock *fluctuated* from a high of 19 to a low of 17.
fluent (*adj.*) 'flü-ənt	ready with a flow of words; speaking or writing easily; articulate; eloquent	Do you have to grope for words, or are you a *fluent* speaker?
fluid (*n.*) 'flü-əd	substance that flows	Air, water, molasses, and milk are all *fluids*.
fluid (*adj.*)	not rigid; changeable; unstable	During November, the military situation remained *fluid,* with advances and retreats by both sides.
flux (*n.*) 'fləks	continuous flow or changing; unceasing change	When prices are in a state of *flux,* many buyers delay purchases until conditions are more settled.
influx (*n.*) 'in-,fləks	inflow; inpouring; inrush	The discovery of gold in California in 1848 caused a large *influx* of settlers from the East.

EXERCISE 5.2: *FIN, FLU, FLUC,* AND *FLUX* WORDS

Fill each blank with the most appropriate word from groups 3 and 4.

1. A diplomat who represents us in Russia should be _____ in Russian.

2. During the late spring, beach resorts ready themselves for the expected _____ of summer visitors.

3. The entire cast appeared on stage after the _____ to acknowledge the applause.

4. Unlike a lower court ruling, which may be reversed on appeal, a Supreme Court decision is _____.

5. There is a(n) _____ among classmates that is often as strong as loyalty to one's family.

5. GEN, GENER, GENIT: "birth," "kind," "class"

degenerate (*v.*)
di-'je-nə-‚rāt
sink to a lower class or standard; worsen; deteriorate
But for the skill of the presiding officer, the debate would have *degenerated* into an exchange of insults.

engender (*v.*)
in-'jen-dər
give birth to; create; generate; produce; cause
Name-calling *engenders* hatred.

genre (*n.*)
'zhän-rə
kind; sort; category
The writer achieved distinction in two literary *genres*—the short story and the novel.

progenitor (*n.*)
prō-'je-nə-tər
ancestor to whom a group traces its birth; forefather; forebear
The Bible states that Adam and Eve were the *progenitors* of the human race.

regenerate (*v.*)
ri-'je-nə-‚rāt
cause to be born again; put new life into; reform completely; revive; reinvigorate
The new manager *regenerated* the losing team and made it a strong contender.

6. GREG: "gather," "flock"

aggregate (*adj.*)
'a-gri-gət
gathered together in one mass; total; collective
The *aggregate* strength of the allies was impressive, though individually some were quite weak.

aggregation (*n.*)
‚a-gri-'gā-shən
gathering of individuals into a body or group; assemblage
At the airport, the homecoming champions were welcomed by a huge *aggregation* of admirers.

congregation (*n.*)
‚kän-gri-'gā-shən
"flock" or gathering of people for religious worship
The minister addressed the *congregation* on the meaning of brotherhood.

gregarious (*adj.*)
gri-'gar-ē-əs
inclined to associate with the "flock" or group; fond of being with others; sociable
Human beings, as a rule, are *gregarious*; they enjoy being with other people.

segregation (*n.*)
‚se-gri-'gā-shən
separation from the "flock" or main body; setting apart; isolation; separation
The warden believes in *segregation* of first offenders from hardened criminals.

📖 **EXERCISE 5.3:** *GEN, GENER, GENIT,* AND *GREG* WORDS

Fill each blank with the most appropriate word from groups 5 and 6.

1. New housing developments, shopping centers, and schools can _____ decadent neighborhoods.

2. Everyone in the _____ rose to sing a hymn.

3. Unless healed soon, these animosities are sure to _____ armed conflict.

4. The box score shows the points scored by each player, as well as the team's _____ score.

5. When I first came here, I had no friends and kept to myself. I was not too _____.

7. HERE, HES: "stick"

adhere (*v.*) ad-'hir	stick; hold fast; cling; be attached	Apply the sticker according to the directions, or it will not *adhere*.
cohere (*v.*) kō-'hir	stick together; hold together firmly	I glued together the fragments of the vase, but they did not *cohere*.
coherence (*n.*) kō-'hir-ən(t)s	state of sticking together; consistency; logical connection	If the relationship between the first sentence and what follows is not clear, the paragraph lacks *coherence*.
cohesion (*n.*) kō-'hē-zhən	act or state of sticking together; union; unity; bond	There can be no real *cohesion* in an alliance if the parties have little in common.
incoherent (*adj.*) ,in-kō-'hir-ənt	not logically connected; disconnected; unintelligible	The speech of a person in a rage may be *incoherent*.
inherent (*adj.*) in-'hir-ənt	(literally, "sticking in") deeply infixed; intrinsic; essential	Because of her *inherent* carefulness, I am sure my sister will be a good driver.

8. LATERAL: "side"

bilateral (*adj.*) bī-'la-tə-rəl	involving two sides	A *bilateral* team of federal and local experts conducted the survey.
collateral (*adj.*) kə-'la-tə-rəl	situated at the side; accompanying; parallel; additional; supplementary	After voting for the road-building program, the legislature took up the *collateral* issue of how to raise the necessary funds.
equilateral (*adj.*) ,ē-kwə-'la-tə-rəl	having all sides equal	If one side of an *equilateral* triangle measures three feet, the other two must also be three feet each.
lateral (*adj.*) 'la-tə-rəl	of or pertaining to the side	The building plan shows both a front and a *lateral* view of the proposed structure.
multilateral (*adj.*) ,məl-ti-'la-tə-rəl	having many sides	A parent plays a *multilateral* role as a nurse, housekeeper, shopper, cook, teacher, etc.
quadrilateral (*n.*) ,kwä-drə-'la-tə-rəl	plane figure having four sides and four angles	A square is a *quadrilateral*.
unilateral (*adj.*) ,yü-ni-'la-tə-rəl	one-sided; undertaken by one side only	Don't judge the matter by my opponent's *unilateral* statement, but wait till you have heard the other side.

EXERCISE 5.4: *HERE, HES,* AND *LATERAL* WORDS

Fill each blank with the most appropriate word from groups 7 and 8.

1. Most city blocks are shaped like a(n) _____.

2. Are you speaking for all the members of your club or giving only your _____ views?

3. Some believe that might is right, but I do not _____ to that doctrine.

4. When we were studying *Johnny Tremain,* our teacher assigned _____ reading on the Revolutionary War.

5. The politician's _____ role as champion of justice, defender of the poor, supporter of education, and friend of business attracted many adherents.

9. LITERA: "letter"

alliteration (*n.*)
ə-,li-tə-'rā-shən

repetition of the same letter or consonant at the beginning of neighboring words

Note the *alliteration* in the line "Sing a song of sixpence."

literacy (*n.*)
'li-tə-rə-sē

state of being lettered or educated; ability to read and write

Research required a high degree of *literacy.*

literal (*adj.*)
'li-tə-rəl

following the letters or exact words of the original; verbatim; word-for-word

We translate "laissez-faire" as "absence of government interference," but its *literal* meaning is "let do."

literary (*adj.*)
'li-tə-,rer-ē

having to do with letters or literature

Willa Cather is one of the great writers of novels in our *literary* history.

literate (*adj.*)
'li-tə-rət

lettered; able to read and write; educated

The teacher's main goal in working with adults who can neither read nor write is to make them *literate.*

10. LUC, LUM: "light"

elucidate (*v.*)
i-'lü-sə-,dāt

throw light upon; make clear; explain; clarify

I asked the teacher to *elucidate* a point that was not clear to me.

lucid (*adj.*)
'lü-səd

(literally, "containing light") clear; easy to understand; comprehensible

To obviate misunderstanding, state the directions in the most *lucid* way possible.

luminary (*n.*)
'lü-mə-,ner-ē

one who is a source of light or inspiration to others; famous person; notable; celebrity

A number of *luminaries,* including a Nobel Prize winner, will be present.

luminous (*adj.*)
'lü-mə-nəs

emitting light; bright; shining; brilliant

With this watch you can tell time in the dark because its hands and dial are *luminous.*

translucent (*adj.*)
tran(t)s-'lü-sᵊnt

letting light through

Lamp shades are *translucent* but not transparent.

EXERCISE 5.5: *LITERA, LUC,* AND *LUM* WORDS

Fill each blank with the most appropriate word from groups 9 and 10.

1. You need not prove that you can read and write. No one doubts your
   _____.

2. _____ paint is used for road signs so that they may be visible to night drivers.

3. Gary tried to _____ the matter, but he only made us more confused.

4. A host of admirers surrounded the sports _____ to ask for her autograph.

5. Did you know that the _____ meaning of Philip is "lover of horses"?

Review Exercises

REVIEW 1: LATIN ROOTS 1–10

In the space before each Latin root in column I, write the *letter* of its definition from column II.

COLUMN I		COLUMN II
___ 1. LATERAL		*a.* light
___ 2. FLU, FLUC, FLUX		*b.* letter
___ 3. AM, AMOR		*c.* birth, kind, class
___ 4. GREG		*d.* side
___ 5. HERE, HES		*e.* flow
___ 6. ANIM		*f.* love, liking, friendliness
___ 7. FIN		*g.* gather, flock
___ 8. LUC, LUM		*h.* end, boundary, limit
___ 9. GEN, GENER, GENIT		*i.* stick
___ 10. LITERA		*j.* mind, will, spirit

REVIEW 2: WORD-BUILDING

Fill in the *prefix* in column I, the *root* in column II, and the *missing letters* of the word in column III. Each blank stands for *one* missing letter.

I PREFIX		II ROOT		III WORD
1. _ _ _ _ _ *through*	+	_ _ _ *light*	=	_ _ _ _ _ _ _ _ ENT *letting light through*
2. _ _ *down from*	+	_ _ _ _ _ *class*	=	_ _ _ _ _ _ _ ATE *sink to a lower class; deteriorate*
3. _ _ *again*	+	_ _ _ _ _ *birth*	=	_ _ _ _ _ _ _ ATE *cause to be born again; reform completely*
4. _ _ _ *together*	+	_ _ _ _ *stick*	=	_ _ _ _ _ _ _ *hold together firmly*
5. _ _ *in*	+	_ _ _ _ *flow*	=	_ _ _ _ _ _ *inflow; inpouring*
6. _ _ _ *one*	+	_ _ _ _ _ _ _ *side*	=	_ _ _ _ _ _ _ _ _ *one-sided*
7. _ _ *in*	+	_ _ _ _ _ *stick*	=	_ _ _ _ _ NT *"sticking in"; deeply infixed; intrinsic*
8. _ _ *apart*	+	_ _ _ _ *flock*	=	_ _ _ _ _ ATION *separation from the flock; isolation*
9. _ _ *together*	+	_ _ _ _ *stick*	=	_ _ _ _ _ ION *act of sticking together, union*
10. _ _ *not*	+	_ _ _ _ _ _ *letter*	=	_ _ _ _ _ _ _ _ TE *unlettered; unable to read or write*

REVIEW 3: SENTENCE COMPLETION

Fill each blank with the word from the list below that best fits the context.

adhere	affinity	alliteration	amateur	amicable
amorous	animosity	cohere	confine	congregation
definitive	degenerate	elucidate	engender	finale
fluent	gregarious	inherent	literary	luminary

1. A boundary dispute had _____ed considerable _____ between the two neighbors who formerly were friends.

2. Dad was once _____ in French, but his proficiency in that language has _____d because he has not used it for twenty years.

3. Being a(n) _____ person, Roy lingered in the auditorium after the _____ of the opera to chat with friends.

4. When he addresses the _____, the spiritual leader is usually—but not always—brief; he does not have to _____ to a time schedule.

5. The _____ who had been invited to the convention announced that she would _____ her oral reading to passages from her prize-winning book.

6. Sheldon is a lawyer by profession, but in painting he is just a(n) _____, though he has a great _____ for that calling.

7. In considering the suitor's proposal, Portia had to decide whether her feelings for him were truly _____, or merely _____.

8. The witness was asked to _____ a statement she made that did not seem to _____ with her earlier testimony.

9. In the line, "The furrow followed free," Samuel T. Coleridge uses the _____ device known as _____.

10. The advice "Never make a generalization" cannot be regarded as _____ because it contains a(n) _____ contradiction: "Never make a generalization" is itself a generalization.

REVIEW 4: SYNONYMS

Avoid repetition by replacing the boldfaced word or expression with a **synonym** from the following words.

amiable	amity	animus	cohesion	fluctuate
literate	luminous	magnanimous	unanimity	unilateral

_____ 1. Many have forgiven and forgotten the suffering that former enemies caused, but others have not been so **forgiving**.

_____ 2. I don't like that ill-tempered grouch; he is not a(n) **likable** person.

_____   3. The moon, which has no brightness of its own, is **bright** at night with light that shines on it from the sun.

_____   4. If many members are resisting goals that a majority in their union supports, there is obviously a lack of **unity**.

_____   5. This is just my **one-sided** opinion; it does not reflect the views of all sides to the dispute.

_____   6. A nation that sets a low priority on education is not likely to have the world's most **educated** population.

_____   7. The 11-to-1 vote shows how strongly the club agrees with your motion. If not for that one negative ballot, we would have had **complete agreement**.

_____   8. There was no **friendship** between us when we were rivals. Lately, however, we have become friends.

_____   9. Last month, there was little movement in stock prices. Usually, they **move up and down** quite a bit.

_____   10. Linda is a person of good will; she has no **ill will** toward any one.

REVIEW 5: ANTONYMS

Enter the word from the list below that is most nearly the **opposite** of the boldfaced word.

amateur	amicable	amity	definitive	degenerate
fluid	flux	literate	lucid	translucent

1. After a long interval of **stability**, we are now in a period of _____.

2. The early results are encouraging but **inconclusive**; more _____ proof is needed before the researchers can claim a medical breakthrough.

3. Ours is a cast of talented _____s, but we are not **professionals**.

4. Immediately after the operation, the patient was on a rigid diet of _____s, with no **solids** whatsoever.

5. At last, the feud is over; _____ has replaced **enmity**.

6. No light penetrates the walls because they are made of **opaque** materials; the windowpanes, of course, are _____.

7. This firm's prospects for recovery have _____d rather than **improved**.

8. Explain what happened in _____ English; don't be **vague**.

9. Earlier in the negotiations, the mood of both parties was _____; now, it has turned **antagonistic**.

10. A bilingual person is _____ in two languages but **illiterate** in all others.

REVIEW 6: SYNONYM SUMMARY

Each line, when completed, should have three words similar in meaning. Enter the missing letters.

1. chang __ __ ble   unst __ ble   flu __ d
2. fr __ __ ndly   n __ __ ghborly   __ mic __ ble
3. fin __ l   concl __ sive   def __ n __ tive
4. w __ rd-for-w __ rd   verb __ t __ m   l __ teral
5. cre __ te   __ ause   __ __ gender
6. sep __ ration   is __ lation   __ __ gregation
7. disc __ __ nected   unintellig __ ble   in __ __ herent
8. __ __ traction   l __ king   __ __ finity
9. __ nion   b __ nd   co __ __ sion
10. accompan __ ing   para __ __ el   c __ __ lateral
11. comp __ sure   equ __ librium   e __ __ animity
12. k __ nd   cat __ gory   __ __ nre
13. ant __ g __ nism   __ __ mity   an __ m __ sity
14. c __ l __ brity   not __ ble   l __ min __ ry
15. g __ n __ rous   chiv __ lrous   mag __ __ nimous
16. tot __ l   c __ __ lective   __ __ gregate
17. __ __ flow   inp __ __ ring   infl __ x
18. __ __ sential   intr __ nsic   __ __ herent
19. __ loquent   artic __ late   fl __ ent
20. wors __ n   deter __ __ rate   __ __ generate

 ## REVIEW 7: CONCISE WRITING

In no more than fifty words, rewrite the following passage, keeping all its ideas. *Hint:* Reduce each boldfaced expression to a single word. The first sentence has been done to get you started. Go on from there.

A Rare Person

Bruce can be **pleasant and agreeable** when others are cranky. When they are unforgiving, he is usually **generous in overlooking injury or insult**. And when they get upset, he maintains his **evenness of mind and temper**. He is a rare person whose moods do not **change continually or vary in an irregular way**. Besides, he is **fond of being with others**. In conversation, he is not only **ready with a flow of words**, but logical and **easy to understand**.

A Rare Person
(concise version)

Bruce can be amiable when others are cranky.

_____

_____

_____

_____

_____

_____

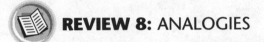 **REVIEW 8:** ANALOGIES

Which lettered pair of words—*a, b, c, d,* or *e*—most nearly expresses the same relationship as the capitalized pair? Write the letter of your answer in the space provided.

___ 1. MALEVOLENT : ANIMUS

    a. blameless : guilt   *b.* circumspect : foresight

    c. indigent : resources   *d.* audacious : manners

    e. trustworthy : deception

___ 2. SQUARE : QUADRILATERAL

    a. hand : digit   *b.* weapon : missile

    c. bulb : socket   *d.* access : passageway

    e. eighth : fraction

___ 3. FLUCTUATION : UNCERTAINTY

    a. defect : malfunction   *b.* pain : inflammation

    c. delay : fog   *d.* boredom : repetition

    e. malnutrition : health

—— 4. GREGARIOUS : COMPANY

    a. reserved : communication   *b.* slovenly : neatness

    c. frugal : waste   *d.* withdrawn : solitude

    e. parsimonious : expenditure

—— 5. INDIVIDUAL : AGGREGATION

    a. particle : dust   *b.* chord : note

    c. head : hair   *d.* oyster : pearl

    e. message : word

—— 6. LUCID : COMPREHEND

    a. complex : grasp   *b.* indelible : erase

    c. versatile : adapt   *d.* inequitable : justify

    e. decadent : regenerate

—— 7. MAGNANIMOUS : PARDON

    a. headstrong : acquiesce   *b.* reasonable : compromise

    c. meek : protest   *d.* insubordinate : obey

    e. persistent : quit

—— 8. TRANSLUCENT : LIGHT

    a. opinionated : ideas   *b.* exclusive : people

    c. airtight : leak   *d.* porous : liquid

    e. conspicuous : attention

REVIEW 9: COMPOSITION

Answer in a sentence or two.

1. Would you probably be magnanimous toward someone you were enamored of? Why?

_____

_____

2. Who are some people you consider to be literary luminaries? Explain your choices.

_____

_____

3. Why was segregation of the races inherently unfair?

_____

_____

4. Do you think a unilateral or a multilateral effort is more likely to bring about the end of a war? Explain.

_____

_____

5. How might an influx of new industries regenerate a city's economy?

_____

_____

LATIN ROOTS 11–20

Pretest 2

Insert the *letter* of the best answer in the space provided.

1. *Video* signals have to do with _____.

    (A) sounds   (B) pictures   (C) music

2. In a *soliloquy,* you would be _____.

    (A) doing most of the   (B) questioning a group   (C) talking to yourself
        talking

3. A *redundant* expression should be _____.

    (A) removed   (B) explained   (C) replaced

4. _____ involves no *manual* operations.

    (A) Dining   (B) Typing   (C) Smiling

5. A *pendant* cannot _____.

    (A) translate   (B) adorn   (C) dangle

6. Now that my *veracity* has been questioned, I feel deeply _____.

    (A) honored   (B) insulted   (C) relieved

7. A *scribe* belongs to the _____ profession.

    (A) teaching   (B) acting   (C) writing

8. We cannot tell whether their interest is *simulated* or _____.

    (A) real   (B) selfish   (C) pretended

9. The new regulation *imposes* additional _____ on all.

    (A) responsibilities   (B) privileges   (C) benefits

10. If you are *insolvent,* you cannot _____.

    (A) vote   (B) pay your debts   (C) think logically

THE ANSWERS ARE

1. B   **2.** C   **3.** A   **4.** C   **5.** A
6. B   **7.** C   **8.** A   **9.** A   **10.** B

Had you known the meaning of the roots *vid, sol, unda, manu, pend, vera, scrib, simul, pos,* and *solv,* you would have had an advantage in the pretest. You will learn about these roots in the following pages.

11. MAN, MANU: "hand"

emancipate (*v.*) i-'man(t)-sə-,pāt	(literally, "take from the hand" or power of another) release from bondage; free; liberate	The washing machine has *emancipated* millions of people from a great deal of drudgery.
manacle (*n.*) 'ma-ni-kəl	handcuff	The *manacles* were removed from the prisoner's wrists.
mandate (*n.*) 'man-,dāt	(literally, something "given into one's hand") 1. authorization to act	The overwhelming vote for the reform slate is regarded as a *mandate* from the people to root out corruption.
	2. command; order; injunction	By a close margin, the workers voted to comply with the court's *mandate* against a strike.
manipulate (*v.*) mə-'ni-pyə-,lāt	1. operate with the hands; handle or manage skillfully; maneuver	In today's lesson I learned how to *manipulate* the steering wheel.
	2. manage unethically to serve a fraudulent purpose; falsify; rig	The defeated candidate charged that the election results had been *manipulated.*
manual (*n.*) 'man-yə-wəl	small, helpful book capable of being carried in the hand; handbook	Each student has a learner's permit and a copy of the "Driver's *Manual.*"
manual (*adj.*)	relating to, or done with, the hands	Milking, formerly a *manual* operation, is now done by machine.
manuscript (*n.*) 'man-yə-,skript	document written by hand, or typewritten	The author's *manuscript* is now at the printer.

12. PEND, PENS: "hang"

append (*v.*) ə-'pend	(literally, "hang on") attach; add as a supplement	If you hand in your report late, *append* a note explaining the reason for the delay.
appendix (*n.*) ə-'pen-diks	(literally, something "hung on") matter added to the end of a book or document	A school edition of a novel usually has an *appendix* containing explanatory notes.
impending (*adj.*) im-'pen-diŋ	(literally, "overhanging") threatening to occur soon; imminent	At the first flash of lightning, we scurried for shelter from the *impending* storm.
pendant (*n.*) 'pen-dənt	hanging ornament	The *pendant* dangling from the chain around her neck looked like a medal, but it was really a timepiece.
pending (*adj.*) 'pen-diŋ	(literally, "hanging") waiting to be settled; not yet decided	Has a date been set for the game, or is the matter still *pending*?
pending (*prep.*)	until	Barbara agreed to conduct the meeting, *pending* the election of a presiding officer.
suspend (*v.*) sə-'spend	1. hang by attaching to something	Would you prefer to attach a lamp to the wall or *suspend* one from the ceiling?
	2. stop temporarily; hold up; make inoperative for a while	Service will be *suspended* from midnight to 4 A.M. to permit repairs.
suspense (*n.*) sə-'spen(t)s	condition of being left "hanging" or in doubt; mental uncertainty; anxiety; apprehension	If you have seen the marks posted, please tell me whether I passed or failed; don't keep me in *suspense*!

EXERCISE 5.6: *MAN, MANU, PEND,* AND *PENS* WORDS

Fill each blank with the most appropriate word from groups 11 and 12.

1. Can you operate this gadget? I don't know how to _____ it.

2. As the enemy approached, the defenders got ready for the _____ attack.

3. Because of a lengthy labor dispute, the city's daily newspapers had to _____ publication.

4. Is it possible to _____ addicts from their bondage to drugs?

5. The retiring manager has agreed to stay on, _____ the choice of a successor.

13. PON, POS: "put"

depose (*v.*)
di-'pōz

1. (literally, "put down") put out of office; dethrone

Did the king abdicate, or was he *deposed*?

2. state under oath; testify; swear

He *deposed* on the witness stand that he had never taken a bribe.

impose (*v.*)
im-'pōz

put on as a burden, duty, tax, etc.; inflict

Cleaning up after the job is the repair crew's responsibility. Don't let them *impose* it on you.

postpone (*v.*)
pōs(t)-'pōn

(literally, "put after") put off; defer; delay

Our instructor has *postponed* the test until tomorrow to give us an extra day to study.

superimpose (*v.*)
,sü-pər-im-'pōz

put on top of or over; attach as an addition

Today's snowfall *superimposed* a fresh two inches on yesterday's accumulation.

transpose (*v.*)
tran(t)s-'pōz

(literally, "put across") change the relative order of; interchange

There is a misspelled word on your paper, "strenght." Correct it by *transposing* the last two letters.

14. SCRIB, SCRIPT: "write"

conscript (*v.*)
kən-'skript

enroll (write down) into military service by compulsion; draft

When there were not enough volunteers for the armed forces, the government had to *conscript* additional men and women.

inscription (*n.*)
in-'skrip-shən

something inscribed (written) on a monument, coin, etc.

The *inscription* on the inside of their wedding bands read, "Nicole and Adam forever."

prescribe (*v.*)
pri-'skrīb

(literally, "write before")
1. order; dictate; direct

The law *prescribes* that aliens may not vote.

2. order as a remedy

Her physician *prescribed* some pills, a light diet, and plenty of rest.

proscribe (*v.*)
prō-'skrīb

condemn as harmful or illegal; prohibit; forbid

The dumping of wastes into the waterways is *proscribed*.

scribe (*n.*)
'skrīb

person who writes; author; journalist

Both candidates used professional *scribes* to prepare their campaign speeches.

script (*n.*) 'skript	1. written text of a play, speech, etc.	How much time did the actors have to memorize the *script*?
	2. handwriting; penmanship	I knew the note was from Mabel because I recognized her *script*.
subscriber (*n.*) səb-'skrī-bər	one who writes his or her name at the end of a document, thereby indicating approval; one who regularly receives a magazine, newspaper, etc.	The petition to nominate Sue for president of the junior class already has forty-three *subscribers*.

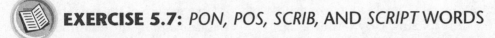

EXERCISE 5.7: *PON, POS, SCRIB,* AND *SCRIPT* WORDS

Fill each blank with the most appropriate word from groups 13 and 14.

1. In his address, the President inserted some remarks that were not in the _____ previously released to the press.

2. The insurgents aim to _____ the dictator and establish a republic.

3. According to the _____ on its cornerstone, this school was erected in 1969.

4. With war impending, the nation hastened to _____ all able-bodied citizens.

5. You cannot _____ your decision much longer; the deadline for submitting applications is Monday.

15. *SIMIL, SIMUL:* "*similar,*" "*like,*" "*same*"

assimilate (*v.*) ə-'si-mə-ˌlāt	1. make similar or like	The letter "n" in the prefix "in-" is often *assimilated* to the following letter. For example, "in" plus "legible" becomes "illegible."
	2. take in and incorporate as one's own; absorb	A bright student *assimilates* knowledge rapidly.
dissimilar (*adj.*) ˌdi(s)-'si-mə-lər	opposite of *similar*; unlike; different	These gloves are not a pair; they are quite *dissimilar*.
similarity (*n.*) si-mə-'lar-ə-tē	likeness; resemblance	The two pills are alike in color and shape, but there the *similarity* ends.
simile (*n.*) 'si-mə-(ˌ)lē	comparison of two different things introduced by *like* or *as*	"What happens to a dream deferred?" asks Langston Hughes in one of his poems. "Does it dry up/ Like a raisin in the sun?" Note that the last six words are a *simile*.

simulate (*v.*) 'sim-yə-,lāt	give the appearance of; feign; imitate	Nancy was the star of the show; she *simulated* the bewildered mother very effectively.
simultaneous (*adj.*) ,sī-məl-'tā-nē-əs	existing or happening at the same time; contemporary; concurrent	The flash of an explosion comes to us before the sound, though the two are really *simultaneous*.

16. SOL, SOLI: "alone," "lonely, "single"

desolate (*v.*) 'de-sə-,lāt	(literally, "make lonely or deprive of inhabitants"); lay waste; ravage; devastate	A large section of the neighborhood was *desolated* by the disastrous fire.
desolate (*adj.*) 'de-sə-lət	left alone; deserted; forlorn; abandoned; forsaken	At 5:30 A.M. the normally crowded intersection looks *desolate*.
sole (*adj.*) 'sōl	one and only; single; lone	Franklin D. Roosevelt was the *sole* candidate to be elected President for a fourth term.
soliloquy (*n.*) sə-'li-lə-kwē	speech made to oneself when alone	What an actor says in a *soliloquy* is heard by no one except the audience.
solitary (*adj.*) 'sä-lə-,ter-ē	opposite of *accompanied*; being or living alone; without companions	A hermit leads a *solitary* existence.
solitude (*n.*) 'sä-lə-,tüd	condition of being alone; loneliness; seclusion	Though I like company, there are times when I prefer *solitude*.
solo (*n.*) 'sō-lō	musical composition (or anything) performed by a single person	Instead of singing a *solo*, Brenda would prefer to join with me in a duet.

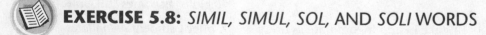

EXERCISE 5.8: *SIMIL, SIMUL, SOL,* AND *SOLI* WORDS

Fill each blank with the most appropriate word from groups 15 and 16.

1. Did you know you were using a(n) _____ when you said I was as sly as a fox?

2. After the chorus sang the first number, Stanley played a violin _____.

3. The closing of the huge factory did not _____ the area, as few of the workers moved away.

4. Don't compare Jane with Peggy; the two are entirely _____.

5. If you speak too rapidly, your audience may be unable to _____ what you are saying.

17. SOLV, SOLU, SOLUT: "loosen"

absolute (*adj.*) 'ab-sə-ˌlüt	1. completely free ("loosened") of constitutional or other restraint; autocratic; despotic	A democratic ruler is restricted by a constitution, a legislature, and courts, but a dictator has *absolute* power.
	2. utter; outright; unquestionable	The sudden rainstorm turned our picnic into an *absolute* mess.
dissolution (*n.*) ˌdi-sə-'lü-shən	act of "loosening" or breaking up into component parts; disintegration; ruin; destruction	When President Lincoln took office, the Union faced imminent *dissolution*.
dissolve (*v.*) di-'zälv	(literally, "loosen apart") 1. break up; disintegrate; disband	Since the members lack mutual interests, the group will probably *dissolve*.
	2. cause to disappear; end	After our quarrel, Grace and I *dissolved* our friendship.
resolution (*n.*) ˌre-zə-'lü-shən	(literally, "act of unloosening") solving; solution; answer	The *resolution* of our air and water pollution problems will be difficult and costly.
resolve (*v.*) ri-'zälv	(literally, "unloosen") break up; solve; explain; unravel	A witness provided the clue that *resolved* the mystery.
soluble (*adj.*) 'säl-yə-bəl	(literally, "able to be loosened") 1. capable of being dissolved or made into a liquid	Sugar is *soluble* in water.
	2. solvable	Someone would have found the answer by now if the problem were *soluble*.
solvent (*n.*) 'säl-vənt	substance, usually liquid, able to dissolve ("loosen") another substance, known as the "solute"	In a saltwater solution, the water is the *solvent* and the salt is the solute.
solvent (*adj.*)	able to pay all one's debts	The examiners found the bank *solvent*, much to the relief of its depositors.

18. UND, UNDA: "wave," "flow"

abound (*v.*) ə-'baund	(literally, "rise in waves" or "overflow") 1. (used with *in* or *with*) be well supplied; teem	Our nation *abounds* in (or with) opportunities for well-educated young men and women.
	2. be plentiful; be present in great quantity	Fish *abound* in the waters off Newfoundland.
abundant (*adj.*) ə-'bən-dənt	(literally, "rising in waves") more than sufficient; plentiful	Before Christmas, the stores have *abundant* supplies of merchandise.
inundate (*v.*) 'i-nən-,dāt	flood; overflow; deluge; overwhelm	On Election Night, the victor's offices were *inundated* by congratulatory messages.
redound (*v.*) ri-'daund	flow back as a result; contribute	The success of so many of its graduates *redounds* to the credit of the school.
redundant (*adj.*) ri-'dən-dənt	(literally, "flowing back") exceeding what is necessary; superfluous; surplus; opposite of *concise*	Remove the last word of the following sentence because it is *redundant*: "My report is longer than Bob's report."

 EXERCISE 5.9: *SOLV, SOLU, SOLUT, UND,* AND *UNDA* WORDS

Fill each blank with the most appropriate word from groups 17 and 18.

1. Mutual suspicion and jealousy led to the eventual _____ of the alliance.

2. The blue whale, once _____ in Antarctic waters, is becoming more and more scarce.

3. The firm is in no danger of bankruptcy; it is completely _____.

4. Several offshore areas _____ in oil.

5. Either of the signers can _____ the agreement by giving thirty days' written notice to the other.

19. VER, VERA, VERI: "true," "truth"

aver (*v.*)
ə-'vər
state to be true; affirm confidently; assert; depose; opposite of *deny*
Two eyewitnesses *averred* they had seen the defendant at the scene.

veracity (*n.*)
və-'ra-sə-tē
truthfulness
Since he has lied to us in the past, he should not wonder that we doubt his *veracity*.

verdict (*n.*)
'vər-,dikt
(literally, something "truly said") decision of a jury; opinion; judgment
A hung jury is one that has been unable to reach a *verdict*.

verify (*v.*)
'ver-ə-,fī
prove to be true; confirm; substantiate; corroborate
So far, the charges have been neither disproved nor *verified*.

veritable (*adj.*)
'ver-ə-tə-bəl
true; actual; genuine; real; authentic
As the pretended heirs of Peter Wilks were disposing of his fortune, the *veritable* heirs arrived.

verity (*n.*)
'ver-ə-tē
truth (of things); something true; true statement
That smoking is injurious to health is a scientifically established *verity*.

20. VID, VIS: "see," "look," "sight"

envision (*v.*)
in-'vi-zhən
foresee; envisage; have a mental picture of (something not yet a reality)
Mr. Brown *envisions* for Marcia a bright career as a fashion designer.

improvise (*v.*)
'im-prə-,vīz
(literally, "do something without having prepared or seen it beforehand") compose, recite, or sing on the spur of the moment; invent offhand; extemporize
Did you prepare your jokes before the program or *improvise* them as you went along?

invisible (*adj.*)
in-'vi-zə-bəl
not able to be seen; imperceptible; indiscernible
The microscope enables us to see organisms *invisible* to the naked eye.

revise (*v.*)
ri-'vīz
look at again to correct errors and make improvements; examine and improve
Before handing in your composition, be sure to *revise* it carefully.

video (*adj.*)
'vi-dē-,ō
having to do with the transmission or reception of what is seen
The audio (sound) and *video* signals of a television program can be recorded on magnetic tape.

videotape (*v.*) 'vi-dē-ō-,tāp	make a videotape recording of an event or TV program	If we *videotape* the party, we can show it later to those who could not attend.
visibility (*n.*) ,vi-zə-'bi-lə-tē	degree of clearness of the atmosphere, with reference to the distance at which objects can be clearly seen	With the fog rolling in and *visibility* approaching zero, it was virtually impossible for planes to land.
visual (*adj.*) 'vi-zhə-wəl	having to do with sight	Radar tells us of an approaching object long before *visual* contact is possible.

EXERCISE 5.10: *VER, VERA, VERI, VID,* AND *VIS* WORDS

Fill each blank with the most appropriate word from groups 19 and 20.

1. I am not much of a student, but Norma is a(n) _____ scholar.

2. Since words alone may fail to convey an idea, teachers often use _____ aids, such as pictures, charts, and films.

3. La Guardia Airport reports low clouds and reduced _____.

4. Since the speaker was not prepared, he had to _____ his talk.

5. You may believe this statement; it comes from a person of unquestionable _____.

Review Exercises

REVIEW 10: WORD-BUILDING

Fill in the *prefix* in column I, the *root* in column II, and the *missing letters* of the word in column III. Each blank stands for *one* missing letter.

I PREFIX	II ROOT	III WORD
1. __ __ __ *apart*	+ __ __ __ __ *loosen*	= __ __ __ __ __ __ ED *separated into parts*
2. __ __ *not*	+ __ __ __ __ *seen*	= __ __ __ __ __ IBLE *not able to be seen*
3. __ __ *on*	+ __ __ __ *put*	= __ __ __ __ __ ED *put on as a burden; inflicted*

4. __ __ __ + __ __ __ __ = __ __ __ __ __ __ __ __ ION

   apart   *loosen*   *act of breaking up; disintegration*

5. __ __ + __ __ __ = __ __ D __ __ __ __ NT

   back   *flow*   *exceeding what is necessary; superfluous*

6. __ __ __ + __ __ __ __ __ = __ __ __ __ __ __ __ __ __ ED

   before   *write*   *ordered as a remedy*

7. __ __ + __ __ __ = __ __ __ __ __ ING

   again   *look*   *looking at again to correct*

8. __ __ + __ __ __ __ = __ __ __ __ __ __ TE

   over   *flow*   *overflow; overwhelm*

9. __ __ __ + __ __ __ __ __ = __ __ __ __ __ __ __ __ __ ER

   under   *write*   *one who writes his or her name at the end of a document*

10. __ __ + __ __ __ = __ __ __ __ __ ED

   down   *put*   *put out of office; dethroned*

 REVIEW 11: LATIN ROOTS 11–20

In the space before each Latin root in column I, write the *letter* of its definition from column II.

COLUMN I	COLUMN II
__ 1. SOL, SOLI	*a.* hang
__ 2. MAN, MANU	*b.* see, look, sight
__ 3. PEND, PENS	*c.* put
__ 4. SOLV, SOLU, SOLUT	*d.* write
__ 5. UND, UNDA	*e.* alone, lonely, single
__ 6. VER, VERA, VERI	*f.* similar, like, same
__ 7. SCRIB, SCRIPT	*g.* wave, flow
__ 8. VID, VIS	*h.* hand
__ 9. SIMIL, SIMUL	*i.* true, truth
__ 10. PON, POS	*j.* loosen

REVIEW 12: SENTENCE COMPLETION

Fill each blank with the word from the list below that best fits the context.

abound	appendix	desolate	dissimilar	manipulate
manual	manuscript	pending	redundant	resolution
resolve	revise	simulate	simile	sole
soliloquy	solitude	veracity	verdict	video

1. Since the _____ on my TV has gone out for the third time this week, I am afraid there may be no early _____ of the problem. The only thing I see is "snow."

2. By closing her door, Jane was able to get the _____ she needed to complete the _____ of her term paper.

3. The owner's _____ explains how to _____ the controls on the air conditioner.

4. Gulliver, the _____ survivor of a shipwreck, landed on an apparently _____ coast, since there were no signs of other humans or dwellings.

5. One thing I had to do when I _____d my paper was to eliminate all _____ words and phrases.

6. Homer's *Iliad* _____s in vivid _____s. Here is a sample: "Achilles ran toward Hector as a hawk swoops for a trembling dove."

7. The _____ to the annual report informs stockholders about _____ lawsuits against the company.

8. The suspect's handwriting and the writing on the ransom note proved to be _____. That was a blow to the detectives trying to _____ the case.

9. Othello thinks Iago is his true friend. However, in a(n) _____ later in the play, Iago reveals that his friendship for Othello is _____d.

10. The jury's "not guilty" _____ shows that they must have had confidence in the _____ of the defense witness's testimony.

REVIEW 13: SYNONYMS

Avoid repetition by replacing the boldfaced word or expression with a **synonym** from the following words.

absolute	abundant	emancipate	impending	postpone
similarity	simultaneous	solvent	suspend	verify

_____ 1. In many respects, the partners do not resemble each other, but there is a striking **resemblance** in their voices.

_____ed **2.** Play will be **temporarily stopped** until it stops raining.

_____ **3.** Her guilt is beyond question; there is **unquestionable** proof that she evaded the law.

_____ **4.** Shouldn't we leave sooner? A storm is **threatening to occur soon**.

_____ **5.** Since the two programs were **on at the same time**, I turned on one and videotaped the other.

_____ **6.** Though the company is indebted to many suppliers, it is still **able to pay its debts**.

_____ **7.** In late summer, there is plenty of fresh corn; the markets get **plentiful** supplies of it daily.

_____ **8.** Several independent researchers are trying to **confirm** the scientist's claims. As yet, there is no confirmation.

_____d **9.** The trial has already been **deferred** twice; now, the defendant is again requesting a deferment.

_____ **10.** The revolution gave the people freedom from tyranny, but it did not **free** them from poverty.

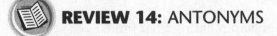 **REVIEW 14:** ANTONYMS

Enter the word from the list below that is most nearly the **opposite** of the boldfaced word or words.

append	aver	depose	impose	inundate
manual	pending	proscribe	simultaneous	soluble

1. Before the clearance sale, the old price tickets were **detached** from the garments, and new ones were _____ed.

2. Now that there is a promising clue, the case thought to be **beyond resolution** may indeed be _____.

3. The legislature voted to **remove** nuisance taxes that it had previously _____d on business.

4. Two witnesses _____ that the suspect tried to intimidate them, but he continues to **deny** that charge.

5. Engineers are working to **drain** the tunnel _____d by last night's heavy rainstorm.

6. Most drivers prefer an **automatic** transmission rather than a(n) _____ one because it allows them to shift gears without using their hands.

7. I can usually answer the telephone and the doorbell if they ring **at different times**, but not if they are _____.

8. Few who had seen the monarch **enthroned** were present when he was
_____d.

9. Is the matter already **decided**, or is it still _____?

10. Most of the dumping that used to be **permitted** is now _____d.

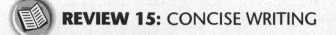 **REVIEW 15:** CONCISE WRITING

Using no more than sixty words, rewrite the following passage, keeping all its
ideas. The first sentence has been rewritten to get you started. Go on from there.

Broker vs. Clients

In one of the cases waiting to be settled, two clients are accusing a broker of managing their
investments in a manner that is not ethical. They say that he has made huge profits, while they
are now not able to pay their debts. The broker insists that he has never acted in a way that is
fraudulent. When he was asked if he wanted to look back over his testimony to correct mis-
statements or make additions, he said "no." The decision of the jury is expected to be out in a
short time.

Broker vs. Clients
(concise version)

In a pending case, two clients are accusing a broker of manipulating their funds.

_____

_____

_____

_____

_____

_____

REVIEW 16: SYNONYM SUMMARY

Each line, when completed, should have three words similar in meaning.
Enter the missing letters.

1. att __ ch   __ dd   app __ nd

2. disint __ grate   d __ sband   d __ __ solve

3. auth __ r   journ __ list   scr __ be

4. lib __ rate   __ ree   eman __ ipate

5. dev __ state   r __ vage   __ __ solate

6. gen __ ine   __ __ thentic   v __ r __ table

7. fl __ __ d   over __ helm   in __ __ date

8. c __ mm __ nd   __ __ thorization   m __ nd __ te

9. d __ rect   d __ ctate   p __ __ scr __ be

10. utt __ r   __ __ __ right   abs __ l __ te

11. h __ nd __ riting   pen __ __ __ ship   __ __ ript

12. test __ fy   __ wear   __ __ pose

13. s __ l __ tion   ans __ er   res __ l __ tion

14. proh __ b __ t   __ __ __ bid   pr __ scribe

15. im __ tate   f __ __ gn   s __ m __ late

16. lon __ l __ ness   s __ cl __ sion   sol __ t __ de

17. anx __ __ ty   appre __ __ __ sion   __ __ __ pense

18. abs __ rb   inc __ rp __ rate   as __ __ milate

19. conf __ rm   substant __ __ te   v __ r __ fy

20. c __ nc __ rr __ nt   __ __ __ temporary   s __ multan __ __ us

REVIEW 17: ANALOGIES

Which lettered pair of words—*a, b, c, d,* or *e*—most nearly expresses the same relationship as the capitalized pair? Write the letter of your answer in the space provided.

___ 1. ACTOR : SCRIPT

    a. physician : prescription   *b.* composer : score

    c. navigator : course   *d.* author : manuscript

    e. dramatist : play

___ 2. GREGARIOUS : SOLITUDE

    a. economical : conservation   *b.* contentious : argument

    c. autocratic : power   *d.* conservative : change

    e. independent : freedom

___ 3. EMANCIPATE : BONDAGE

    a. indict : accusation   *b.* promote : rank

    c. enlighten : ignorance   *d.* commission : task

    e. laud : commendation

___ **4.** APPEND : DETACH

    a. prohibit : ban   *b.* frustrate : circumvent

    c. debilitate : weaken   *d.* heed : mind

    e. curtail : protract

___ **5.** ENIGMA : RESOLVE

    a. ball : roll   *b.* smoke : rise

    c. perfection : achieve   *d.* rumor : spread

    e. fish : swim

___ **6.** INSOLVENT : CURRENCY

    a. magnanimous : generosity   *b.* amiable : cordiality

    c. undaunted : courage   *d.* arrogant : pride

    e. solitary : company

___ **7.** POSTPONEMENT : DEFERRAL

    a. scarcity : abundance   *b.* exploit : feat

    c. redundancy : conciseness   *d.* calamity : boon

    e. impasse : resolution

___ **8.** PERJURER : VERACITY

    a. bulldog : tenacity   *b.* celebrity : renown

    c. jack-of-all-trades : versatility   *d.* upstart : resources

    e. monopolist : competition

___ **9.** EARRING : PENDANT

    a. water : solvent   *b.* ornament : ring

    c. moisture : sponge   *d.* vegetable : asparagus

    e. animal : deer

___ **10.** IMPROVISE : EXTEMPORANEOUS

    a. obey : insubordinate   *b.* lurk : conspicuous

    c. conspire : clandestine   *d.* rage : rational

    e. sneeze : voluntary

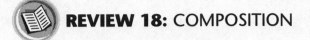

REVIEW 18: COMPOSITION

Answer in a sentence or two.

1. Why is revising a manuscript for redundant words a useful thing to do?

_____

_____

2. Why does the resolution of a story usually end the suspense?

_____

_____

3. Is a magazine with many subscribers likely to be dissolved? Why?

_____

_____

4. Would tourists abound in a desolated region? Explain.

_____

_____

5. Why is veracity an important trait for a scribe?

_____

_____

6

Enlarging Vocabulary Through Greek Word Elements

Why study Greek word elements?

English contains a substantial and growing number of words derived from Greek. Some of these words are general words in everyday use, e.g., *authentic, chronological, economical, homogeneous,* etc. Others are used in specialized fields. Certainly you have heard terms like *antibiotic, orthopedic,* and *pediatrician* in the field of medicine; *astronaut, protoplasm,* and *thermonuclear* in science; and *autonomous, demagogue,* and *protocol* in government.

These important words, and others like them in this chapter, are constructed from Greek word elements. Once you know what a particular word element means, you have a clue to the meaning of words derived from it. When, for example, you have learned that *PAN* or *PANTO* means "complete" or "all," you are better able to understand—and remember—that a *panacea* is a "remedy for *all* ills," a *panorama* is a "*complete* and unobstructed view in *all* directions," and a *pantomime* is "*all* gestures and signs, i.e., a performance without words."

Purpose of this chapter

This chapter aims to enlarge your vocabulary by acquainting you with twenty Greek word elements and some English words derived from them. As you study each word group, make it a special point to memorize the meaning of the word element so that you will be able to recognize it in derivatives.

GREEK WORD ELEMENTS 1–10

Pretest 1

Insert the *letter* of the best answer in the space provided.

1. In a *plutocracy,* _____ govern.
   (A) technical experts   (B) the wealthy   (C) the nobles

2. A *pedagogue is* mainly concerned with _____.
   (A) politics   (B) medicine   (C) teaching

3. *Pandemonium* is a condition of _____.
   (A) wild disorder   (B) poor nourishment   (C) absolute peace

4. People who lack *autonomy* are _____.
   (A) unreliable   (B) selfish   (C) not self-ruled

5. You study *orthography* mainly in your _____ classes.
   (A) English   (B) mathematics   (C) social studies

6. A mistake in _____ order is a mistake in *chronology.*
   (A) word   (B) alphabetical   (C) time

7. In a *homogeneous* group, the members are of _____ ability.
   (A) similar   (B) varied   (C) high

8. A *kleptomaniac* is a menace mainly to _____.
   (A) liberty   (B) property   (C) life

9. The *odometer* on your automobile dashboard measures _____.
   (A) distance   (B) speed   (C) motor temperature

10. A *demagogue* stirs up the people _____.
    (A) when they forget   (B) to protect democratic   (C) for personal advantage
        their responsibilities   principles

THE ANSWERS ARE
1. B   2. C   3. A   4. C   5. A
6. C   7. A   8. B   9. A   10. C

Each italicized word in the pretest came from a different word element: *plutocracy* from CRACY, meaning "government"; *pedagogue* from PED, meaning "child," etc. You will now study ten such word elements and some words derived from them.

1. AUT, AUTO: "self"

WORD	MEANING	TYPICAL USE
authentic (*adj.*) ȯ-'then-tik	(literally, "from the master himself") genuine; real; reliable; trustworthy	When you withdraw money, the bank may compare your signature with the one in its files to see if it is *authentic*.
autobiography (*n.*) ,ȯ-tō-bī-'ä-grə-fē	story of a person's life written by the person himself or herself	In her *autobiography* THE STORY OF MY LIFE, Helen Keller tells how unruly she was as a young child.
autocrat (*n.*) 'ȯ-tə-,krat	ruler exercising self-derived, absolute power; despot; dictator	The *autocrat* was replaced by a ruler responsible to the people.
autograph (*n.*) 'ȯ-tə-,graf	person's signature written by himself or herself	The baseball star wrote his *autograph* for an admirer who came up to him with a pencil and scorecard.
automatic (*adj.*) ,ȯ-tə-'ma-tik	acting by itself; self-regulating	Some cars require the driver to shift gears manually, while others have an *automatic* transmission.
automation (*n.*) ,ȯ-tə-'mā-shən	technique of making a process self-operating by means of built-in electronic controls	Many workers have lost their jobs as a result of *automation*.
automaton (*n.*) ȯ-'tä-mə-tən	(literally, "self-acting thing") purely mechanical person following a routine; robot	An autocrat prefers subjects who are *automatons* rather than intelligent human beings.
autonomous (*adj.*) ȯ-'tä-nə-məs	self-governing; independent; sovereign	The Alumni Association is not under the control of the school. It is a completely *autonomous* group.
autonomy (*n.*) ȯ-'tä-nə-mē	right of self-government; independence; sovereignty	After World War II, many former colonies were granted *autonomy* and became independent nations.
autopsy (*n.*) 'ȯ-,täp-sē	(literally, "a seeing for oneself") medical examination of a dead body to determine the cause of death; postmortem examination	The cause of the celebrity's sudden death will not be known until the *autopsy* has been performed.

📖 **EXERCISE 6.1:** *AUT, AUTO* WORDS

Fill each blank with the most appropriate word from group 1.

1. Some members want to censure the president for ignoring the club's constitution and behaving like an _____.

2. You are no better than an _____ if you act mechanically without using your intelligence.

3. The prime minister left her life story to others, for she had neither the time nor the desire to write an _____.

4. The camera has a built-in _____ flash, which works whenever there's not enough light.

5. For generations, colonial peoples who asked for _____ were usually told that they were not ready to govern themselves.

2. CRACY: "government"

aristocracy (*n.*) ‚ar-ə-'stä-krə-sē	1. (literally, "government by the best") government or country governed by a small privileged upper class	Before 1789, France was an *aristocracy*.
	2. ruling class of nobles; nobility; privileged class; gentry	When the Revolution of 1789 began, many members of the French *aristocracy* fled to other lands.
autocracy (*n.*) ȯ-'tä-krə-sē	government. or country governed by one individual with self-derived, unlimited power	Germany under Adolf Hitler was an *autocracy*.
bureaucracy (*n.*) byü-'rä-krə-sē	government by bureaus or groups of officials; administration characterized by excessive red tape and routine	The mayor was criticized for setting up an inefficient *bureaucracy* unresponsive to the needs of the people.
democracy (*n.*) di-'mä-krə-sē	government or country governed by the people; rule by the majority	The thirteen colonies developed into the first *democracy* in the Western Hemisphere.
plutocracy (*n.*) plü-'tä-krə-sē	government or country governed by the rich	If only millionaires can afford to run for office, we may soon become a *plutocracy*.
technocracy (*n.*) tek-'nä-krə-sē	government or country governed by technical experts	In a *technocracy*, the governing class would consist largely of engineers.

The form *crat* at the end of a word means "advocate of a type of government," "member of a class," or, if the word is capitalized, "member of a political party." Examples:

aristocrat (*n.*) ə-'ris-tə-,krat	1. advocate of aristocracy	An *aristocrat* would like to see members of the upper class in control of the government.
	2. member of the aristocracy; noble; patrician	Winston Churchill was born an *aristocrat*; he was the son of Sir Randolph Churchill.
Democrat (*n.*) 'de-mə-,krat	member of the Democratic Party	The senator used to be a Republican, but she is now a *Democrat*.

Also: **bureaucrat, plutocrat, technocrat**

EXERCISE 6.2: *CRACY* WORDS

Fill each blank with the most appropriate word from group 2.

1. It was most unusual for a member of the _____ to marry someone not belonging to the nobility.

2. If you believe that only the affluent are fit to govern, you must be a(n) _____.

3. In a(n) _____, the ruler has absolute and unlimited power.

4. How can you call yourself a(n) _____ if you do not believe in majority rule?

5. Many are opposed to a(n) _____ because they do not wish to be ruled by technical experts.

3. DEM, DEMO: *"people"*

| demagogue (*n.*)
'de-mə-,gäg | political leader who stirs up the people for personal advantage; rabble-rouser | No responsible leader, only a *demagogue,* would make campaign speeches promising to solve all the people's problems. |
| democratic (*adj.*)
de-mə-'kra-tik | based on the principles of democracy, or government by the people | A nation cannot be considered democratic unless its leaders are chosen by the people in free elections. |

democratize (*v.*) di-'mä-krə-‚tīz	make democratic	The adoption of the 19th Amendment, giving women the franchise, greatly *democratized* our nation.
epidemic (*adj.*) ‚e-pə-'de-mik	(literally, "among the people") affecting many people in an area at the same time; widespread	Greater federal and state aid is needed in areas where unemployment is *epidemic*.
epidemic (*n.*)	outbreak of a rapidly spreading, contagious disease affecting many people at the same time; plague; rash	The high rate of absenteeism was caused by the flu *epidemic*.

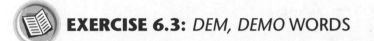 **EXERCISE 6.3:** *DEM, DEMO* WORDS

Fill each blank with the most appropriate word from group 3.

1. Millions of people died in the 14th century as the result of a(n) _____ known as the Black Death.

2. The election was not _____ because some people voted more than once and others were prevented from voting.

3. An intelligent voter can distinguish the unselfish political leader from the _____.

4. To _____ the country, a new constitution was drawn up, giving equal rights to all segments of the population.

5. It is more _____ for a governor to be chosen by the people than to be appointed by the king.

4. PAN, PANTO: "all," "complete"

panacea (*n.*) ‚pa-nə-'sē-ə	remedy for all ills; cure-all; universal remedy; elixir	The international treaty will reduce tensions, but it will not resolve all conflict. It is no *panacea*.
Pan-American (*adj.*) ‚pa-nə-'mer-ə-kən	of or pertaining to all the countries of North, South, and Central America	The *Pan-American* Highway links all the countries of the Western Hemisphere from Alaska to Chile.
pandemonium (*n.*) ‚pan-də-'mō-nē-əm	(literally, "abode of all the demons," i.e., hell) wild uproar; very noisy din; wild disorder; tumult; racket	The huge crowds in Times Square grew noisier as the old year ticked away, and when midnight struck there was *pandemonium*.

panoply (*n.*) ʹpa-nə-plē	complete suit of armor; complete covering or equipment; magnificent array	The opposing knights, mounted and in full *panoply,* awaited the signal for the tournament to begin.
panorama (*n.*) ˌpa-nə-ʹra-mə	complete, unobstructed view	From the Verrazano-Narrows Bridge, you can get an excellent *panorama* of New York's harbor.
pantomime (*n.*) ʹpan-tə-ˌmīm	dramatic performance that is all signs and gestures without words	Not until THE GREAT DICTATOR did Charlie Chaplin play a speaking part. All his previous roles were in *pantomime.*

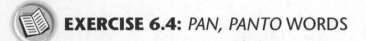

EXERCISE 6.4: *PAN, PANTO* WORDS

Fill each blank with the most appropriate word from group 4.

1. When Karen scored the tie-breaking goal with five seconds left to play, _____ broke out.

2. Many regard education as the _____ that will cure all of society's ills.

3. The top of 3605-foot Mt. Snow in Vermont offers a fine _____ of the Green Mountains.

4. In a _____, the actors express themselves only by facial expressions, bodily movements, and gestures.

5. The woods in their full _____ of autumn color are a breathtaking sight.

5. CHRON, CHRONO: *"time"*

anachronism (*n.*) ə-ʹna-krə-ˌni-zəm	error in chronology or time order	The actor playing the Roman gladiator forgot to remove his wristwatch, creating an amusing *anachronism.*
chronicle (*n.*) ʹkrä-ni-kəl	historical account of events in the order of time; history; annals	One of the earliest accounts of King Arthur occurs in a 12th-century *chronicle* of the kings of Britain by Geoffrey of Monmouth.
chronological (*adj.*) ˌkrä-nə-ʹlä-ji-kəl	arranged in order of time	The magazines in this file are not in *chronological* order. I found the February issue after the October one.

chronology (*n.*) krə-'nä-lə-jē	arrangement of data or events in order of time of occurrence	In the *chronology* of American Presidents, Ulysses S. Grant comes after Andrew Johnson.
synchronize (*v.*) 'siŋ-krə-,nīz	cause to agree in time; make simultaneous	The clocks in the library need to be *synchronized*; one is a minute and a half behind the other.

EXERCISE 6.5: *CHRON, CHRONO* WORDS

Fill each blank with the most appropriate word from group 5.

1. Can you recall the World Series champions of the last five years in the correct _____?

2. To say that the ancient Greeks watched the siege of Troy on television would be an amusing _____.

3. The film begins near the climax and then goes back to the hero's childhood, violating the usual _____ order.

4. The townspeople used to _____ their timepieces with the clock outside the village bank.

5. The current *World Almanac* gives a(n) _____ of last year's events.

6. *MANIA: "madness," "insane impulse," "craze"*

kleptomania (*n.*) ,klep-tə-'mā-nē-ə	insane impulse to steal	The millionaire arrested for shoplifting was found to be suffering from *kleptomania*.
mania (*n.*) 'mā-nē-ə	1. madness; insanity	For a student with an A average to quit school two months before graduation is sheer *mania*.
	2. excessive fondness; craze	Though I still read science fiction, I no longer have the *mania* for it that I originally had.
maniac (*n.*) 'mā-nē-,ak	raving lunatic; mad or insane person; crackpot	The deranged behavior of the narrator in "The Tell-Tale Heart" leaves little doubt that he is a *maniac*.
maniacal (*adj.*) mə-'nī-ə-kəl	characterized by madness; insane; raving	You protested in such a loud, violent, and *maniacal* manner that onlookers must have thought you had lost your sanity.

pyromania (*n.*) ˌpī-rō-'mā-nē-ə	insane impulse to set fires	The person charged with setting the fire had been suspected of *pyromania* on two previous occasions.

The form *maniac* at the end of a word means "person affected by an insane impulse or craze." Examples: **kleptomaniac, pyromaniac.**

EXERCISE 6.6: *MANIA* WORDS

Fill each blank with the most appropriate word from group 6.

1. The weird, _____ shrieks and groans coming from the house might have made one believe that it was inhabited by a raving lunatic.

2. Sharon has a _____ for chocolates; she will finish a whole box in no time at all if not restrained.

3. Herb can't help taking things belonging to others; he is a _____.

4. Officials believe the recent series of small fires to be the work of a _____.

5. The spoiled brat raved like a _____ when he didn't get his way.

7. PED: *"child"*

encyclopedia (*n.*) in-ˌsī-klə-'pē-dē-ə	(literally, "well-rounded rearing of a child") work offering alphabetically arranged information on various branches of knowledge	There are four different *encyclopedias* in the reference section of our school library.
orthopedic (*adj.*) ˌȯr-thə-'pē-dik	(literally, "of the straight child") having to do with *orthopedics*, the science dealing with the correction and prevention of deformities, especially in children	Patients recovering from broken limbs are treated in the hospital's *orthopedic* ward.
pedagogue (*n.*) 'pe-də-ˌgäg	(literally, "leader of a child") teacher of children	The new teacher received a great deal of help from the more experienced *pedagogues*.
pedagogy (*n.*) 'pe-də-ˌgō-jē	art of teaching	Dr. Dworkin's lessons are usually excellent. She is a master of *pedagogy*.
pediatrician (*n.*) ˌpē-dē-ə-'tri-shən	physician specializing in the treatment of babies and children	When the baby developed a fever, the parents telephoned the *pediatrician*.

| pediatrics (*n.*)
ˌpē-dē-ʹa-triks | branch of medicine dealing with the care, development, and diseases of babies and children | From the number of baby carriages outside the office, you can tell that Dr. Enders specializes in *pediatrics*. |

📖 EXERCISE 6.7: *PED* WORDS

Fill each blank with the most appropriate word from group 7.

1. _____ deals with diseases that afflict the young.

2. You can now purchase an entire twenty-two-volume _____ on one CD, saving a considerable amount of space in your home.

3. A teacher's professional training includes courses in _____ .

4. Until the age of six months, the baby was taken to the _____ every month.

5. A(n) _____ specialist performed the operation to correct the deformity of the child's spinal column.

8. ORTHO: "straight," "correct"

orthodontist (*n.*) ˌȯr-thə-ʹdän-tist	dentist specializing in orthodontics, a branch of dentistry dealing with straightening and adjusting of teeth	A teenager wearing braces is obviously under the care of an *orthodontist*.
orthodox (*adj.*) ʹȯr-thə-ˌdäks	(literally, "correct opinion") generally accepted, especially in religion; conventional; approved; conservative	There was no religious liberty in the Massachusetts Bay Colony. Roger Williams, for example, was banished because he did not accept *orthodox* Puritan beliefs.
orthography (*n.*) ȯr-ʹthä-grə-fē	(literally, "correct writing") correct spelling	American and English *orthography* are very much alike. One difference, however, is in words like "honor" and "labor," which the English spell "honour" and "labour."
orthopedist (*n.*) ˌȯr-thə-ʹpē-dist	physician specializing in the correction and prevention of deformities, especially in children	A deformity of the spine is a condition that requires the attention of an *orthopedist*.
unorthodox (*adj.*) ˌən-ʹȯr-thə-ˌdäks	not orthodox; not in accord with accepted, standard, or approved belief or practice; unconventional; heretical	Vaccination was rejected as *unorthodox* when Dr. Jenner first suggested it.

EXERCISE 6.8: *ORTHO* WORDS

Fill each blank with the most appropriate word from group 8.

1. It is _____ to begin a meal with the dessert.

2. Phyllis has won the spelling bee again. She excels in _____.

3. The young patient is under the care of a well-known _____ for a leg deformity.

4. The infant gets up at 4 A.M. We should prefer him to wake at a more _____ hour, such as 7 A.M.

5. Laura's parents have been assured by an _____ that her teeth can be straightened.

9. GEN, GENO, GENEA: "race," "kind," "birth"

genealogy (*n.*) ˌjē-nē-'ä-lə-jē	(literally, "account of a race or family") history of the descent of a person or family from an ancestor; lineage; pedigree	Diane can trace her descent from an ancestor who fought in the Mexican War. I know much less about my own *genealogy*.
genesis (*n.*) 'je-nə-səs	birth or coming into being of something; origin	According to legend, the Trojan War had its *genesis* in a dispute among three Greek goddesses.
heterogeneous (*adj.*) ˌhe-tə-rə-'jē-nē-əs	differing in kind; dissimilar; not uniform; varied	Many different racial and cultural groups are to be found in the *heterogeneous* population of a large American city.
homogeneous (*adj.*) ˌhō-mə-'jē-nē-əs	of the same kind; similar; uniform	All the dancers in the ballet corps wore the same costume to present a *homogeneous* appearance.
homogenize (*v.*) hō-'mä-jə-ˌnīz	make homogeneous	If dairies did not *homogenize* milk, the cream would be concentrated at the top instead of being evenly distributed.

EXERCISE 6.9: *GEN, GENO, GENEA* WORDS

Fill the blank with the appropriate word from group 9.

1. The class consists of intermediate and advanced dancers, as well as a few beginners. It is a _____ group.

2. A family Bible in which births, marriages, and deaths have been recorded for generations is a source of information about a person's _____.

3. There are always lumps in the cereal when you cook it. You don't know how to _____ it.

4. When every house on the block has the same exterior, the result is a _____ dullness.

5. Democracy is not an American creation; it had its _____ in ancient Greece.

10. METER, METR: *"measure"*

barometer (*n.*) bə-ʹrä-mə-tər	instrument for measuring atmospheric pressure as an aid in determining probable weather changes	When the *barometer* indicates a rapid drop in air pressure, it means a storm is coming.
chronometer (*n.*) krə-ʹnä-mə-tər	instrument for measuring time very accurately	Unlike ordinary clocks and watches, *chronometers* are little affected by temperature changes or vibration.
diameter (*n.*) dī-ʹa-mə-tər	(literally, "measure across") straight line passing through the center of a body or figure from one side to the other; length of such a line; thickness; width	Some giant redwood trees measure up to 30 feet (9.14 meters) in *diameter*.
meter (*n.*) ʹmē-tər	1. device for measuring	When water *meters* are installed, it will be easy to tell how much water each home is using.
	2. unit of measure in the metric system; 39.37 inches	A *meter* is 3.37 inches longer than a yard.
odometer (*n.*) ō-ʹdä-mə-tər	instrument attached to a vehicle for measuring the distance traversed	All eyes, except the driver's, were fastened on the *odometer* as it moved from 9,999.9 to 10,000 miles.

photometer (*n.*)
fō-ʼtä-mə-tər

instrument for measuring intensity of light

The intensity of a source of light, such as an electric lightbulb, can be measured with a *photometer*.

speedometer (*n.*)
spi-ʼdä-mə-tər

instrument for measuring speed; tachometer

I advised Ann to slow down, as we were in a 30-mile-an-hour zone and her *speedometer* registered more than 40.

symmetry (*n.*)
ʼsi-mə-trē

correspondence in measurements, shape, etc., on opposite sides of a dividing line; well-balanced arrangement of parts; harmony; balance

As the planes passed overhead, we were impressed by the perfect *symmetry* of their V-formation.

 ## EXERCISE 6.10: *METER, METR* WORDS

Fill each blank with the most appropriate word from group 10.

1. Every apple in this package has a(n) _____ of no less than 2¼ inches.

2. We couldn't tell how fast we were going because the _____ was out of order.

3. Notice the _____ of the human body. The right side is the counterpart of the left.

4. You can tell how many miles a car has been driven since its manufacture if you look at its _____.

5. In the 100-_____ dash, the course is more than 100 yards long.

Review Exercises

 ## REVIEW 1: GREEK WORD ELEMENTS 1–10

In the space before each Greek word element in column I, write the *letter* of its correct meaning from column II.

COLUMN I

___ **1.** ORTHO

___ **2.** MANIAC

___ **3.** GEN, GENO, GENEA

___ **4.** CHRON, CHRONO

COLUMN II

a. child

b. all; complete

c. madness; insane impulse; craze

d. straight; correct

___ 5. CRAT   *e.* government

___ 6. AUT, AUTO   *f.* race; kind; birth

___ 7. METER, METR   *g.* people

___ 8. PAN, PANTO   *h.* advocate of a type of government

___ 9. MANIA   *i.* measure

___ 10. CRACY   *j.* self

___ 11. PED   *k.* time

___ 12. DEM, DEMO   *l.* person affected by an insane impulse

 REVIEW 2: WORD-BUILDING

Fill in the missing letters of the word at the right. Each dash stands for one missing letter.

DEFINITION	WORD
1. arranged in order of time	__ __ __ __ __ __ LOGICAL
2. technique of making a process self-operating	__ __ __ __ MATION
3. instrument for measuring atmospheric pressure	BARO __ __ __ __ __
4. remedy for all ills	__ __ __ ACEA
5. differing in kind	HETERO __ __ __ EOUS
6. person affected by an insane impulse to set fires	PYRO __ __ __ __ __ __
7. government by small privileged upper class	ARISTO __ __ __ __ __
8. dentist specializing in straightening teeth	__ __ __ __ __ DONTIST
9. teacher of children	__ __ __ AGOGUE
10. self-governing	__ __ __ __ NOMOUS
11. correspondence in shape, size, measurements, etc.	SYM __ __ __ __ Y
12. complete equipment	__ __ __ OPLY
13. contrary to approved or conservative practice	UN __ __ __ __ __ DOX
14. physician specializing in treatment of children	__ __ __ IATRICIAN
15. member of wealthy ruling class	PLUTO __ __ __ __
16. of the same kind	HOMO __ __ __ EOUS
17. affecting many people in an area at the same time	EPI __ __ __ IC

18. characterized by madness   — — — — — CAL

19. cause to agree in time   SYN — — — — — IZE

20. government by the people   — — — — CRACY

REVIEW 3: SENTENCE COMPLETION

Fill each blank with the word from the list below that best fits the context.

anachronism	aristocracy	authentic	autobiography	autocrat
autograph	chronological	democracy	encyclopedia	genesis
heterogeneous	homogeneous	maniacal	panacea	pandemonium
pedagogue	pedagogy	pyromaniac	synchronize	unorthodox

1. In his _____, the famous teacher describes some personal experiences that taught him the art of _____.

2. When the home team won the championship, _____ broke out, and thousands of _____ fans charged the goal posts to knock them down.

3. A handwriting expert was called in to determine whether the _____ of Babe Ruth on the old baseball was _____.

4. Hoping to oust the _____ ruling the country with an iron fist, the conspirators _____d their watches and moved cautiously toward the palace.

5. The psychiatrist treating the _____ is trying to discover the _____ of his urge to set fires.

6. Only if I were a "walking _____" could I have recited the names of all the kings and queens of England in perfect _____ order.

7. The _____ explained to her class that the striking of the clock in *Julius Caesar* is a(n) _____, since the play is set in ancient Rome.

8. Though the young man had grown up among the _____, his father had instilled in him the principles of _____.

9. The _____ candidate readily admitted to the voters that she had no _____ for their problems.

10. The athletes participating in the international meet were _____ in ethnic origin, but _____ in their quest for glory.

REVIEW 4: SYNONYMS

Avoid repetition by replacing the boldfaced word or expression with a **synonym** from the following words.

automatic	automaton	autonomous	chronology	diameter
genealogy	kleptomania	orthography	pantomime	pediatrician

_____ 1. The helper was a(n) **purely mechanical person** who mechanically repeated everything that the boss said.

_____ 2. Posts with a **thickness** of six inches are much sturdier than those that are only four inches thick.

_____s 3. **Physicians who specialize in the treatment of children** see more cases of measles than most other physicians.

_____ 4. Once we set the temperature, the heating system is **self-regulating**; we don't have to regulate it.

_____ 5. Most colonies governed by a mother country eventually became **self-governing**.

_____ 6. Jack would be a better speller if he learned some of the rules of **spelling**.

_____ 7. If you say that something happened at an earlier time than it really did, you are making an error in **time sequence**.

_____ 8. The defendant claims she took to stealing not because of greed, but because of **an insane impulse to steal**.

_____ 9. From history and from conversations with your grandparents and great-grandparents, you may learn a good deal about your **family history**.

_____ 10. Not a word was spoken; the performers used **signs and gestures, but no words**.

REVIEW 5: ANTONYMS

Enter the word from the list below that is most nearly the **opposite** of the boldfaced word or words.

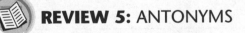

aristocrat	authentic	automatic	democratic	genesis
heterogeneous	homogeneous	maniac	symmetry	unorthodox

1. In the olden days, it was rare for a **commoner** to marry a(n) _____.

2. The insurgents hope to topple the **authoritarian** regime and replace it with a(n) _____ government.

3. From its _____ to its **cessation**, the epidemic took a heavy toll.

4. Is the car equipped with a(n) _____ transmission, or a **manual** one?

5. It is hard to believe that a **sane person** could suddenly turn into a(n) _____.

6. Is the class _____, or does it consist of students of **dissimilar** ability?

7. An occasional **lack of balance** in the marching formations somewhat marred the _____ of the parade.

8. The documents would have seemed _____ to most people, but experts knew they were **false**.

9. The establishment favors **conventional** ways of dealing with the crisis and frowns on _____ approaches.

10. We looked through a(n) _____ assortment of lamps reduced for final sale, in which no two were **of the same kind**.

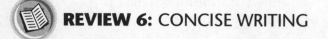

REVIEW 6: CONCISE WRITING

In no more than eighty words, rewrite the following passage, keeping all its ideas. *Hint:* Reduce each boldfaced expression to a single word.

The Peloponnesian War: 431–404 B.C.

In 431 B.C., Athens, a small **country governed in accordance with the wishes of the majority of its citizens**, went to war with Sparta, a **nation governed by a small privileged upper class**. Athens would have won if not for two misfortunes. First, it was devastated in 430-428 B.C. by a **rapidly spreading contagious disease** that killed a quarter of its population. Then, because of **political leaders who stirred up the people for their own selfish advantage**, it undertook reckless offensives on which it squandered its finest troops. As a result, Athens lost not only the war, but its **right to govern itself**.

Most of the above facts were recorded by Thucydides in his **historical account of the events, in the order of time**, of the Peloponnesian War.

The Peloponnesian War: 431–404 B.C.
(concise version)

_____

_____

_____

_____

_____

_____

_____

REVIEW 7: SYNONYM SUMMARY

Each line, when completed, should have three words similar in meaning.
Enter the missing letters.

1. dictat __ r   d __ spot   __ __ tocrat

2. ins __ ne   r __ ving   __ __ niacal

3. b __ rth   __ rigin   genes __ __

4. w __ dth   th __ ckness   d __ ameter

5. tr __ stworthy   gen __ ine   aut __ __ ntic

6. l __ natic   cr __ ckp __ t   man __ __ c

7. ind __ pend __ nt   self-gov __ __ ning   aut __ n __ mous

8. sim __ l __ r   un __ form   homogen __ __ us

9. n __ b __ lity   g __ ntry   a __ __ __ tocracy

10. __ __ sanity   m __ dness   __ __ nia

11. b __ lance   harm __ ny   s __ __ metry

12. convent __ __ nal   __ __ __ servative   __ __ thodox

13. t __ mult   r __ cket   __ __ __ demonium

14. __ __ story   ann __ ls   chr __ n __ cle

15. ped __ gree   lin __ __ ge   gene __ logy

16. n __ ble   patri __ __ an   __ r __ st __ crat

17. __ __ dependence   sover __ __ gnty   aut __ n __ my

18. __ __ conventional   h __ retical   __ __ ortho __ __ __

19. plag __ __   r __ sh   ep __ d __ mic

20. __ __ __ similar   v __ ried   h __ t __ r __ geneous

REVIEW 8: ANALOGIES

Which lettered pair of words—*a, b, c, d,* or *e*—most nearly expresses the same relationship as the capitalized pair? Write the letter of your answer in the space provided.

___ 1. DUCHESS : ARISTOCRACY

    a. retiree : staff
    b. student : faculty
    c. voter : electorate
    d. employment : management
    e. alien : citizenry

___ 2. PANDEMONIUM : HEARING

    a. glare : sight
    b. praise : learning
    c. abundance : scarcity
    d. fog : collision
    e. disharmony : agreement

Hint: **pandemonium** makes **hearing** difficult.

___ 3. DEMAGOGUE : POLITICS

    a. civilian : warfare
    b. quack : medicine
    c. amateur : sports
    d. clown : circus
    e. apprentice : trade

Hint: A **demagogue** is an unscrupulous person in **politics**.

___ 4. AUTHENTIC : ACCEPTANCE

    a. futile : effort
    b. corrupt : contempt
    c. incredible : belief
    d. insignificant : concern
    e. demagogic : trust

___ 5. AUTOMATION : PRODUCTIVITY

    a. rest : fatigue
    b. air conditioning : temperature
    c. bickering : amity
    d. resentment : achievement
    e. refrigeration : shelf life

___ 6. SUBJUGATE : AUTONOMY

    a. demote : authority
    b. initiate : membership
    c. vindicate : innocence
    d. gag : censorship
    e. elevate : prestige

___ 7. BIOGRAPHY : CHRONOLOGICAL

    a. height : vertical
    b. index : alphabetical
    c. novel : fictional
    d. width : horizontal
    e. news story : factual

___ 8. ORTHODONTICS : DENTISTRY

    a. astronomy : physics   *b.* orthopedics : fractures

    c. biology : zoology   *d.* pyrotechnics : fireworks

    e. pediatrics : childhood

___ 9. GENESIS : BEGINNING

    a. diagnosis : disease   *b.* prognosis : recovery

    c. crisis : downfall   *d.* status : promotion

    e. metamorphosis : change

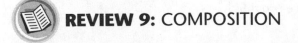

REVIEW 9: COMPOSITION

Answer in a sentence or two.

1. Would you prefer to live in an autocracy or a democracy? Explain your choice.

  _____

  _____

2. How might the outbreak of a deadly and unknown new epidemic cause pandemonium in a city?

  _____

  _____

3. Would most pediatricians see and cure cases of pyromania on a regular basis? Why or why not?

  _____

  _____

4. Why does chronology play an important role in most genealogies?

  _____

  _____

5. Are most pedagogues more interested in automation or orthography? Tell why you think so.

  _____

  _____

GREEK WORD ELEMENTS 11–20

Pretest 2

Insert the *letter* of the best answer in the space provided.

1. If a product is *synthetic,* it was not made by _____.
   (A) hand
   (B) nature
   (C) humans

2. A *thermostat* _____.
   (A) regulates temperature
   (B) keeps liquids warm
   (C) provides heat

3. The reference mark _____ is called an *asterisk.*
   (A) [;]
   (B) [']
   (C) [*]

4. An *anonymous* poem is _____.
   (A) by an unknown author
   (B) humorous
   (C) a nursery rhyme

5. The _____ in a series of similar things is the *prototype.*
   (A) latest
   (B) first
   (C) best

6. Usually, a *nemesis* brings _____.
   (A) defeat
   (B) luck
   (C) victory

7. A *phenomenon* can be _____.
   (A) a ghost or a shadow only
   (B) an extraordinary fact only
   (C) any observable fact or event

8. A *dermatologist* is a _____ specialist.
   (A) skin
   (B) foot
   (C) heart

9. If you have an *antipathy* to a subject, you have a(n) _____ for it.
   (A) enthusiasm
   (B) dislike
   (C) talent

10. The word _____ is an *anagram* of "meat."
    (A) "meet"
    (B) "flesh"
    (C) "team"

THE ANSWERS ARE
1. B   2. A   3. C   4. A   5. B
6. A   7. C   8. A   9. B   10. C

Each italicized word in the pretest came from a different word element: *synthetic* from THET, meaning "put"; *thermostat* from THERMO, meaning "heat," etc. In the following pages you will learn about ten such word elements and some of their derivatives.

11. ANT, ANTI: "against," "opposite"

antagonist (*n.*)
an-'ta-gə-,nist
one who is against, or contends with, another in a struggle, fight, or contest; opponent; adversary; foe
Great Britain was our *antagonist* in the War of 1812.

antibiotic (*n.*)
,an-tē-,bī-'ä-tik
substance obtained from tiny living organisms that works against harmful bacteria
The *antibiotic* penicillin stops the growth of bacteria that cause pneumonia, tonsillitis, and certain other diseases.

antibody (*n.*)
'an-ti-,bä-dē
substance manufactured in the body that works against germs or poisons produced by germs
When the body is invaded by foreign agents, such as bacteria or viruses, the *antibodies* go to work against them.

antidote (*n.*)
'an-ti-,dōt
1. remedy that acts against the effects of a poison
By telephone, the physician prescribed the exact *antidote* to be given immediately to the poison victim.

2. countermeasure
Heavy fines are an *antidote* to illegal parking.

antihistamine (*n.*)
,an-tē-'his-tə-,mən
drug used against certain allergies and cold symptoms
The *antihistamine* prescribed for my cold was not too effective.

antipathy (*n.*)
an-'ti-pə-thē
feeling against; distaste; repugnance; dislike; enmity
A few of the neighbors have an *antipathy* to dogs, but most are fond of them.

antiseptic (*n.*)
,an-tə-'sep-tik
(literally, "against decaying") substance that prevents infection by checking the growth of microorganisms; germicide
The wound was carefully washed; then hydrogen peroxide was applied as an *antiseptic*.

antitoxin (*n.*)
,an-ti-'täk-sən
substance formed in the body as the result of the introduction of a toxin (poison) and capable of acting against that toxin
We are injected with diphtheria *antitoxin* produced in horses because the *antitoxin* manufactured by our bodies may not be enough to prevent diphtheria.

antonym (*n.*)
'an-tə-,nim
word meaning the opposite of another word; opposite
"Temporary" is the *antonym* of "permanent."

EXERCISE 6.11: *ANT, ANTI* WORDS

Fill each blank with the most appropriate word from group 11.

1. An _____ prescribed by a physician may give temporary relief to some cold and allergy sufferers.

2. Our armed forces must be capable of defending us against any foreign _____.

3. Streptomycin, an _____ developed from living microorganisms, is used in the treatment of tuberculosis.

4. The infection would not have developed if an _____ had been used.

5. I have had an _____ to ship travel ever since I became seasick on a lake cruise.

12. ONYM, ONOMATO: *"name," "word"*

acronym (*n.*) 'a-krə-,nim	name formed from the first letter or letters of other words	The word "radar" is an *acronym* for *RA*dio *D*etecting *A*nd *R*ange.
anonymous (*adj.*) ə-'nä-nə-məs	nameless; unnamed; unidentified	An *anonymous* American killed in combat in World War I lies in the Tomb of the Unknowns.
homonym (*n.*) 'hä-mə-,nim	word that sounds like another but differs in meaning	"Fair" and "fare" are *homonyms*.
onomatopoeia (*n.*) ,ä-nə-,ma-tə-'pē-ə	use of words whose sound suggests their meaning	Notice the *onomatopoeia* in these lines by the poet John Dryden: "The double, double, double beat/ Of the thundering drum."
pseudonym (*n.*) 'sü-dᵊn-,im	(literally, "false name") fictitious name used by an author; pen name; alias	Because of antipathy to female authors in her time, Mary Ann Evans wrote under the *pseudonym* "George Eliot."
synonym (*n.*) 'si-nə-,nim	word having the same meaning as another word	"Building" is a *synonym* for "edifice."

EXERCISE 6.12: *ONYM, ONOMATO* WORDS

Fill each blank with the most appropriate word from group 12.

1. "Deer" and "dear" are _____s.

2. There is no need to use a(n) _____, unless you wish to conceal your identity.

3. Scuba is a(n) _____ for "self-contained underwater breathing apparatus."

4. I was embarrassed when the _____ test paper my teacher spoke about turned out to be mine. I had forgotten to put my name on it.

5. "Hiss," "mumble," and "splash" are good one-word examples of _____.

13. *DERM, DERMATO: "skin"*

dermatologist (*n.*) dər-mə-'tä-lə-jist	physician specializing in *dermatology,* the science dealing with the skin and its diseases	The patient with the skin disorder is under the care of a *dermatologist.*
dermis (*n.*) 'dər-məs	inner layer of the skin	The tiny cells from which hairs grow are located in the *dermis.*
epidermis (*n.*) ,e-pə-'dər-məs	outer layer of the skin	Although very thin, the *epidermis* protects the underlying dermis.
hypodermic (*adj.*) ,hī-pə-'dər-mik	beneath the skin	A *hypodermic* syringe is used for injecting medication beneath the skin.
taxidermist (*n.*) 'tak-sə-,dər-mist	one who practices *taxidermy,* the art of preparing, stuffing, and mounting the skins of animals in lifelike form	The lifelike models of animals that you see in museums are the work of skilled *taxidermists.*

EXERCISE 6.13: *DERM, DERMATO* WORDS

Fill each blank with the most appropriate word from group 13.

1. The _____ stretched the skin over a plastic cast of the animal's body.

2. Was the antibiotic taken by mouth or administered by _____ injection?

3. There are numerous tiny openings, or pores, in the _____, or outer layer of the skin.

4. It took three visits for the _____ to remove Rita's painful wart in the skin of her left sole.

5. The sweat glands are located in the _____, or inner layer of the skin.

14. NOM, NEM: "management," "distribution," "law"

agronomy (*n.*)
ə-'grä-nə-mē

(literally, "land management") branch of agriculture dealing with crop production and soil management; husbandry

The science of *agronomy* helps farmers obtain larger and better crops.

astronomical (*adj.*)
,as-trə-'nä-mi-kəl

1. having to do with *astronomy* (literally, "distribution of the stars"); the science of the sun, moon, planets, stars, and other heavenly bodies

The first *astronomical* observations with a telescope were made by the Italian scientist Galileo.

2. inconceivably large

It is difficult to conceive of so *astronomical* a sum as a trillion dollars.

economic (*adj.*)
,e-kə-'nä-mik

having to do with *economics* (literally, "household management"); the social science dealing with production, distribution, and consumption

The President's chief *economic* adviser expects that production will continue at the same rate for the rest of the year.

economical (*adj.*)
,e-kə-'nä-mi-kəl

managed or managing without waste; thrifty; frugal; sparing

Which is the most *economical* fuel for home heating—gas, electricity, or oil?

gastronome (*n.*)
'gas-trə-,nōm

one who follows the principles of *gastronomy*, the art or science of good eating (literally, "management of the stomach"); lover of good food; epicure; gourmet

Being a *gastronome*, my uncle is well-acquainted with the best restaurants in the city.

nemesis (*n.*)
'ne-mə-səs

(from *Nemesis*, the Greek goddess of vengeance who distributes or deals out what is due)
1. person that inflicts just punishment for evil deeds; avenger; scourge

The tyrant Macbeth was invincible in combat until he faced Macduff, who proved to be his *nemesis*.

2. formidable and usually victorious opponent

We would have ended the season without a defeat if not for our old *nemesis*, Greeley High.

EXERCISE 6.14: *NOM, NEM* WORDS

Fill each blank with the most appropriate word from group 14.

1. The villain had engineered several robberies before encountering his _____ in the person of Sherlock Holmes.

2. Overproduction is a serious _____ problem.

3. Some museums and art collectors have gone to _____ expense to acquire famous paintings.

4. Underdeveloped nations are trying to improve the yield and quality of their crops by applying the principles of _____.

5. The acknowledged _____ cheerfully aided her dining companions in making their selections from the menu.

15. *PHAN, PHEN: "show," "appear"*

cellophane (*n.*) 'se-lə-,fān	cellulose substance that "shows" through or permits seeing through; transparent cellulose substance used as a wrapper	When used as a wrapper, *cellophane* lets the purchaser see the contents of the package.
diaphanous (*adj.*) dī-'a-fə-nəs	of such fine texture as to permit seeing through; sheer; transparent	Pedestrians on the sidewalk could see some of the inside of the restaurant through its *diaphanous* curtains.
fancy (*n.*) 'fan-sē	imagination; illusion	We must be able to distinguish between fact and *fancy*.
fantastic (*adj.*) fan-'tas-tik	based on fantasy rather than reason; imaginary; unreal; odd; unbelievable	Robert Fulton's proposal to build a steamboat was at first regarded as *fantastic*.
fantasy (*n.*) 'fan-tə-sē	illusory image; play of the mind; imagination; fancy	Selma is not sure whether she saw a face at the window. Perhaps it was only a *fantasy*.
phantom (*n.*) 'fan-təm	something that has appearance but no reality; apparition; ghost; specter	The *phantom* of the slain Caesar appeared to Brutus in a dream.
phenomenal (*adj.*) fi-'nä-mə-n°l	extraordinary; remarkable; exceptional; unusual	Bernadine has a *phenomenal* memory; she never forgets a face.

| **phenomenon** (*n.*) fə-'nä-mə-,nän | (literally, "an appearance") 1. any observable fact or event | We do not see many adults traveling to work on bicycles, but in some foreign cities it is a common *phenomenon*. |
| | 2. extraordinary person, event, or thing; wonder; prodigy | Renowned as a composer and performer while yet in his teens, Mozart was a musical *phenomenon*. |

EXERCISE 6.15: *PHAN, PHEN* WORDS

Fill each blank with the most appropriate word from group 15.

1. Sarah Bernhardt was no ordinary actress; she was a _____.

2. Though these conclusions may seem _____, I can show you they are based on reason.

3. If the apples are in a _____ bag, you can tell how many there are without opening it.

4. Joan was sure someone was behind the door, but no one was there. It was just a

   _____.

5. Mrs. Potter thought Christine's performance was _____, but I found nothing extraordinary or remarkable in it.

16. THERM, THERMO: "heat"

diathermy (*n.*) 'dī-ə-,thər-mē	generation of heat in body tissues through high-frequency electric currents for medical purposes	*Diathermy* may be used to treat arthritis, bursitis, and other conditions requiring heat treatment.
thermal (*adj.*) 'thər-məl	pertaining to heat; hot; warm	At Lava Hot Springs in Idaho, visitors may bathe in the *thermal* mineral waters.
thermometer (*n.*) thər-'mä-mə-tər	instrument for measuring temperature	At 6 A.M. the *thermometer* registered 32° Fahrenheit (0° Celsius).
thermonuclear (*adj.*) ,thər-mō-'nü-klē-ər	having to do with the fusion (joining together), at an extraordinarily high temperature, of the nuclei of atoms (as in the hydrogen bomb)	It is believed that the sun gets its energy from *thermonuclear* reactions constantly taking place within it.

thermostat (*n.*) 'thər-mə-,stat	automatic device for regulating temperature	You can set the *thermostat* to shut off the heat when the room reaches a comfortable temperature.

EXERCISE 6.16: *THERM, THERMO* WORDS

Fill each blank with the most appropriate word from group 16.

1. The room was cold because the _____ had been set for only 59° Fahrenheit (19° Celsius).

2. If you have a _____ mounted outside your window, you don't need to go outside to learn what the temperature is.

3. The unbelievably intense heat required to start the _____ reaction in a hydrogen bomb is obtained by exploding an atomic bomb.

4. Drugs, hot baths, and _____ are some of the means used to relieve the pain of arthritis.

5. Hot Springs, Arkansas, derives its name from its numerous _____ springs.

17. PROT, PROTO: "first"

protagonist (*n.*) prō-'ta-gə-,nist	the leading ("first") character in a play, novel, or story	Brutus is the *protagonist* in William Shakespeare's JULIUS CAESAR, and Anthony is the antagonist.
protocol (*n.*) 'prō-tə-,kȯl	1. first draft or record (of discussions, agreements, etc.) from which a treaty is drawn up; preliminary memorandum	The *protocol* initiated by the representatives of the three nations is expected to lead to a formal treaty.
	2. rules of etiquette of the diplomatic corps, military services, etc.	It is a breach of *protocol* for a subordinate publicly to question the judgment of a superior officer.
protoplasm (*n.*) 'prō-tə-,pla-zəm	(literally, "first molded material") fundamental substance of which all living things are composed	The presence of *protoplasm* distinguishes living from nonliving things.
prototype (*n.*) 'prō-tə-,tīp	first or original model of anything; model; pattern	The crude craft in which the Wright brothers made the first successful flight in 1903 was the *prototype* of the modem airplane.
protozoan (*n.*) ,prō-tə-'zō-ən	(literally, "first animal") animal consisting only of a single cell	The tiny *protozoan* is believed to be the first animal to have appeared on earth.

EXERCISE 6.17: *PROT, PROTO* WORDS

Fill the blank with the appropriate word from group 17.

1. At the opening game of the baseball season in Washington, D.C., the President, according to _____, is invited to throw out the first ball.

2. The amoeba, a one-celled animal living in ponds and streams, is a typical _____.

3. Our Constitution has served as the _____ of similar documents in democratic nations all over the world.

4. The movie star will not accept a minor part; she wants the role of the _____.

5. Living plants and animals consist of _____.

18. *THESIS, THET: "set," "put"*

antithesis (*n.*) an-'ti-thə-səs	(literally, "a setting against") direct opposite; contrary; reverse	I cannot vote for a candidate who stands for the *antithesis* of what I believe.
epithet (*n.*) 'e-pə-,thet	(literally, something "placed on" or "added") characterizing word or phrase; descriptive name or title	Anna Mary Robertson Moses earned the *epithet* "Grandma" because she did not begin to paint until her late seventies.
hypothesis (*n.*) hī-'pä-thə-səs	(literally, "a placing under" or "supposing") supposition or assumption made as a basis for reasoning or research	When Columbus first presented his *hypothesis* that the earth is round, very few believed it.
synthesis (*n.*) 'sin(t)-thə-səs	(literally, "putting together") combination of parts or elements into a whole	Much of the rubber we use is not a natural product but a *synthesis* of chemicals.
synthetic (*adj.*) sin-'the-tik	(literally, "put together") artificial; factitious; not of natural origin	Cotton is a natural fiber, but rayon and nylon are *synthetic*.

| thesis (*n.*)
'thē-səs | (literally, "a setting down")
1. claim put forward; proposition; statement; contention | Do you agree with Ellen's *thesis* that a student court would be good for our school? |
| | 2. essay written by a candidate for an advanced degree | Candidates for Ph.D. degrees usually must write a *thesis* based on original research. |

Note: To form the plural of a word ending in *is,* change the *is* to *es.* Examples: *antitheses, hypotheses, theses,* etc.

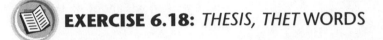

EXERCISE 6.18: *THESIS, THET* WORDS

Fill each blank with the most appropriate word from group 18.

1. _____ rubber is superior to natural rubber in some respects and inferior in others.

2. Jonathan's jalopy is a(n) _____ of parts from several old cars.

3. In the *Odyssey,* you will often find the _____ "wily" before Ulysses' name because he had a reputation for cunning.

4. Anyone who undertakes to write a(n) _____ must know how to do research.

5. Their leader, timid, complaining, and weak, is the _____ of what a leader should be.

19. ASTER, ASTR, ASTRO: *"star"*

aster (*n.*) 'as-tər	plant having small, starlike flowers	Most *asters* bloom in the fall.
asterisk (*n.*) 'as-tə-,risk	(literally, "little star") star-shaped mark (*) used to call attention to a footnote, omission, etc.	The *asterisk* after "Reduced to $9.95" refers the shopper to a footnote reading "Small and medium only."
asteroid (*n.*) 'as-tə-,ròid	1. very small planet resembling a star in appearance	Compared to planet Earth, some *asteroids* are tiny, measuring less than a mile in diameter.
	2. starfish	If an *asteroid* loses an arm to an attacker, it can grow back the missing arm.

astrologer (*n.*) ə-'strä-lə-jər	person who practices *astrology,* a study professing to interpret the supposed influence of the moon, sun, and stars on human affairs	An *astrologer* would have people believe that their lives are regulated by the movements of the stars, planets, sun, and moon.
astronaut (*n.*) 'as-trə-ˌnȯt	(literally, "star sailor") traveler in outer space	Yuri Gagarin, the world's first *astronaut,* orbited the earth in an artificial satellite on April 12, 1961.
astronomer (*n.*) ə-'strä-nə-mər	expert in *astronomy,* science of the stars, planets, sun, moon, and other heavenly bodies	Because the stars are so far away, as*tronomers* measure their distance from Earth in "light-years" (one light-year equals about six trillion miles).
disaster (*n.*) di-'zas-tər	(literally, "contrary star") sudden or extraordinary misfortune; calamity; catastrophe	The attack on Pearl Harbor was the worst *disaster* in the history of the U.S. Navy.

EXERCISE 6.19: *ASTER, ASTR, ASTRO* WORDS

Fill each blank with the most appropriate word from group 19.

1. Some _____s are regarded as pests because they feed on oysters.

2. _____s claim that your life is influenced by the position of the stars at the moment of your birth.

3. _____s undergo a long and difficult period of training that equips them for the challenges of space travel.

4. Nations that continue to spend beyond their means are headed for economic _____.

5. A(n) _____ alerts the reader to look for additional information at the foot of the page.

20. GRAM, GRAPH: "letter," "writing"

anagram (*n.*) 'a-nə-ˌgram	word or phrase formed from another by transposing the letters	"Moat" is an *anagram* for "atom."
cartographer (*n.*) kär-'tä-grə-fər	(literally, "map writer") person skilled in *cartography,* the science or art of mapmaking	Ancient *cartographers* did not know of the existence of the Western Hemisphere.
cryptogram (*n.*) 'krip-tə-ˌgram	something written in secret code	Military leaders, diplomats, and industrialists use *cryptograms* to relay secret information.

electrocardiogram (*n.*) i-,lek-trō-'kär-dē-ə-,gram	"writing" or tracing made by an *electrocardiograph,* an instrument that records the amount of electricity the heart muscles produce during the heartbeat	After reading Henrietta's *electrocardiogram,* the physician assured her that her heart was working properly.
epigram (*n.*) 'e-pə-,gram	(literally, something "written on" or "inscribed") bright or witty thought concisely and cleverly expressed	"The more things a man is ashamed of, the more respectable he is" is one of George Bernard Shaw's *epigrams.*
graphic (*adj.*) 'gra-fik	written or told in a clear, lively manner; vivid; picturesque	The reporter's *graphic* description made us feel that we were present at the scene.
graphite (*n.*) 'gra-,fīt	soft black carbon used in lead pencils	"Lead" pencils do not contain lead, but rather a mixture of clay and *graphite.*
monogram (*n.*) 'mä-nə-,gram	(literally, "one letter") person's initials interwoven or combined into one design	*My monogram* appears on the front of my warm-up jacket.
monograph (*n.*) 'mä-nə-,graf	written account of a single thing or class of things	For her thesis, my sister wrote a *monograph* on the life of an obscure 19th-century composer.
stenographer (*n.*) stə-'nä-grə-fər	person skilled in, or employed to do, *stenography* (literally, "narrow writing") the art of writing in shorthand	A court *stenographer* has to be able to take down more than 250 words a minute.
typographical (*adj.*) ,tī-pə-'gra-fi-kəl	pertaining to or occurring in printing or *typography* (literally, "writing with type")	Proofs submitted by the printer should be carefully checked to eliminate *typographical* errors.

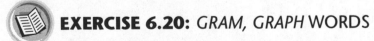

EXERCISE 6.20: *GRAM, GRAPH* WORDS

Fill each blank with the most appropriate word from group 20.

1. Modern _____s use aerial photography to aid in mapmaking.

2. There is a(n) _____ account of London in the 1580s in Marchette Chute's *Shakespeare of London.*

3. The patient's physicians cannot be certain that a heart attack has occurred until they have studied his _____.

4. "Reform" is a(n) _____ for "former."

5. I knew it was Annabel's handkerchief because her _____ was on it.

Review Exercises

REVIEW 10: GREEK WORD ELEMENTS 11–20

In the space before each Greek word element in column I, write the *letter* of its correct meaning from column II.

COLUMN I	COLUMN II
___ 1. NOM, NEM	*a.* heat
___ 2. ASTER, ASTR, ASTRO	*b.* first
___ 3. THERM, THERMO	*c.* skin
___ 4. ANT, ANTI	*d.* management, distribution, law
___ 5. DERM, DERMATO	*e.* name, word
___ 6. GRAM, GRAPH	*f.* star
___ 7. ONYM, ONOMATO	*g.* show, appear
___ 8. THESIS, THET	*h.* against, opposite
___ 9. PROT, PROTO	*i.* letter, writing
___ 10. PHAN, PHEN	*j.* set, place, put

REVIEW 11: WORD-BUILDING

Fill in the missing letters of the word at the right. Each dash stands for one missing letter.

DEFINITION	WORD
1. putting together of parts into a whole	SYN __ __ __ __ __ __
2. remedy against the effects of a poison	__ __ __ __ DOTE
3. punishment distributor	__ __ __ ESIS
4. outer layer of the skin	EPI __ __ __ __ IS
5. skilled writer of shorthand	STENO __ __ __ __ __ ER
6. of unnamed origin	AN __ __ __ __ OUS
7. first draft leading to a treaty	__ __ __ __ __ COL
8. feeling against	__ __ __ __ PATHY

9. expert in the science of the stars   __ __ __ __ __ NOMER

10. any observable fact or event   __ __ __ __ OMENON

11. automatic temperature-regulating device   __ __ __ __ __ __ STAT

12. managing without waste   ECO __ __ __ ICAL

13. first or original model   __ __ __ __ __ TYPE

14. small star-resembling planet   __ __ __ __ __ OID

15. use of words whose sound suggests their meaning   __ __ __ __ __ __ __ POEIA

16. something having appearance but no reality   __ __ __ __ TOM

17. word formed of transposed letters of another   ANA __ __ __ __

18. characterizing name added to ("put on") a person   EPI __ __ __ __

19. pertaining to heat   __ __ __ __ __ AL

20. beneath the skin   HYPO __ __ __ __ IC

REVIEW 12: SENTENCE COMPLETION

Fill each blank with the word from the list below that best fits the context.

anonymous	antagonist	antidote	antipathy	antithesis
asterisk	asteroid	astrology	astronomy	epigram
gastronome	homonym	hypodermic	nemesis	phenomenal
protagonist	protocol	pseudonym	thesis	typographical

1. Henry's _____ in the finals was the longtime _____ who had defeated him in all six of their previous matches.

2. Nadine is the _____ of a(n) _____; she doesn't go to fancy restaurants, and she will eat any food that is wholesome and nourishing.

3. Pip, the _____ of *Great Expectations,* has his education financed by a(n) _____ benefactor who later identifies himself as Abel Magwitch.

4. The _____ of this article is that dinosaurs became extinct after the earth collided with a(n) _____.

5. Unfortunately, many people know more about the false science of _____ than about the true science of _____.

6. Because the author has a(n) _____ to being in the public eye, she wrote her best-selling novels under a(n) _____.

7. The sentence ends with *mens sana in corpore sano.** The _____ leads to a footnote explaining that the words are a Latin _____ meaning "a healthy mind in a healthy body."

8. Because of a(n) _____ error in the phonetic spelling of *wary* in my dictionary, I pronounced it as if it were a(n) _____ of weary.

9. The patient who had accidentally swallowed the poisonous liquid was given a(n) _____ injection of the appropriate _____.

10. Sending an undersecretary to greet the visiting foreign potentate was a breach of _____, as well as a(n) _____ diplomatic blunder.

REVIEW 13: SYNONYMS

Avoid repetition by replacing the boldfaced word or expression with a **synonym** from the following words.

antiseptic	astronomical	cryptogram	disaster	epithet
graphic	hypothesis	phenomenon	prototype	synthetic

_____ 1. The flowers were artificial. The fruit in the basket was artificial. The whole place had a(n) **artificial** appearance.

_____ 2. If no **substance to prevent infection** is applied, the wound may become infected.

_____ 3. Our enormous national debt keeps growing larger and larger; it has become **inconceivably large**.

_____ 4. Dealers had catastrophic losses in the fall. If sales had not picked up before Christmas, the year would have ended in financial **catastrophe**.

_____ 5. What **descriptive title** can better describe America than "the Beautiful"?

_____s 6. Their **coded messages** were undecipherable only so long as no one else knew their code.

_____ 7. Her **lively** manner of expression makes everything she describes come to life.

_____ 8. The return of spring is truly a(n) **extraordinary event**. Unfortunately, some people are so used to it that they rarely think it is extraordinary.

_____ 9. Sometimes a movie is so successful that it becomes the **original model** on which a series of later films is modeled.

_____ 10. The alchemists assumed that a way could be found to turn base metals into gold, but they were never able to verify their **assumption**.

REVIEW 14: ANTONYMS

Enter the word from the list below that is most nearly the **opposite** of the boldfaced word or words.

anonymous	antagonist	antipathy	antonym	economical
fancy	homonym	phenomenal	protagonist	synthetic

1. When those that we have befriended become intolerable, our **affection** for them may turn to _____.

2. Since last summer's drought, we have reduced our **extravagant** uses of water and become more _____.

3. When we read fairy tales, we leave **reality** and enter the realm of _____.

4. "Authentic" is a **synonym** of "genuine," and "fraudulent" is one of its _____s.

5. The soles are made of **natural** leather, but the heels are _____.

6. In last year's play, Sheila was a **minor character**, but in this one she is the _____.

7. Joan of Arc had an **ordinary** peasant background, but she provided France with _____ leadership.

8. **Words that do not sound alike** cannot be called _____s.

9. The donors have asked not to be **named**; they prefer to remain _____.

10. Many a nation that was once our _____ in the United Nations is now our **supporter**.

REVIEW 15: CONCISE WRITING

Express the thought of each sentence below in **no more than four words**, as in 1, below.

1. What assumption did you make as a basis for reasoning?

   What was your hypothesis? _____

2. No one can predict when sudden or extraordinary misfortunes will strike.

   _____

3. Is he the one with whom you have been contending?

   _____

4. Letters that do not disclose the name of the writer are not worthy of trust.

_____

5. No one who practices the art of good eating devours food.

_____

6. Everyone enjoys witty thoughts that are concisely and cleverly expressed.

_____

7. Gail is taking courses in crop production and soil management.

_____

8. Amebas are animals that consist of only a single cell.

_____

9. People who do not conform to generally accepted patterns of behavior pay no attention to the rules of etiquette.

_____

10. Our bodies manufacture substances that counteract the effects of disease-causing germs and their poisons.

_____

 REVIEW 16: SYNONYM SUMMARY

Each line, when completed, should have three words similar in meaning. Enter the missing letters.

1. unbel __ __ vable   __ __ real   __ __ __ tastic

2. fr __ g __ l   sp __ ring   eco __ __ __ ical

3. __ __ ponent   advers __ ry   __ __ tagonist

4. w __ rm   h __ t   th __ rm __ l

5. rev __ rse   opp __ s __ te   __ __ __ __ __ thesis

6. v __ v __ d   pictur __ __ que   gr __ ph __ c

7. artifi __ __ al   facti __ __ ous   syn __ __ etic

8. __ nmity   rep __ gn __ nce   __ __ tipathy

9. s __ pposition   as __ __ __ ption   __ __ pothesis

10. n __ meless   __ __ identified   an __ __ ymous

11. w __ nder   pr __ d __ gy   phe __ __ __ enon

12. c __ l __ mity   __ __ tastrophe   dis __ __ ter

13. sh __ __ r   transp __ rent   __ __ aphanous

14. m __ del   patt __ rn   __ __ ototype

15. app __ r __ tion   __ host   ph __ nt __ m

16. r __ m __ dy   c __ __ ntermeasure   an __ __ dote

17. ill __ sion   __ magination   f __ __ cy

18. prop __ s __ tion   cont __ ntion   th __ s __ s

19. g __ __ rmet   ep __ c __ re   gastr __ n __ me

20. av __ nger   sc __ __ rge   n __ m __ sis

 REVIEW 17: ANALOGIES

Which lettered pair of words—*a, b, c, d,* or *e*—most nearly expresses the same relationship as the capitalized pair? Write the letter of your answer in the space provided.

___ 1. ASTEROID : PLANET
   a. skyscraper : edifice   *b.* deluge : shower
   c. crowd : gathering   *d.* microbe : organism
   e. age : interval

___ 2. FANTASY : FACT
   a. significance : meaning   *b.* warmth : cordiality
   c. antipathy : affection   *d.* celerity : speed
   e. equity : justice

___ 3. DERMATOLOGY : SKIN
   a. chronology : story   *b.* psychology : mind
   c. anthology : volume   *d.* biology : science
   e. apology : blame

___ 4. ASTRONOMICAL : LARGE
   a. immature : old   *b.* nominal : significant
   c. extraordinary : common   *d.* priceless : cheap
   e. infinitesimal : small

___ 5. STEEL : STEAL
   a. ribbon : bow   *b.* here : there
   c. friend : foe   *d.* peace : piece
   e. flaw : defect

___ 6. SYNTHETIC : ARTIFICIAL

    a. restive : restful   *b.* healthful : deleterious

    c. partial : objective   *d.* toxic : antiseptic

    e. sagacious : wise

___ 7. PROTAGONIST : STORY

    a. standard-bearer : cause   *b.* tenor : opera

    c. finalist : tournament   *d.* professor : faculty

    e. soprano : choir

___ 8. PHANTOM : EXISTENCE

    a. river : source   *b.* progenitor : descendant

    c. statue : mobility   *d.* cryptogram : solution

    e. chaos : disorder

___ 9. THERMOSTAT : COMFORT

    a. alarm : security   *b.* pandemonium : harmony

    c. digression : direction   *d.* defection : unity

    e. lamp : electricity

   Hint: A **thermostat** provides **comfort**.

___ 10. HYPOTHESIS : REASONING

    a. unpacking : moving   *b.* landing : flying

    c. review : learning   *d.* rebuttal : debating

    e. soil preparation : planting

REVIEW 18: COMPOSITION

Answer in a sentence or two.

1. Why would an anonymous poet not have a monogram?

_____

_____

2. In which might you find a typographical error—an epithet or a gastronome? Give your reason.

_____

_____

3. Why would most people feel antipathy toward their nemesis?

   _____

   _____

4. Would a dermatologist or a protagonist be more likely to offer you antibiotics? Why?

   _____

   _____

5. Is a diaphanous robe likely to provide thermal value?

   _____

   _____

Expanding Vocabulary Through Derivatives

Suppose you have just learned a new word—*literate,* meaning "able to read and write; educated." If you know how to form derivatives, you have in reality learned not one new word but several: *literate, illiterate,* and *semiliterate; literately, illiterately,* and *semiliterately; literacy, illiteracy,* and *semiliteracy,* etc.

This chapter will help you to expand your vocabulary by teaching you how to form and spell important derivatives.

What is a derivative?

A derivative is a word formed by adding a prefix, a suffix, or both, to a word or root.

PREFIX		WORD		DERIVATIVE
with *(back)*	+	hold	=	withhold *(hold back)*

PREFIX		ROOT		DERIVATIVE
in *(in)*	+	flux *(flow)*	=	influx *(inflow; inpouring)*

WORD		SUFFIX		DERIVATIVE
literate *(educated)*	+	ly *(manner)*	=	literately *(in an educated manner)*

ROOT		SUFFIX		DERIVATIVE
leg *(read)*	+	ible *(able to be)*	=	legible *(able to be read)*

PREFIX		WORD		SUFFIX		DERIVATIVE
semi *(half, partly)*	+	literate	+	ly	=	semiliterately *(in a partly educated manner)*

PREFIX		ROOT		SUFFIX		DERIVATIVE
il *(not)*	+	leg	+	ible	=	illegible *(not able to be read)*

Terms used in this chapter

A derivative may be a noun, an adjective, a verb, or an adverb.

A **noun** is a word naming a person, place, thing, or quality. In the following sentences, all the italicized words are nouns:

1. The enthusiastic *student* very quickly read the partially finished *composition* to the amused *class*.
2. *Knowledge* is *power*.

An **adjective** is a word that modifies (describes) a noun. The following words in sentence 1 are adjectives: *enthusiastic, finished, amused*.

A **verb** is a word that expresses action or a state of being. The verbs in the sentences above are *read* (sentence 1) and *is* (sentence 2).

An **adverb** is a word that modifies a verb, an adjective, or another adverb. In sentence 1 above, *quickly* is an adverb because it modifies the verb "read"; *partially* is an adverb because it modifies the adjective "finished"; and *very* is an adverb because it modifies the adverb "quickly."

Vowels are the letters *a, e, i, o,* and *u.*

Consonants are all the other letters of the alphabet.

FORMING DERIVATIVES BY ATTACHING PREFIXES AND SUFFIXES

1. Attaching Prefixes

When you add the prefix *mis* to the word *spelled,* does the new word have one *s* or two? For help with problems of this sort, learn the following rule:

Rule: Do not add or omit a letter when attaching a prefix to a word. Keep *all* the letters of the prefix and *all* the letters of the word. Examples:

PREFIX		WORD		DERIVATIVE
mis	+	spelled	=	misspelled
mis	+	informed	=	misinformed

 **EXERCISE 7.1**

In column III write the derivative formed by attaching the prefix to the word.

I. PREFIX		II. WORD		III. DERIVATIVE
1. over	+	ripe	=	_____
2. dis	+	integrate	=	_____
3. un	+	necessary	=	_____
4. anti	+	aircraft	=	_____
5. in	+	audible	=	_____
6. under	+	rated	=	_____
7. fore	+	seen	=	_____
8. extra	+	ordinary	=	_____
9. un	+	noticed	=	_____
10. with	+	held	=	_____
11. e	+	migrate	=	_____
12. mis	+	spent	=	_____
13. over	+	estimated	=	_____
14. dis	+	interred	=	_____
15. semi	+	circle	=	_____
16. un	+	nerve	=	_____
17. pre	+	existence	=	_____
18. dis	+	solution	=	_____
19. extra	+	curricular	=	_____
20. un	+	navigable	=	_____
21. over	+	run	=	_____
22. in	+	appropriate	=	_____
23. semi	+	autonomous	=	_____
24. dis	+	satisfied	=	_____
25. un	+	abridged	=	_____

2. Attaching the Prefix IN

Sometimes, the N in the prefix IN changes to another letter. To learn when this occurs, study the following rule:

Rule: Before *l*, IN becomes IL, as in *illegal, illiterate*, etc.
Before *m* or *p*, IN becomes IM, as in *immature, impure*, etc.
Before *r*, IN becomes IR, as in *irrational, irregular*, etc.

EXERCISE 7.2

Make the word in column II negative by attaching *in, il, im,* or *ir* in column I. Then write the complete negative word in column III. (The first line has been done for you as an example.)

I. NEGATIVE PREFIX		II. WORD		III. NEGATIVE WORD
1. in	+	gratitude	=	ingratitude
2. _____	+	patiently	=	_____
3. _____	+	responsible	=	_____
4. _____	+	equitable	=	_____
5. _____	+	moderate	=	_____
6. _____	+	literacy	=	_____
7. _____	+	replaceable	=	_____
8. _____	+	consistently	=	_____
9. _____	+	personal	=	_____
10. _____	+	legible	=	_____
11. _____	+	plausible	=	_____
12. _____	+	articulate	=	_____
13. _____	+	material	=	_____
14. _____	+	reversible	=	_____
15. _____	+	security	=	_____
16. _____	+	liberal	=	_____
17. _____	+	perceptibly	=	_____
18. _____	+	flexible	=	_____
19. _____	+	relevant	=	_____
20. _____	+	moral	=	_____

3. Attaching Suffixes

What happens when you add the suffix *ness* to *stubborn*? Does the new word have one *n* or two? Questions of this sort will never bother you once you have learned this simple rule:

Rule: Do not omit, add, or change a letter when attaching a suffix to a word—unless the word ends in *y* or silent *e*. Keep *all* the letters of the word and *all* the letters of the suffix. Examples:

WORD		SUFFIX		DERIVATIVE
stubborn	+	ness	=	stubbornness
conscious	+	ness	=	consciousness
punctual	+	ly	=	punctually
anonymous	+	ly	=	anonymously
disagree	+	able	=	disagreeable

 EXERCISE 7.3

Fill in column III.

I. WORD		II. SUFFIX		III. DERIVATIVE
1. govern	+	ment	=	_____
2. tail	+	less	=	_____
3. synonym	+	ous	=	_____
4. radio	+	ed	=	_____
5. unilateral	+	ly	=	_____
6. embarrass	+	ment	=	_____
7. sudden	+	ness	=	_____
8. room	+	mate	=	_____
9. ski	+	er	=	_____
10. foresee	+	able	=	_____

4. *Attaching Suffixes to Words Ending in Y*

Final *y* can be troublesome. Sometimes it changes to *i*; sometimes it does not change at all. To learn how to deal with final *y*, follow these helpful rules:

Rule 1: If the letter before final *y* is a consonant, change the *y* to *i* before attaching a suffix.

WORD		SUFFIX		DERIVATIVE
comply	+	ed	=	complied
sturdy	+	est	=	sturdiest
costly	+	ness	=	costliness
ordinary	+	ly	=	ordinarily

Exception A: Except before *ing*.

comply	+	ing	=	complying

Exception B: Learn these special exceptions: *dryly, dryness, shyly, shyness, baby-ish, jellylike.*

Rule 2: If the letter before final *y* is a vowel, do *not* change the *y* before attaching a suffix.

destroy	+	ed	=	destroyed
play	+	ful	=	playful

Exceptions: laid, paid, said, and their compounds (*mislaid, underpaid, unsaid,* etc.); *daily.*

EXERCISE 7.4

In column III, write the derivatives. Watch your spelling.

I. WORD		II. SUFFIX		III. DERIVATIVE
1. decay	+	ed	=	_____
2. fancy	+	ful	=	_____
3. stealthy	+	ly	=	_____
4. foolhardy	+	ness	=	_____
5. magnify	+	ing	=	_____
6. plucky	+	est	=	_____
7. defy	+	ance	=	_____

8. overpay	+	ed	=	_____
9. accompany	+	ment	=	_____
10. costly	+	ness	=	_____
11. ceremony	+	ous	=	_____
12. deny	+	al	=	_____
13. momentary	+	ly	=	_____
14. crafty	+	er	=	_____
15. display	+	ed	=	_____
16. bury	+	al	=	_____
17. shy	+	ly	=	_____
18. oversupply	+	ing	=	_____
19. harmony	+	ous	=	_____
20. disqualify	+	ed	=	_____

 EXERCISE 7.5

Four words have been omitted from each line except the first. Complete each of the other lines so that it will correspond to the first.

I. ADJECTIVE	II. ADJECTIVE ENDING IN ER	III. ADJECTIVE ENDING IN EST	IV. ADVERB ENDING IN LY	V. NOUN ENDING IN NESS
1. clumsy	clumsier	clumsiest	clumsily	clumsiness
2. _____	noisier	_____	_____	_____
3. _____	_____	sturdiest	_____	_____
4. _____	_____	_____	uneasily	_____
5. _____	_____	_____	_____	greediness
6. flimsy	_____	_____	_____	_____
7. _____	wearier	_____	_____	_____
8. _____	_____	heartiest	_____	_____
9. _____	_____	_____	warily	_____
10. _____	_____	_____	_____	unhappiness

5. *Attaching Suffixes to Words Ending in Silent E*

When you add a suffix to a word ending in silent *e*, what happens to the *e*? Is it kept or dropped? Here are the rules:

Rule 1: Drop silent *e* if the suffix begins with a vowel.

WORD		SUFFIX		DERIVATIVE
blame	+	able	=	blamable
secure	+	ity	=	security
innovate	+	or	=	innovator

Exception A: If the word ends in *ce* or *ge*, and the suffix begins with *a* or *o*, keep the *e*.

service	+	able	=	serviceable
courage	+	ous	=	courageous

Exception B: Learn these special exceptions: *acreage, mileage, singeing, canoeing, hoeing, shoeing.*

Rule 2: Keep silent *e* if the suffix begins with a consonant.

hope	+	ful	=	hopeful
profuse	+	ly	=	profusely
postpone	+	ment	=	postponement

Exceptions: argument, awful, duly, truly, wholly, ninth.

EXERCISE 7.6

In column III, write the derivatives. Watch your spelling.

I. WORD		II. SUFFIX		III. DERIVATIVE
1. depreciate	+	ion	=	_____
2. survive	+	al	=	_____
3. suspense	+	ful	=	_____
4. fatigue	+	ing	=	_____
5. censure	+	able	=	_____
6. acquiesce	+	ent	=	_____
7. nine	+	th	=	_____

8. hostile	+	ity	=	_____
9. malice	+	ious	=	_____
10. dawdle	+	er	=	_____
11. reverse	+	ible	=	_____
12. immaculate	+	ly	=	_____
13. spine	+	less	=	_____
14. outrage	+	ous	=	_____
15. demote	+	ion	=	_____
16. homogenize	+	ed	=	_____
17. recharge	+	able	=	_____
18. abate	+	ment	=	_____
19. emancipate	+	or	=	_____
20. dispute	+	able	=	_____
21. whole	+	ly	=	_____
22. provoke	+	ing	=	_____
23. argue	+	ment	=	_____
24. fragile	+	ity	=	_____
25. replace	+	able	=	_____

6. Attaching the Suffix LY

Rule: To change an adjective into an adverb, add *ly*.

ADJECTIVE		SUFFIX		ADVERB
close	+	ly	=	closely
firm	+	ly	=	firmly
usual	+	ly	=	usually

Exception A: If the adjective ends in *y*, remember to change *y* to *i* before adding *ly*.

easy	+	ly	=	easily

Exception B: If the adjective ends in *ic*, add *al* plus *ly*.

tragic	+	al	+	ly	=	tragically
heroic	+	al	+	ly	=	heroically

However, *public* can be either:

public + ly = publicly or public + al + ly = publically

Exception C: If the adjective ends in *le* preceded by a consonant, simply change the *le* to *ly.*

ADJECTIVE	ADVERB
able	ably
simple	simply
idle	idly

 EXERCISE 7.7

Change the following adjectives into adverbs.

ADJECTIVE   ADVERB

1. overwhelming   _____

2. normal   _____

3. interscholastic   _____

4. mutual   _____

5. ample   _____

6. conspicuous   _____

7. economic   _____

8. outspoken   _____

9. graphic   _____

10. incontrovertible   _____

11. punctual   _____

12. exclusive   _____

13. unwary   _____

14. chronic   _____

15. synthetic   _____

16. intermittent   _____

17. manual   _____

18. heavy   _____

19. infallible   _____

20. frantic   _____

📖 **EXERCISE 7.8**

For each noun in column I, write an adjective ending in *ic* and an adverb ending in *ally*. Two examples are given.

I. NOUN	II. IC ADJECTIVE	III. ALLY ADVERB
democracy	democratic	democratically
history	historic	historically
1. autocracy		
2. stenography		
3. antagonist		
4. pedagogy		
5. economics		
6. astronomy		
7. diplomacy		
8. bureaucracy		
9. autobiography		
10. symmetry		

7. Doubling Final Consonants Before Suffixes

Why is the *r* in *defer* doubled (deferred) when *ed* is added, whereas the *r* in *differ* is not (differed)? Why is the *n* in *plan* doubled (planning) before *ing,* whereas the *n* in *burn* is not (burning)?

To clear up these matters, review two rules for doubling final consonants.

Rule 1: In a one-syllable word, double the final consonant before a suffix beginning with a vowel.

WORD		SUFFIXES		DERIVATIVES
plan	+	ing, er	=	planning, planner
stop	+	ed, age	=	stopped, stoppage
big	+	er, est	=	bigger, biggest

Exception A: If the final consonant comes right after two vowels, do not double it.

| fail | + | ed, ing | = | failed, failing |
| stoop | + | ed, ing | = | stooped, stooping |

Exception B: If the final consonant comes right after another consonant, do not double it.

| warm | + | er, est | = | warmer, warmest |
| last | + | ed, ing | = | lasted, lasting |

Rule 2: In a word of two or more syllables, double the final consonant only if it is in an *accented* syllable before a suffix beginning with a vowel.

| deFER′ | + | ed, ing, al | = | deferred, deferring, deferral |
| resubMIT′ | + | ed, ing | = | resubmitted, resubmitting |

Note carefully that the rule does not apply if the final consonant is in an *unaccented* syllable.

| DIF′fer | + | ed, ing, ent | = | differed, differing, different |
| BEN′efit | + | ed, ing | = | benefited, benefiting |

Exception A: The rule does not apply if the final consonant comes right after two vowels.

| obTAIN′ | + | ed, ing | = | obtained, obtaining |
| conCEAL′ | + | ed, ing | = | concealed, concealing |

Exception B: The rule does not apply if the final consonant comes right after another consonant.

| abDUCT′ | + | ed, ing, or | = | abducted, abducting, abductor |
| comMEND′ | + | ed, ing, able | = | commended, commending, commendable |

Exception C: The rule does not apply if the accent shifts back to the first syllable.

conFER′	+	ence	=	CON′ference
preFER′	+	ence	=	PREF′erence
reFER′	+	ence	=	REF′erence

However: exCEL′ + ence = EX′cellence

EXERCISE 7.9

Write the derivatives in column III, paying careful attention to the spelling.

I. WORD		II. SUFFIX		III. DERIVATIVE
1. concur	+	ing	=	_____
2. entail	+	ed	=	_____
3. abhor	+	ent	=	_____

4. flat   +   er   =   _____

5. retract   +   able   =   _____

6. refer   +   al   =   _____

7. dispel   +   ed   =   _____

8. deter   +   ent   =   _____

9. ungag   +   ed   =   _____

10. drum   +   er   =   _____

11. elicit   +   ing   =   _____

12. imperil   +   ed   =   _____

13. absorb   +   ent   =   _____

14. defer   +   ence   =   _____

15. propel   +   ant   =   _____

16. inter   +   ing   =   _____

17. append   +   age   =   _____

18. covet   +   ous   =   _____

19. discredit   +   ed   =   _____

20. adapt   +   able   =   _____

21. cower   +   ing   =   _____

22. disinter   +   ed   =   _____

23. pilfer   +   er   =   _____

24. slim   +   est   =   _____

25. excel   +   ent   =   _____

 EXERCISE 7.10

For each word at the left, form the three derivatives indicated.

1. regret   _____ing   _____ed   _____ful

2. sin   _____ing   _____ed   _____er

3. control   _____ing   _____ed   _____er

4. occur   _____ing   _____ed   _____ence

5. adjourn   _____ing   _____ed   _____ment

6. flip   _____ing   _____ed   _____ant

	ing		ed		er
7. transmit	_____ing		_____ed		_____er
8. profit	_____ing		_____ed		_____able
9. defer	_____ing		_____ed		_____ment
10. dissent	_____ing		_____ed		_____er
11. protract	_____ing		_____ed		_____or
12. spot	_____ing		_____ed		_____er
13. commit	_____ing		_____ed		_____ment
14. excel	_____ing		_____ed		_____ence
15. recur	_____ing		_____ed		_____ent

8. Troublesome Suffixes

Why should *dispensable* end in *able* but *sensible* in *ible*? Why should *foreigner* end in *er* but *debtor* in *or*? Unhappily, there are no simple rules to guide you in these matters. You will have to learn individually each word with a troublesome suffix and consult the dictionary when in doubt. The following review should prove helpful:

1. Attaching *able* or *ible*. Study the following adjectives:

ABLE	IBLE
amiable	accessible
changeable	credible
equitable	fallible
formidable	flexible
hospitable	illegible
impregnable	incompatible
indomitable	incontrovertible
lovable	invincible
noticeable	reversible
unquenchable	visible

Note that adjectives ending in *able* become nouns ending in *ability*. On the other hand, adjectives ending in *ible* become nouns ending in *ibility*.

ADJECTIVE	NOUN	ADJECTIVE	NOUN
incapable	incapability	audible	audibility
pliable	pliability	resistible	resistibility

2. Attaching suffixes meaning "one who" or "that which": *er, or, ent,* or *ant.* Study these nouns:

ER	OR	ENT	ANT
abstainer	aggressor	adherent	assistant
abuser	benefactor	antecedent	consultant
commuter	bisector	belligerent	contestant
contender	collaborator	correspondent	defendant
dispenser	duplicator	current	deodorant
retainer	exhibitor	dependent	immigrant
typographer	interceptor	insurgent	inhabitant
underseller	precursor	opponent	participant
withholder	reflector	precedent	pendant
wrangler	transgressor	proponent	tenant

3. Attaching *ant* or *ent.* Study these adjectives:

ANT	ENT
defiant	adjacent
discordant	affluent
dormant	coherent
extravagant	decadent
hesitant	fluent
ignorant	imminent
incessant	latent
irrelevant	negligent
reliant	permanent
vigilant	vehement

Note that adjectives ending in *ant* become nouns ending in *ance* or *ancy.* On the other hand, adjectives ending in *ent* become nouns ending in *ence* or *ency.*

ADJECTIVE	NOUN	ADJECTIVE	NOUN
defiant	defiance	coherent	coherence
dormant	dormancy	fluent	fluency
hesitant	hesitance, hesitancy	permanent	permanence, permanency

 **EXERCISE 7.11**

Fill in the missing letter.

1. inflex ___ ble

2. ten ___ ncy

3. vehem ___ nce

4. benefact ___ r

5. self-reli ___ nce

6. vis ___ bility

7. dispens ___ r

8. relev ___ nce

9. infall ___ bility

10. unchange ___ ble

11. collaborat ___ r

12. impregn ___ bility

13. reflect ___ r

14. curr ___ ncy

15. correspond ___ nce

16. contend ___ r

17. imperman ___ nt

18. irrevers ___ ble

19. inaccess ___ bility

20. semidepend ___ nt

 **EXERCISE 7.12**

For each noun, write the corresponding adjective. (The first adjective has been filled in as an example.)

NOUN	ADJECTIVE
1. capability	capable
2. urgency	
3. resistance	
4. infallibility	
5. subservience	
6. compatibility	
7. eminence	
8. truancy	
9. audibility	
10. opulence	
11. inconstancy	
12. malevolence	
13. indefatigability	

14. observance   _____

15. cogency   _____

16. adaptability   _____

17. incandescence   _____

18. unavailability   _____

19. compliance   _____

20. transiency   _____

Review Exercises

 REVIEW 1

Two words have been omitted from each line except the first. Complete each of the other lines so that it will correspond to the first.

I. VERB	II. NOUN ENDING IN ER, OR, ENT, OR ANT	III. NOUN ENDING IN ION, ENCE, OR ANCE
1. transgress	**transgressor**	**transgression**
2. _____	_____	dependence
3. _____	correspondent	_____
4. consult	_____	_____
5. _____	_____	exhibition
6. _____	observer	_____
7. intercept	_____	_____
8. _____	_____	opposition
9. _____	immigrant	_____
10. collaborate	_____	_____

REVIEW 2

Two words have been omitted from each line except the first. Complete each of the other lines so that it will correspond to the first.

I. NOUN	II. ADJECTIVE	III. ADVERB
1. happiness	**happy**	**happily**
2. _____	courageous	_____
3. _____	_____	amicably
4. immaturity	_____	_____
5. _____	original	_____
6. _____	_____	coherently
7. benevolence	_____	_____
8. _____	harmonious	_____
9. _____	_____	stubbornly
10. proficiency	_____	_____
11. _____	legible	_____
12. _____	_____	unanimously
13. shyness	_____	_____
14. _____	weary	_____
15. _____	_____	insecurely
16. autonomy	_____	_____
17. _____	logical	_____
18. _____	_____	outrageously
19. consistency	_____	_____
20. _____	hostile	_____

📖 REVIEW 3

Five words have been omitted from each set except the first. Complete each of the other sets so that it will correspond to the first.

ADJECTIVE AND OPPOSITE	ADVERB AND OPPOSITE	NOUN AND OPPOSITE
1. mature	**maturely**	**maturity**
immature	**immaturely**	**immaturity**
2. impatient		
3. _____	dependently	
4. _____		
	incompetently	
5. _____	_____	plausibility
6. _____	_____	
		irresponsibility
7. legible		
8. _____		
inflexible		
9. _____	formally	
10. _____		
	unimportantly	

Chapter

8

Understanding Word Relationships and Word Analogies

Word Relationships

ROBIN : BIRD

What relationship is there between *robin* and *bird*? Obviously, a *robin* is a *bird*. So, too, is a sparrow, a woodpecker, a crow, a gull, a pigeon, a blue jay, etc. *Bird,* clearly, is the large category of which *robin* is one member.

If we call *robin* word A and *bird* word B, we may express the *robin : bird* relationship by saying "A is a member of the B category."

Here are some additional pairs of words with an explanation of the relationship in each pair. As in the above, let us call the first word A and the second B.

MINE : COAL

Mine is the source from which we obtain the substance *coal*. To express the *mine : coal* relationship, we may say "A is the source of B."

SPADE : DIGGING

A *spade* is a kind of shovel that is used for *digging*. The relationship here is "A is used for B."

TEMPERATURE : THERMOMETER

Temperature is measured by a *thermometer*. The relationship in this pair is "A is measured by B."

MEEK : SUBMIT

Anyone who is *meek* ("yielding without resentment when ordered about") will usually *submit* ("give in"). We may express this relationship as "An A person is likely to B."

To find the relationship between a pair of words, go through the kind of reasoning shown in the preceding paragraphs. When you have determined the relationship, sum it up in a very short sentence using A and B, as in the following examples:

WORD PAIR	RELATIONSHIP
PAUPER : MEANS	A lacks B.
FOUNDATION : EDIFICE	A supports B.
SECURITY GUARD : THEFT	A guards against B.
BLINDFOLD : VISION	A interferes with B.
LITERATE : READ	One who is A can B.
ILLNESS : ABSENCE	A may cause B.
SEIZING : TAKING	A is a sudden, forcible form of B.
GREGARIOUS : COMPANY	One who is A likes B.
PEBBLE : STONE	A is a small B.
PAINTER : EASEL	A uses B.

Word Analogy Questions

So far, we have been dealing only with one relationship at a time. A *word analogy question,* however, tests your ability to see that the relationship between one pair of words is the same as the relationship between another pair of words. Here is a typical word analogy question.

Directions: In the space at the right, write the *letter* of the pair of words related to each other in the same way that the capitalized words are related to each other.

PREFACE : INDEX :: _____

    (A) tool : drill   (D) appetizer : dessert

    (B) departure : trip   (E) water : well

    (C) famine : drought

Solution: The first step is to find the relationship in the capitalized pair *preface : index.* Since a *preface* comes at the beginning of a book, and an *index* at the end, the relationship here is "A begins that which B ends."

The next step is to analyze the five suggested answers to see which has the same relationship as *preface : index.* Since an *appetizer* comes at the beginning of dinner and a *dessert* at the end, the correct answer is obviously D.

EXERCISE 8.1

Select the lettered pair that best expresses a relationship similar to that expressed in the capitalized pair. Write the *letter* A, B, C, D, or E in the blank space.

1. NEEDLE : STITCH :: _____

    (A) shears : prune   (D) stake : bush

    (B) rake : mow   (E) wrench : soak

    (C) spade : level

2. FATHOM : DEPTH :: _____

    (A) temperature : calorie   (D) dive : surface

    (B) search : treasure   (E) base : height

    (C) minute : time

3. DAM : FLOW :: _____

    (A) research : information   (D) autocracy : liberty

    (B) laws : justice   (E) education : opportunity

    (C) reporters : news

4. FOREST : TIMBER :: _____

    (A) magnet : filings   (D) clay : earth

    (B) art : museum   (E) zoo : spectators

    (C) quarry : stone

5. NECK : BOTTLE :: _____

    (A) bonnet : head   (D) metal : leather

    (B) rim : wheel   (E) chain : link

    (C) roof : cellar

6. TYRO : EXPERIENCE :: _____

    (A) despot : power   (D) coward : courage

    (B) razor : sharpness   (E) farewell : welcome

    (C) artisan : skill

7. GRAVEL : PIT :: _____

    (A) oil : well   (D) asphalt : road

    (B) cement : sand   (E) crest : mountain

    (C) tunnel : cave

8. FACULTY : TEACHER :: _____

    (A) congregation : clergy   (D) choir : singer

    (B) crew : captain   (E) election : candidate

    (C) act : play

9. KITTEN : CAT :: _____

    (A) ewe : lamb   (D) fawn : deer

    (B) tiger : cub   (E) napkin : towel

    (C) seedling : flower

10. MICROSCOPE : BIOLOGIST :: _____

    (A) horoscope : scientist   (D) telescope : astronomer

    (B) medicine : druggist   (E) spectacles : optometry

    (C) lens : photography

11. LIEUTENANT : OFFICER :: _____

    (A) actor : understudy   (D) sophomore : undergraduate

    (B) moon : planet   (E) passenger : conductor

    (C) veteran : newcomer

12. BIRTH : DECEASE :: _____

    (A) takeoff : flight   (D) dawn : sunset

    (B) negligence : dismissal   (E) competition : defeat

    (C) opera : finale

13. FOG : VISION :: _____

    (A) superstition : ignorance   (D) rain : overflow

    (B) evidence : testimony   (E) vigilance : safety

    (C) malnutrition : growth

14. PLANT : HARVEST :: _____

    (A) factory : equipment   (D) clump : shrub

    (B) launch : decommission   (E) mishap : carelessness

    (C) sow : irrigate

15. COD : FISH :: _____

    (A) immunity : disease   (D) penalty : offense

    (B) band : trumpet   (E) pneumonia : illness

    (C) mutiny : authority

Working Backwards in Completing Analogies

Sometimes you may find it difficult to determine the exact relationship between word A and word B in a given pair. In such cases it is advisable to work backwards from the five choices suggested for the answer. The chances are that one of these choices will lead you to the A : B relationship. Consider the following question:

BANKRUPTCY : PROFIT :: _____

    (A) population : housing   (D) memory : knowledge

    (B) fatigue : effort   (E) flood : thaw

    (C) congestion : space

Suppose you are having trouble finding the relationship between *bankruptcy* and *profit*. Try the back door: find the relationship of each suggested pair and discover which relationship applies also to the capitalized pair. This method is illustrated below.

BANKRUPTCY : PROFIT ::

    (A) population : housing. The relationship is "A needs B" (*population needs housing*). But bankruptcy does not need profit; once bankruptcy has occurred, it is too late for profit to be of help. Therefore, choice A is incorrect.

BANKRUPTCY : PROFIT ::

    (B) fatigue : effort. The relationship is "A results from too much B" (*fatigue results from too much effort*). Since bankruptcy does not result from too much profit, choice B is incorrect.

BANKRUPTCY : PROFIT ::

    (C) congestion : space. The relationship is "A results from a lack of B" (*congestion results from a lack of space*). Bankruptcy results from a lack of profit. Choice C looks correct, but let's test the remaining choices.

BANKRUPTCY : PROFIT ::

    (D) memory : knowledge. The relationship is "A stores B" (*memory stores knowledge*). Since bankruptcy does not store profit, choice D is incorrect.

BANKRUPTCY : PROFIT ::

    (E) flood : thaw. The relationship is "A may result from B" (*a flood may result from a thaw*). But bankruptcy does not result from profit. Therefore, choice E is incorrect.

Answer: C

 **EXERCISE 8.2**

The following questions are more difficult than those in the previous exercise. If you cannot readily find the relationship between word A and word B in the given pair, try the "working backwards" method described above.

1. SOLVENT : PAY :: _____

    (A) indigent : thrive   (D) punctual : tardy

    (B) innocent : acquit   (E) lavish : economize

    (C) loyal : adhere

2. ANTISEPTIC : BACTERIA :: _____

    (A) soldier : nation

    (B) hair : scalp

    (C) pseudonym : author

    (D) prescription : cure

    (E) education : ignorance

3. INTERMEDIARY : SETTLEMENT :: _____

    (A) belligerent : peace

    (B) prosecutor : conviction

    (C) adherent : pact

    (D) strife : recess

    (E) rumor : discovery

4. GENEROUS : FORGIVE :: _____

    (A) pliable : yield

    (B) spineless : resist

    (C) opinionated : change

    (D) conspicuous : hide

    (E) impatient : delay

5. DISTANCE : ODOMETER :: _____

    (A) weight : scale

    (B) heat : barometer

    (C) quiz : knowledge

    (D) map : compass

    (E) clock : time

6. GUILTLESS : BLAME :: _____

    (A) unbiased : prejudice

    (B) bankrupt : debt

    (C) sincere : honesty

    (D) apprehensive : worry

    (E) verdict : acquittal

7. AUTOMATON : ORIGINALITY :: _____

    (A) ambassador : goodwill

    (B) pioneer : foresight

    (C) hothead : equanimity

    (D) guest : hospitality

    (E) benefactor : generosity

8. CONJUNCTION : CLAUSES :: _____

    (A) barrier : neighbors

    (B) paragraph : phrases

    (C) door : hinges

    (D) bridge : shores

    (E) preposition : nouns

9. IRREVOCABLE : ALTER :: _____

    (A) irreproachable : trust

    (B) available : obtain

    (C) audible : hear

    (D) intelligible : comprehend

    (E) pressing : defer

10. SMOG : POLLUTANTS :: _____

    (A) fog : travel

    (B) wars : destruction

    (C) ambition : diligence

    (D) contagion : disinfectants

    (E) exhaustion : overwork

11. MANACLE : MOVEMENT :: ____
        (A) sailor : crew   (D) manual : information
        (B) pendant : chain   (E) invalid : vigor
        (C) gag : speech

12. EROSION : WATER :: ____
        (A) earthquake : destruction   (D) aging : time
        (B) ocean : wind   (E) solid : liquid
        (C) inauguration : presidency

13. ARISTOCRAT : COUNT :: ____
        (A) flower : leaf   (D) civilian : soldier
        (B) senator : voter   (E) insect : ant
        (C) professional : amateur

14. DESPOTIC : DOMINEER :: ____
        (A) disgruntled : rejoice   (D) aggressive : tremble
        (B) cordial : rebuff   (E) malcontent : cooperate
        (C) timorous : withdraw

15. HOLD : VESSEL :: ____
        (A) tail : airplane   (D) garage : vehicle
        (B) vault : security   (E) basement : house
        (C) site : edifice

Alternate-Type Analogy Questions

    In the following alternate type of analogy question, you are given the first pair and the first word of the second pair. You are asked to complete the second pair by selecting one of five suggested words.

 **EXERCISE 8.3**

Write the *letter* of the word that best completes the analogy.

1. *Justice* is to *judge* as *health* is to _____.
        (A) lawyer   (C) physician   (E) jury
        (B) nutrition   (D) disease

2. *Dentist* is to *teeth* as *dermatologist* is to _____.

    (A) heart   (C) eyes   (E) lungs

    (B) feet   (D) skin

3. *Quart* is to *gallon* as *week* is to _____.

    (A) pint   (C) liquid   (E) measure

    (B) year   (D) month

4. *Horse* is to *stable* as *dog* is to _____.

    (A) leash   (C) bone   (E) kennel

    (B) curb   (D) muzzle

5. *Pear* is to *potato* as *peach* is to _____.

    (A) carrot   (C) nectarine   (E) tomato

    (B) cucumber   (D) melon

6. *Composer* is to *symphony* as *playwright* is to _____.

    (A) essay   (C) novel   (E) copyright

    (B) cast   (D) drama

7. *Friction* is to *rubber* as *repetition* is to _____.

    (A) skill   (C) literacy   (E) knowledge

    (B) novelty   (D) memory

8. *Pond* is to *lake* as *asteroid* is to _____.

    (A) moon   (C) planet   (E) meteor

    (B) comet   (D) orbit

9. *Bear* is to *fur* as *fish* is to _____.

    (A) seaweed   (C) scales   (E) gills

    (B) fins   (D) water

10. *Condemn* is to *criticize* as *scald* is to _____.

    (A) praise   (C) freeze   (E) burn

    (B) heat   (D) thaw

11. *Pearl* is to *oyster* as *ivory* is to _____.

    (A) piano   (C) tusks   (E) tortoise

    (B) crocodile   (D) elephant

12. *Sheep* is to *fold* as *bluefish* is to _____.

    (A) boat   (C) bait   (E) shore

    (B) line   (D) school

13. *Drama* is to *intermission* as *conflict* is to _____.

     (A) feud   (C) reconciliation   (E) stage

     (B) truce   (D) intervention

14. *War* is to *hawk* as *peace* is to _____.

     (A) eagle   (C) dove   (E) owl

     (B) gull   (D) falcon

15. *Ballistics* is to *projectiles* as *genealogy* is to _____.

     (A) exploration   (C) minerals   (E) missiles

     (B) lineage   (D) causes

16. *Pistol* is to *holster* as *airliner* is to _____.

     (A) fuselage   (C) runway   (E) landing

     (B) hangar   (D) fuel

17. *Frugal* is to *waste* as *infallible* is to _____.

     (A) dread   (C) criticize   (E) err

     (B) save   (D) prosper

18. *Toothpaste* is to *tube* as *graphite* is to _____.

     (A) pencil   (C) coal   (E) tar

     (B) lead   (D) cable

19. *State* is to *traitor* as *plant* is to _____.

     (A) soil   (C) leaf   (E) moisture

     (B) absorption   (D) pest

20. *Spot* is to *immaculate* as *name* is to _____.

     (A) autonomous   (C) anonymous   (E) illegible

     (B) illiterate   (D) dependent

Dictionary of Words Taught in This Text

The following pages contain a partial listing of the words presented in this book. The words included are those likely to offer some degree of difficulty. The definitions given have in many cases been condensed.

The numeral following a definition indicates the page on which the word appears. Roman type (e.g., abate, 61) is used when the word appears in the first column on that page. Italic type (e.g., abandon, *34*) is used when the word appears in the second column.

Use this dictionary as a tool of reference and review. It is a convenient means of restudying the meanings of words that you may have missed in the exercises. It is also a useful device for a general review before an important vocabulry test. Bear in mind, however, that you will get a fuller understanding of these words from the explanations and exercises of the foregoing chapters.

abandon: give up completely *34*
abate: become less; make less 61
abduct: carry off by force 153
abhor: hate 153, *184*
abnormal: unusual 153
abode: home *115*
abound: be well supplied; be plentiful 232
abrasion: scraping or wearing away of the skin by friction 153
abroad: in or to a foreign land or lands 114
abrupt: broken off 153
abscond: steal off and hide 153
absolute: free from control or restriction 231

absolve: set free from some duty or responsibility; declare free from guilt or blame 154
absorbing: extremely interesting 154
abstain: withhold oneself from doing something 154
abundant: plentiful *5*, 232
abut: be in contact with *155*
accede: agree 92
accessible: easy to approach *181*
accommodate: hold without crowding or inconvenience; do a favor for 51
accord: agreement; agree 61, 92
accumulate: pile up 82
acquiesce: accept, agree, or give implied consent by keeping silent or by not making objections 92, 117
acquiescent: disposed to acquiesce *117*
acquit: exonerate; absolve *14*
acronym: name formed from the first letter or letters of other words 264
adapt: adjust; make suitable for a different use 155
adaptable: capable of changing so as to fit a new or specific use or situation *117*
addicted: given over (to a habit) 155
adept: highly skilled or trained *200*
adequate: enough; sufficient *6*, 155
adhere: stick *52*, 215
adherent: faithful supporter 155
adjacent: lying near 155
adjoin: be next to 155
adjourn: close a meeting 14, 155
adroit: expert in using the hands 80
adroitness: skill in the use of the hands 77
advantageous: helpful *182*
advent: approach 155
adversary: opponent 155, *264*
adverse: unfavorable 155

advocate: supporter *201*

affinity: sympathy 212

affirm: declare to be true *233*

affluence: abundance of wealth or property 82

affluent: very wealthy 81

aggravate: make worse 61

aggregate: gathered together in one mass 214

aggregation: gathering of individuals into a body or group 214

aggression: unprovoked attack 32

aggressor: person or nation that begins a quarrel 32

agitate: disturb 198

agronomy: branch of agriculture dealing with crop production and soil management 266

alertness: watchfulness *107*

alias: assumed name; otherwise called 90, *264*

alienate: turn (someone) from affection to dislike or enmity; make hostile or unfriendly *94*

allegiance: loyalty 117

alleviate: lessen; relieve 5

alliteration: repetition of the same letter or consonant at the beginning of consecutive words 217

altercation: noisy, angry dispute 93

alternative: choice 70

altitude: height; elevation 32

amass: pile up 82

amateur: person who follows a particular pursuit because he likes it, rather than as a profession; person who performs rather poorly 211

ambidextrous: able to use both hands equally well 80

ambush: trap in which concealed persons lie in wait to attack by surprise 91

amiable: lovable 211

amicable: characterized by friendliness rather than antagonism 211

amity: friendship 211

amorous: having to do with love 211

amplify: enlarge *43*

anachronism: error in chronology or time order 248

anagram: word or phrase formed from another by transposing the letters 272

ancestry line of descent *71*

animosity: violent hatred 211

animus: ill will 211

annals: record of events arranged in yearly sequence *248*

annul: cancel *52*

anonymous: of unnamed or unknown origin 264

antagonist: one who is against, or contends with, another in a struggle, fight, or contest; main opponent of the principal character in a play, novel, or story *155*, 263

antagonize: make an enemy of 93

antecedents: ancestors 156

antechamber: an outer room leading to another usually more important room *156*

antedate: assign a date before the true date; precede 156

ante meridiem: before noon 156

anteroom: room placed before and forming an entrance to another 156

antibiotic: substance obtained from tiny living organisms that works against harmful bacteria 263

antibody: substance in the blood or tissues that works against germs or poisons produced by germs 263

anticipate: foresee *51*

antidote: remedy that acts against the effects of a poison 263

antihistamine: drug used against certain allergies and cold symptoms 263

antipathy: dislike 263

antiseptic: substance that prevents infection 263

antithesis: direct opposite 270

antitoxin: substance formed in the body as the result of the introduction of a toxin and capable of acting against that toxin 263

antonym: word meaning the opposite of another word 263

anxiety: painful uneasiness of mind usually over an anticipated ill *107*, 227

apathy: lack of interest or concern *140*

apparition: ghost *267*

append: attach 227

appendix: matter added to the end of a book or document 227

apprehend: anticipate with fear; arrest 51

apprehension: alarm; uneasiness 51, 227

apprehensive: expecting something unfavorable 51, 83

apprentice: person learning an art or trade under a skilled worker *5*, 80

apprise: inform 91

appropriate: fitting; proper 15

aptitude: talent; bent 80

archetype: prototype; original 5

aristocracy: government or country governed by a small privileged upper class; ruling class of nobles 245

aristocrat: advocate of aristocracy; member of the aristocracy 246

articulate: able to speak effectively *213*

artisan: skilled worker *80*

aspersion: discredit *34*

assailant: one who attacks violently with blows or words *32*

assemblage: gathering *214*

assent: agree 92

assert: maintain as true *42*, *233*

assimilate: make similar; take in and incorporate as one's own 229

aster: plant having small starlike flowers 271

asterisk: star-shaped mark (*) used to call attention to a footnote, omission, etc. 271

asteroid: very small planet resembling a star in appearance; starfish 271

astrologer: person who practices astrology 272

astrology: study dealing with the supposed influence of the stars and planets on human affairs *272*

astronaut: outer-space traveler 272

astronomer: expert in astronomy 272

astronomical: having to do with the science of the sun, moon, planets, stars, and other heavenly bodies; inconceivably large 266

astronomy: science of the sun, moon, planets, stars, and other heavenly bodies *266, 272*

astute: shrewd; wise 14

audacious: bold; too bold 83

audacity: nerve; rashness 83

authentic: genuine *5, 233,* 244

autobiography: story of a person's life written by the person 244

autocracy: government, or country governed, by one individual with self-derived, unlimited power 245

autocrat: ruler exercising self-derived, absolute power 244

autocratic: ruling with absolute power and authority *23, 231*

autograph: person's signature 244

automation: technique of making a process self-operating by means of built-in electronic controls 244

automaton: robot 244

autonomous: self-governing 244

autonomy: right of self-government 244

autopsy: medical examination of a dead body to determine the cause of death *157,* 244

avarice: excessive desire for wealth 81

avaricious: greedy 81

aver: state to be true 233

averse: opposed 154, 244

avert: turn away 154, *197*

avocation: hobby *154*

avowal: open acknowledgment *91*

ban: forbid *15*

banish: compel to leave *168*

barometer: instrument for measuring atmospheric pressure as an aid in determining probable weather changes 253

beguile: deceive by means of flattery or by a trick or lie *130*

belittle: speak of in a slighting way *184*

belligerent: fond of fighting *42,* 61

benediction: blessing 182

benefactor: person who gives kindly aid, money, or a similar benefit 182

beneficial: productive of good 182

beneficiary: person receiving some good, advantage, or benefit 182

benevolent: disposed to promote the welfare of others 182

beverage: drink 70

bewilder: confuse *185, 198*

bicameral: consisting of two chambers or legislative houses 157

bicentennial: two-hundredth anniversary 157

bicker: quarrel in a petty way 94

biennial: occurring every two years 157

bilateral: having two sides 158, 216

bilingual: speaking two languages equally well; written in two languages 158

bimonthly: occurring every two months 158

bipartisan: representing two political parties 158

bisect: divide into two equal parts 158

blunder: mistake caused by stupidity or carelessness 70, *130*

brawl: quarrel noisily 94

breach: violation of a law or duty *116*

bulwark: wall-like defensive structure 105

bureaucracy: government by bureaus or groups of officials 245

bureaucrat: member of a bureaucracy 246

cache: hiding place to store something 23

calamitous: disastrous 32

calamity: great misfortune 32, *272*

capsize: overturn 42

captivated: charmed *211*

cartographer: person skilled in the science or art of mapmaking 272

catastrophe: great misfortune *272*

category: kind; sort *214*

cautious: wary; circumspect *107, 195*

cede: relinquish *34*

celerity: speed *44*

cellophane: transparent cellulose substance 267

censure: act of blaming; find fault with 14, 15

chasm: split; division *93*

check: hold back *24*

chivalrous: generous and high-minded *211*

chronic: marked by long duration and frequent recurrence; having a characteristic, habit, disease, etc., for a long time 118

chronicle: historical account of events in the order of time 248

chronological: arranged in order of time 248

chronology: arrangement of data or events in order of time of occurrence *248*

chronometer: instrument for measuring time very accurately 253

chum: crony; associate *33*

circumference: distance around a circle or rounded body 195

circumlocution: roundabout way of speaking 195

circumnavigate: sail around 195

circumscribe: draw a line around; limit 195

circumspect: careful to consider all circumstances and possible consequences 195

circumvent: go around   195
citadel: fortress   105
civilian: person not a member of the armed forces, or police, or fire-fighting forces   4
clandestine: carried on in secrecy and concealment   91
cleavage: split   93
cleave: stick   52
cling: stick   *52, 215*
coalesce: grow together   196
coerce: force; compel   30
cogent: convincing   105
cogitation: thought   *34*
cohere: stick together   215
coherence: state of sticking together   215
coherent: sticking together   196
cohesion: act or state of sticking together   215
coincide: agree   *4*
collaborate: work together   196
collateral: situated at the side   216
collective: of a group of individuals as a whole   *214*
collusion: secret agreement for a deceitful purpose   196
colossal: huge   102
combative: eager to fight   *61*
comestible: eatable   *95*
commencing: beginning   *118*
commend: praise   23
commodious: spacious and comfortable   102
commute: travel back and forth daily, as from a home in the suburbs to a job in the city   114
commuter: person who travels back and forth daily   114
compact: agreement   92
compatible: able to exist together harmoniously   92
compelling: forceful   92
compete: take part in a contest   *42*
complex: hard to analyze or solve   *4*
complicated: hard to understand   4
comply: act in accordance with another's wishes or in obedience to a rule   *92, 117*
comprehensible: understandable   *217*
compulsory: required by authority   119
con: against; opposing argument   170
conclusive: final   *212*
concord: state of being together in heart or mind   196
concur: agree   4
concurrent: occurring at the same time   118, *230*
concurrently: at the same time   *44*
condiment: something added to or served with food to enhance its flavor   95
confine: keep within limits   212
confirm: state or prove the truth of   5
confirmation: proof   5
confirmed: habitual   *118*
conform: be in agreement or harmony with   92

congenial: agreeable; pleasant   92
congenital: existing at birth   196
congregate: come together into a crowd   32
congregation: gathering of people for religious worship   214
conscientious: having painstaking regard for what is right   *107*
conscript: enroll into military service by compulsion   228
conservative: tending or disposed to maintain existing views, conditions, or institutions   *251*
consistency: harmony   *215*
consistent: keeping to the same principles throughout   92, *196*
consonant: in agreement   *92*
conspicuous: noticeable   61, *167, 200*
conspiracy: plot   *196*
constant: steady; unchanging   *118*
contemplate: consider carefully and for a long time   *52*
contend: take part in a contest; argue   42
content: satisfied   52
contentious: inclined to argue   *24,* 42
contraband: merchandise imported or exported contrary to law   171
contrary: opposite   *270*
contravene: go or act contrary to   171
controversy: dispute   70, 171
convene: meet in a group for a specific purpose   32, 196
convention: treaty; agreement   32
conventional: customary   *251*
cordial: warm and friendly   32
cordiality: friendliness   32
correspond: be in harmony   93, 196
corroborate: confirm   *233*
counter: contrary   171
countermand: cancel (an order) by issuing a contrary order   171
covenant: agreement   *92*
covert: secret   *91*
covet: crave, especially something belonging to another   81
cow: make afraid   *33,* 83
cower: draw back tremblingly   83
craft: skill; cunning   61
craftsperson: skilled worker   80
crafty: clever   *14,* 61
craven: cowardly; coward   61, *83*
craze: fad   *249*
cringe: shrink in fear   *83*
crony: close companion   33
crouch: cower   *83*
cryptogram: something written in secret code   272
culprit: one guilty of a fault or crime   52
cunning: clever   *14, 61*
cupidity: greediness   81
cur: worthless dog   23
curb: hold back   *24, 144*
cure-all: remedy for all ills   *247*

disperse: scatter *70*

disputatious: contentious; controversial 24, *70*

dispute: argue about 24

disregard: pay no attention to *106*

disrepair: bad condition 185

dissension: discord; conflict; strife 14, *93*

dissent: differ in opinion 14, 93, 185

dissident: not agreeing 185

dissimilar: unlike 229, *252*

dissolution: act of breaking up into component parts 231

dissolve: break up; cause to disappear 231

distinguish: tell apart 43

distract: draw away (the mind or attention) 185

divert: turn the attention away *185*

divulge: make known 43, 91

docile: easily taught 117

domain: region; sphere of influence *52*

domicile: home 115

domineering: ruling in an overbearing way *23, 132*

dormant: inactive, as if asleep 71, *91*

dovetail: to fit together with, so as to form a harmonious whole 93

dowry: money, property, etc., that a bride brings to her husband 81

draft: enroll into military service 228

drought: long period of dry weather 43

dubious: doubtful 33

duplicate: copy 62

dynamic: forceful 105

economic: having to do with the social science dealing with production, distribution, and consumption 266

economical: thrifty; frugal *81,* 266

economics: the social science dealing with production, distribution, and consumption 266

economize: reduce expenses 81

edible: fit for human consumption 95

edifice: building, especially a large or impressive building 24

eject: force out; expel 168

elaborate: complex; intricate *4*

electrocardiogram: tracing showing the amount of electricity the heart muscles produce during the heartbeat 273

electrocardiograph: instrument that records the amount of electricity the heart muscles produce during the heartbeat *273*

elevation: height 32

elicit: draw forth 91, 167

eliminate: get rid of 52

elucidate: make clear 217

emancipate: set free 226

embroil: involve in conflict 94

emigrate: move out of a country or region to settle in another 167

eminence: a natural elevation 32

eminent: standing out 167

enamored: inflamed with love 211

encyclopedia: work offering alphabetically arranged information on various branches of knowledge 250

endurance: ability to withstand strain, suffering, or hardship *63, 84*

endure: hold out; last *144, 198*

enduring: lasting *118, 198*

enervate: lessen the vigor or strength of 104, *140, 167*

enfeeble: weaken *104, 167*

engender: give birth to 214

engrave: cut or carve on a hard surface *167*

engrossing: taking up the whole interest of *154*

enigma: puzzle 91

enigmatic: puzzling 91

enlighten: shed the light of truth and knowledge upon 91

enmity: hatred *183, 211, 263*

enrage: fill with anger *43*

entail: involve as a necessary consequence 119

entomb: bury 5

envisage: have a mental picture of especially in advance of realization *233*

envision: foresee 233

ephemeral: not lasting; passing soon *16*

epicure: person with sensitive or discriminating tastes in food or wine *266*

epidemic: affecting many people in an area at the same time; outbreak of a disease affecting many people at the same time 247

epidermis: outer layer of the skin 265

epigram: bright or witty thought concisely and cleverly expressed 273

epithet: characterizing word or phrase 270

epoch: age; period *24*

equanimity: evenness of mind or temper 211

equilateral: having all sides equal 216

equilibrium: emotional balance *211*

equitable: fair to all concerned 14

era: historical period 24

eradicate: remove by or as if by uprooting *143*

erosion: gradual wearing away 167

essence: most necessary or significant part, aspect, or feature 119

essential: necessary *120, 215*

estrange: turn from affection to dislike or enmity 94

evidence: show 92

evident: clear; obvious 92

evoke: bring out 91, 167

excise: cut out 167

exclude: shut out *52*

exclusive: shutting out, or tending to shut out, others; not shared with others 71, 168

exclusively: without sharing with others 71

haunt: come to mind frequently   *197*
heed: pay attention   107
heedless careless   106, *140*
heterogeneous: differing in kind   252
hibernate: spend the winter   33
hinder: hold back; obstruct   *62, 197*
hindrance: something that obstructs or impedes   *197*
hoard: save and conceal   82
homogeneous: of the same kind   252
homogenize: make uniform   252
homonym: word that sounds like another but differs in meaning   264
horde: great crowd   *24*
hospitable: kind to guests and strangers   *181*
host: person who receives or entertains a guest or guests; large number   33
hostile: of or relating to an enemy or enemies; unfriendly   5, *155*
husbandry: agriculture   *266*
hypodermic: beneath the skin   265
hypothesis: supposition or assumption made as a basis for reasoning or research   270

ignore: disregard; overlook   106
illegible: not able to be read; very hard to read   15, 180
illiterate: unable to read and write   180
illogical: not observing the rules of correct reasoning   181
illuminate: light up   43
immaculate: spotless   62, 181
immature: not fully grown or developed   181
immigrate: move into a foreign country or region as a permanent resident   167
imminent: about to happen   118, 167, 227
immoderate: too great   *103*
immunity: condition of being not susceptible   *71, 181*
impartial: fair   14, *185*
impatient: not willing to bear delay   5
impede: block   *199*
impediment: obstruction   *197*
impel: drive on   168
impending: threatening to occur soon   167, 227
imperative: not to be avoided   119
imperil: endanger   *43,* 71
impetuous: impulsive   *84*
implicate: show to be part of or connected with   168
impose: put on as a burden, duty, tax, etc.   *197,* 228
impoverish: make very poor   81
impregnable: incapable of being taken by assault   105
impromptu: without previous thought or preparation   *15*
improvise: compose, recite, or sing on the spur of the moment   233

improvised: composed, recited, or sung on the spur of the moment   *15*
impudent: marked by a bold disregard of others   83
impugn: call in question   168
impunity: freedom from punishment, harm, loss, etc.   *71,* 181
inaccessible: not able to be reached   181
inadvertent: careless   106
inadvertently: not done on purpose   15
inappropriate: not fitting   15
inaudible: incapable of being heard   43
inborn: born in or with one   *196*
incapacitate: render incapable or unfit   104
incarcerate: put into prison   168
incense: make extremely angry   43, 201
incessant: not ceasing   *118,* 181
incipient: beginning to show itself   118
incise: cut into   168
inclusive: including the limits mentioned   168
incoherent: unintelligible   215
incompatible: not capable of being brought together in harmonious or agreeable relations   *94, 181*
inconsistency: lack of agreement or harmony   *93,* 265
incontrovertible: not able to be disputed   171
incumbent: imposed as a duty   119
indifference: lack of interest; dislike   *140*
indigence: poverty   81
indigent: needy   *81*
indispensable: absolutely necessary   120
indisputable: unquestionable   *171*
indomitable: incapable of being subdued   84
induct: lead in   *24*
inept: lacking in skill or aptitude   *80*
inequitable: unfair   14
inexhaustible: plentiful enough not to give out or be used up   *103*
inextinguishable: unquenchable   *140*
infallible: incapable of error   52
infinite: without ends or limits   103
infinitesimal: so small as to be almost nothing   103
infirmity: weakness   104
infixed: implanted   215
inflate: swell with air or gas   103
inflexible: not easily bent   181
inflict: cause (something disagreeable) to be borne; impose   *228*
influx: inflow   213
infraction: breaking (of a law, regulation, etc.)   116
infrequent: seldom happening or occurring   119
infringe: violate   *171*
infuriate: fill with rage   *43*
ingratitude: state of being not grateful   181
inherent: belonging by nature   215

inhibit: hold in check 168

inhospitable: not showing kindness to guests and strangers 181

initial: beginning; introductory 5

initiate: begin; admit into a club by special ceremonies 24

initiation: installation as a member 24

inmate: person confined in an institution, prison, hospital, etc. 115

innate: inborn *196*

inordinate: much too great 103

inscribe: write, engrave, or print to create a lasting record 168

inscription: something written on a monument, coin, etc. 228

insignificant: of little importance *103*

insolent: lacking in respect for rank or position 83

insoluble: not capable of being solved; not capable of being dissolved 181

insubordinate: not submitting to authority 116, *168*

insurgent: one who rises in revolt against established authority; rebellious 116, 168

insurrection: uprising against established authority 116, *186*

integrate: make into a whole *185*

intensify: make more acute *61*

inter: bury 5

intercede: interfere to reconcile differences *62*, 171

intercept: stop or seize on the way from one place to another 171

interdict: forbid; prohibit *15*

interlinear: inserted between lines already printed or written 172

interlude: anything filling the time between two events 172

intermediary: go-between 172

interminable: continual; endless *181*

intermission: pause between periods of activity 172

intermittent: coming and going at intervals 118

intersect: cut by passing through or across 172

interurban: between cities or towns 172

interval: space of time between events or states *172*

intervene: occur between; come between to help settle a quarrel *62*, 172

intervention: intercession; interference 62

intimidate: frighten 33, 83

intramural: within the walls or boundaries 170

intraparty: within a party 170

intrastate: within a state 170

intravenous: within or by way of the veins 170

intrepid: fearless and daring *83*

intricate: not simple or easy 4

intrinsic: belonging to the essential nature or constitution of a thing *215*

intrude: come or go in without invitation or welcome *197*

inundate: flood 43, 232

invigorate: give life and energy to 105

invincible: unconquerable *84, 105*

invisible: imperceptible 233

invoke: call on for help or protection 167

involve: draw in as a participant *168*

iota: very small quantity 103

irrational: illogical; fallacious *181*

irreconcilable: unable to be brought into friendly accord or understanding 94, 181

irrelevant: off the topic *169*, 181

irrevocable: incapable of being recalled 181

isolate: set apart from others *186*

isolated: infrequent 119

isolation: the act or condition of being set apart from others; segregation *214*

jeopardize: expose to danger 43, *71*

jeopardy: danger 43

Jolly Roger: pirates' flag 24

journalist: editor of or writer for a periodical *228*

jurisdiction: territory within which authority may be exercised *52*

jut: stick out; protrude *201*

kinship: sense of oneness 212

kleptomania: insane impulse to steal 249

latent: present but not showing itself 91

lateral: of or pertaining to the side 216

lavish: too free in giving, using, or spending; given or spent too freely 82, *200*

lax: careless *106*

legible: capable of being read *15*

lettered: able to read and write *217*

liberate: set free *140, 226*

lineage: descent 71, *252*

literacy: ability to read and write 217

literal: following the letters or exact words of the original 217

literary: having to do with letters or literature 217

literate: able to read and write 217

litigation: lawsuit 94

loathe: detest; abhor *153*

logic: correct reasoning *181*

logical: observing the rules of correct reasoning *196*

loiter: hang around idly *118*

lucid: clear 217

lucrative: profitable 15, 82

luminary: famous person 217

luminous: shining 217

lurk: be hidden 91

luscious: delicious 95
luxurious: extravagantly elegant and comfortable 82

magnanimous: showing greatness or nobility of mind 211
magnify: cause to be or look larger 43
magnitude: size 103
major: greater 71
maladjusted: out of harmony with one's environment 183
maladroit: clumsy 80
malcontent: discontented person 116
malediction: curse 182
malefactor: evildoer 182
malevolence: ill will 183
malevolent: showing ill will 183
malice: ill will 183
malign: speak evil of; slander *168*
malnutrition: poor nourishment 183
maltreat: treat badly or roughly 183
mammoth: of very great size *102*
manacle: handcuff 226
mandate: territory entrusted to the administration of another country; authoritative command 226
maneuver: handle; engineer 226
mania: madness; excessive fondness 249
maniac: raving lunatic 249
maniacal: characterized by madness 249
manifest: show; plain 92
manipulate: operate with the hands 226
manual: small, helpful book capable of being carried in the hand; relating to, or done with, the hands 226
manuscript: document written by hand, or typewritten 226
means: wealth 82
mediate: intervene between conflicting parties or viewpoints to reconcile differences *172*
mediator: impartial third party who acts as a go-between in a dispute in order to arrange a peaceful settlement *172*
meditate: consider carefully and for a long time *52*
meek: submissive 117
meter: device for measuring; 39.37 inches 253
meticulous: extremely or excessively careful about small details 107
migrate: move from one place to settle in another; move from one place to another with the change of season 115
mind: pay attention to *107*
miniature: small 62
misbelief: wrong or erroneous belief 130
mischance: piece of bad luck 130
misdeed: bad act 130
misfire: fail to be fired or exploded properly 130
misgiving: uneasy feeling 114, 130
mishap: bad happening 130

mislay: put or lay in an unremembered place 130
mislead: lead astray 130
misstep: wrong step 130
mitigate: make less severe 5
moderate: make less violent, severe, or intense *61*
modify: make changes in *155*
momentary: lasting only a moment 16
monetary: having to do with money 81
monogram: person's initials interwoven or combined into one design 273
monograph: written account of a single thing or class of things 273
multilateral: having many sides 216
multitude: crowd 24, *33*
multitudinous: numerous 24
municipal: of a city or town 43
mutineer: rebel; insurgent *168*
mutinous: rebellious *116, 168*

native: person born in a particular place; born or originating in a particular place 115
necessitate: make necessary 120
neglect: give little or no attention to; lack of proper care or attention 106
negligence: carelessness *106*
nemesis: person that inflicts just punishment for evil deeds; formidable and usually victorious opponent 266
neophyte: beginner; novice 5
noble: aristocrat 246
nomad: member of a tribe that has no fixed home but wanders from place to place 115
nomadic: roaming from place to place 115
nonconformist: not agreeing; dissenting *185*
notable: standing out *200, 217*
noteworthy: remarkable *167*
notwithstanding: in spite of 144
novice: one who is new to a field or activity 5, *80*

objective: goal; involving facts, rather than personal feelings or opinions *14,* 71
obligatory: required *119*
oblige: compel 120
obliterate: remove all traces of 197
obscure: not clear *91, 132*
obsess: trouble the mind of 197
obstacle: something standing in the way 197
obstruct: be in the way of 197
obtrude: thrust forward without being asked 197
obviate: make unnecessary 120, 197
obvious: not obscure; evident 92
odometer: instrument attached to a vehicle for measuring the distance traversed 253
offhand: without previous thought *15*
omen: foreboding; presentiment 114
onomatopoeia: use of words whose sound suggests their meaning 264

opinionated: unduly attached to one's own opinion 71

opulence: wealth 82

opulent: wealthy *81*

origin: coming into being; genesis *252*

original: a work created firsthand and from which copies are made; belonging to the beginning 5

originality: freshness; novelty 5

originate: begin *24*

orthodontics: branch of dentistry dealing with the straightening and adjusting of teeth *251*

orthodontist: dentist specializing in the straightening and adjusting of teeth 251

orthodox: generally accepted, especially in religion 251

orthography: correct spelling 251

orthopedic: having to do with the correction and prevention of deformities, especially in children 250

orthopedics: the science dealing with the correction and prevention of deformities, especially in children *250*

orthopedist: physician specializing in the correction and prevention of deformities, especially in children 251

outfox: outwit *131*

outgrow: grow too large for 131

outlandish: looking or sounding as if it belongs to a foreign land 131

outlast: last longer than 131

outlive: live longer than *131*

outlook: a looking beyond 131

output: a yield or product 131

outrun: run faster than 131

outspoken: speaking out freely or boldly 131

outweigh: exceed in weight, value, or importance *132*

outwit: get the better of by being more clever 131

overawe: subdue by awe *33*

overbearing: domineering over others 132

overburden: place too heavy a load on 132

overconfident: too sure of oneself 132

overdose: too big a dose 132

overestimate: overrate 132

overhasty: too hasty *84*

overpower: overcome by superior force *132*

overshadow: cast a shadow over 132

oversupply: too great a supply 132

overt: open to view 92

overtax: put too great a burden or strain on *132*

overvalue: set too high a value on *132*

overwhelm: overpower 132, *232*

palatable: agreeable to the taste 95

panacea: remedy for all ills 247

Pan-American: of or pertaining to all the countries of North, South, and Central America 247

pandemonium: wild uproar 247

panoply: complete suit of armor 247

panorama: complete, unobstructed view 247

pantomime: dramatic performance that is all signs and gestures without words 247

parallel: running alongside *216*

passionate: showing strong feeling *185*

patrician: member of the aristocracy 246

pauperize: make very poor; impoverish 81

pecuniary: having to do with money *81*

pedagogue: teacher of children 250

pedagogy art of teaching 250

pediatrician: physician specializing in the treatment of babies and children 250

pediatrics: the branch of medicine dealing with the care, development, and diseases of babies and children 250

pedigree: ancestral line *252*

pendant: hanging ornament 227

pending: waiting to be settled; until 227

penetrate: pass into or through *198*

penury: poverty; indigence 81

perceive: become aware of through the senses 24

perception: idea; conception 24

perennial: continuing through the years; plant that lives through the years 118, *198*

perforate: make a hole or holes through *43*, *198*

peril: exposure to injury, loss, or destruction *43*

perimeter: the whole outer boundary of a body or area *195*

periodic: happening repeatedly *118*

permanent: enduring; perennial 15, *118*

permeate: pass through 198

perplex: confuse thoroughly 198

persevere: keep at something in spite of difficulties or opposition *198*

persist: continue in spite of opposition; continue to exist 198

pertinent: connected with the matter under consideration 198

perturb: disturb thoroughly or considerably 198

pervade: spread through; penetrate *198*

perverse: obstinate (in opposing what is right or reasonable) 116

petty: small and of no importance *103*

phantom: something that has appearance but no reality 267

phenomenal: extraordinary 267

phenomenon: any observable fact or event; extraordinary person or thing 268

photometer: instrument for measuring intensity of light 254

picayune: concerned with trifling matters 103

pilfer: steal (in small amounts) 52

pittance: small amount 103

pliable: easily bent or influenced 117

pluck: courage *84*
plucky: courageous 84
plutocracy: government or country governed by the rich 245
plutocrat: member of wealthy class 246
portal: door; entrance 24
postdate: assign a date after the true date 156
postgraduate: having to do with study after graduation from high school or college 156
post meridiem: after noon 156
postmortem: thorough examination of a body after death 157, 244
postscript: note added to a completed letter 157
potential: capable of becoming real *91*
precede: come or go before *33, 156,* 199
precise: very exact *107*
preclude: put a barrier before *120,* 199
precocious: showing mature characteristics at an early age 199
preconceive: form an opinion of beforehand without adequate evidence 199
predecessor: ancestor; forebear *156*
prefabricate: construct beforehand 199
preface: introduction; introduce with a foreword 33, *129,* 199
premature: before the proper or usual time 199
premeditate: consider beforehand 199
preoccupy: engage the attention of *197*
prerequisite: something required beforehand 120
prescribe: order; order as a remedy 228
presentiment: feeling that something will, or is about to, happen 114
presently: in a short time 71
pressing: requiring immediate attention 120
presume: take for granted without proof 200
preview: view of something before it is shown to the public 200
procrastinate: put things off 71, 118, 200
prodigal: profuse; lavish 82
prodigious: extraordinary in size, quantity, or extent 72
prodigy: extraordinary person or thing 72, *268*
profession: vocation; occupation *53*
proficient: well advanced in any subject or occupation 200
profuse: pouring forth freely *82,* 200
progenitor: ancestor to whom a group traces its birth 214
prohibit: forbid; proscribe 15, *228*
project: throw or cast forward 200
prologue: introduction *33, 129*
prominent: readily noticeable *61,* 200
prompt: on time *15*
propel: drive onward 201
prophecy: prediction 114
prophesy: predict *33*

proponent: person who puts forth a proposal or argues in favor of something 201
prospect: thing looked forward to 201
prospects: chances 201
protagonist: the leading character in a play, novel, or story 269
protocol: first draft or record from which a treaty is drawn up; rules of etiquette of the diplomatic corps, military services, etc. 269
protoplasm: fundamental substance of which all living things are composed 269
prototype: first or original model of anything *5,* 269
protozoan: animal consisting of only a single cell 269
protract: draw out 72, 118, 201
protrude: thrust forth 201
province: proper business or duty 52
provoke: call forth; make angry 201
prudence: skill and good sense in taking care of oneself or of one's affairs *129*
prudent: shrewd in the management of practical affairs *195*
pseudonym: fictitious name used by an author 264
punctual: on time 15
punctuality: promptness 15
puncture: make a hole with a pointed object 43, *198*
puny: slight or inferior in size, power, or importance 103
pusillanimous: cowardly *61*
pyromania: insane impulse to set fires 250

quadrilateral: plane figure having four sides and four angles 216
quench: put out; satisfy *95*
questionable: not certain 33
quintet: group of five 62

rabble-rouser: one who stirs up the people, especially to hatred or violence *246*
ramble: aimless walk *25*
rampart: broad bank or wall used as a fortification or protective barrier 105
ransack: search thoroughly 44
rarity: something uncommon, infrequent, or rare 5
rash: taking too much risk 84, *140*
ravage: lay waste 230
ravenous: voracious *95*
raze: tear down; destroy *14,* 184
rebel: one who opposes or takes arms against the government or ruler *116, 168*
rebuke: express disapproval of 14, 15
reckless: foolishly bold *84, 106*
recoil: draw back because of fear *6,* 34
reconcilable: able to be brought into friendly accord *181*
reconcile: cause to be friends again 62, 93
recurrent: returning from time to time *118*

spine: backbone   25

spineless: cowardly   25

sporadic: occurring occasionally or in scattered instances   119

stable: enduring; not changing   *15*

stamina: endurance   63

stealthy: secret in action or character   91

stenographer: person employed chiefly to take and transcribe dictation   273

stenography: the art of writing in shorthand   *273*

stress: emphasize; underscore   *141*

strife: bitter conflict   *93*

stroll: idle and leisurely walk   25

stronghold: fortified place   *105*

sturdy: strong and vigorous   *105*

submissive: meek   *117*

submit: yield to another's will, authority, or power   117

subscriber: one who writes his or her name at the end of a document, thereby indicating approval   229

subsequently: later   44

substantiate: provide evidence for   *5, 233*

succulent: full of juice   95

suffice: be enough   6

sumptuous: involving large expense   82

superabundance: excessive abundance   103

superfluous: beyond what is necessary or desirable   53, 120, *232*

superimpose: put on top of or over   228

supplement: something that makes an addition   227

supplementary: additional   *216*

surmount: conquer   53

surplus: excess   *53, 103, 120, 232*

survive: live longer than   44, *131*

suspend: hang by attaching to something; stop temporarily   227

suspense: mental uncertainty   227

swarm: great crowd   *24*

swindle: cheat   82

symmetry: correspondence in measurements, shape, etc., on opposite sides of a dividing line   254

synchronize: cause to agree in time   249

synonym: word having the same meaning as another word   264

synthesis: combination of parts or elements into a whole   270

synthetic: artificially made   270

tachometer: instrument for measuring speed   *254*

tally: match   *196*

taxidermist: one who prepares, stuffs, and mounts the skins of animals in lifelike form   265

taxidermy: the art of preparing, stuffing, and mounting the skins of animals in lifelike form   *265*

technocracy: government or country governed by technical experts   245

teem: be present in large quantity   *232*

temerity: nerve; audacity   *83*

tenacious: holding fast or tending to hold fast   *72*, 105

testify: state under oath   *228*

thermal: pertaining to heat   268

thermonuclear: having to do with the fusion, at an extraordinarily high temperature, of the nuclei of atoms   268

thermostat: automatic device for regulating temperature   269

thesis: claim put forward; essay written by a candidate for a college degree   271

thrifty: inclined to save   *81, 266*

throng: great crowd   *24, 33*

timid: lacking courage or self-confidence   *25, 83*

timorous: full of fear   25, *83*

tolerable: endurable   34

tolerate: endure   34

toxin: poison   *263*

tractable: easily controlled, led, or taught   117

transgress: go beyond the set limits of   116

transient: not lasting; visitor or guest staying for only a short time   16

transitory: short-lived   16

translucent: letting light through   217

transpose: change the relative order of   228

traverse: pass across, over, or through   44

trepidation: nervous agitation   83

trespass: encroach on another's rights, privileges, property, etc.   116

trustworthy: worthy of confidence   *244*

tuition: payment for instruction   25

typographical: pertaining to or occurring in printing   243

typography: use of type for printing   243

tyrannical: domineering   *23*

tyro: beginner   *5, 80*

unabridged: not made shorter   139

unanimity: complete agreement   212

unanimous: in complete accord   212

unbiased: not prejudiced in favor of or against   *14,* 139

unblemished: spotless   *62*

uncommunicative: not inclined to talk   *24*

unconcern: lack of concern, anxiety, or interest   140

undeceive: free from deception or mistaken ideas   140

underbrush: shrubs, bushes, etc., growing beneath large trees in a wood   141

underdeveloped: insufficiently developed because of a lack of capital and trained personnel for exploiting natural resources   141

undergraduate: student in a college or university who has not yet earned his or her first degree   141

underhand: marked by secrecy and deception *91*

underpayment: insufficient payment 141

underprivileged: deprived through social or economic oppression of some of the fundamental rights supposed to belong to all 141

underscore: draw a line beneath 141

undersell: sell at a lower price than 141

undersigned: person or persons who sign at the end of a letter or document 141

understatement: restrained statement in mocking contrast to what might be said 141

understudy: one who "studies under" and learns the part of a regular performer so as to be his or her substitute if necessary 142

ungag: remove a gag from 140

unilateral: one-sided 216

unintelligible: incomprehensible *215*

unity: act of sticking together; cohesion *215*

unmindful: careless 106

unnerve: deprive of nerve or courage 140

unorthodox: not in accord with accepted, standard, or approved belief or practice *251*

unquenchable: not capable of being satisfied 140

unravel: solve *231*

unscramble: restore to intelligible form 140

unshackle: set free from restraint 140

unsubstantial: lacking firmness, strength, or substance *104*

untimely: before the proper time *199*

unwarranted: uncalled for 119

unwary: not alert 140

unyielding: firm and determined *105*

upcoming: being in the near future 142

update: bring up to date 142

upgrade: raise the grade or quality of 142

upheaval: violent heaving up 142

upkeep: maintenance 142

uplift: elevate; raise 142

upright: standing up straight on the feet 143

uproot: pull up by the roots 143

upset: overturn *42*, 140

upstart: person who has suddenly risen to wealth and power, especially if he or she is conceited and unpleasant 143

upturn: upward turn toward better conditions 143

urban: having to do with cities or towns 53

usher in: preface; introduce *33*

vacancy: job opening; unoccupied apartment 6

vacant: empty 6

valiant: courageous *83*

valor: courage *84*

valorous: courageous *84*

vanguard: troops moving at the head of an army *129*

at variance: in disagreement *94*

variation: change in form, position, or condition *93, 185*

vehement: showing strong feeling 105

velocity: speed 44

veracity: truthfulness 233

verbiage: excessive wordiness *195*

verdict: decision of a jury 233

verification: proof; confirmation 5

verify: prove to be true *5*, 233

veritable: true 233

verity: truth 233

versatile: capable of doing many things well 80

version: account from a particular point of view; translation 25

vicinity: neighborhood 53

video: having to do with the transmission or reception of what is seen 233

vie: strive for superiority *42*

vigilance: alert watchfulness to discover and avoid danger 107

vigilant: alertly watchful, especially to avoid danger *107*

vigor: active strength or force *63*, 105

visibility: degree of clearness of the atmosphere, with reference to the distance at which objects can be clearly seen 234

visual: having to do with sight 233

vocal: inclined to express oneself freely 131

vocation: occupation 53

volition: act of willing or choosing 63

voracious: having a huge appetite 95

wary: on one's guard against danger, deception, etc. 107

wayward: following one's own and usually improper way *116*

wily: cunning; astute *14*

wince: draw back involuntarily *6, 34*

withdraw: take or draw back or away *24*, 143

withdrawal: act of taking back or drawing out from a place of deposit 143

withdrawn: drawn back or removed from easy approach *24*, 144

withhold: hold back 144

withholding tax: sum withheld or deducted from wages for tax purposes 144

withstand: stand up against 144

witty: cleverly amusing in speech or writing 52

wrangle: quarrel noisily *93*, 94